University of Michigan Publications
HISTORY AND POLITICAL SCIENCE

VOLUME XVI

DETROIT'S FIRST AMERICAN DECADE
1796 to 1805

(Courtesy of the Historical Society of Pennsylvania)

DETROIT'S FIRST AMERICAN DECADE
1796 to 1805

By F. CLEVER BALD

ANN ARBOR · UNIVERSITY OF MICHIGAN PRESS
LONDON · GEOFFREY CUMBERLEGE, OXFORD UNIVERSITY PRESS

1948

COPYRIGHT 1948
BY THE UNIVERSITY OF MICHIGAN

Paperback ISBN: 978-0-472-75015-3

PREFACE

VERY little has been printed about Detroit during the first decade of American occupation. Anyone who has had occasion to search books for information on that period knows how few facts can be found; and, if he is acquainted with the sources, he will soon discover that some of the "facts" are legendary.

Historians have neglected the years 1796 to 1805, perhaps because they seemed to be unimportant. Detroit was a frontier village, far from the seat of the national government and the populous cities of the eastern seaboard. Except for rumors of wars that kept the officials at Philadelphia aware of the necessity of maintaining a garrison in Fort Lernoult, there were no developments of national significance at Detroit. Nevertheless, if one wants to understand the later history of the city, he must begin at the beginning—at least at the beginning of the American régime and, after surveying the earlier background, study the old town with its French and British inhabitants under the impact of the new American element which now appears.

The first American decade lends itself well to treatment as a separate subject, for it is a natural unit. It opens with the occupation of Fort Lernoult by American troops and the proclamation of Wayne County, Northwest Territory, in 1796; it closes with the arrival at Detroit of the Governor and the other officers of the newly established Michigan Territory in 1805. The complete destruction of the town by fire, in the same year, also marked the end of a period and made possible a new beginning on a grander scale.

This book is intended to bridge the historical gap between the British régime and the establishment of Michigan Territory. Its basic theme is the slow development of American institutions and influence in a community which was essentially French, but which contained also a strong British element.

The organization of the material is chronological. This method of presentation avoids the frequent repetitions which must occur when the topical arrangment is used. Besides, it permits the reader to see developments in various fields of human endeavor in their relations to each other.

Many people have generously contributed to the making of this book. I am especially indebted to my good friend Dr. Milo M. Quaife, formerly secretary of the Burton Historical Collection, Detroit Public Library, for his expert guidance during my research, and for his criticism of the manuscript while it was in preparation.

The materials for the book were found in many depositories. The most important of them was the Burton Historical Collection. To Miss Gracie B. Krum, former chief, to Mrs. Elleine Stones, the present chief, to Miss Louise Rau, curator of manuscripts, and to all the members of the staff I owe a great debt of gratitude for their invaluable assistance and their untiring labors in my behalf over a period of several years.

The rich store of historical resources on the campus of the University of Michigan provided much valuable information. Dr. Lewis G. Vander Velde, director of the Michigan Historical Collections, Dr. Randolph G. Adams, director of the William L. Clements Library, and Dr. Hobart Coffey, director of the Law Library, placed at my disposal the materials in their collections. Mr. Henry D. Brown, director of the Detroit Historical Society, Mr. Howard Peckham, director of the Indiana Historical Bureau, and Mr. Colton Storm, assistant-director of the Clements Library, helped by locating documents pertinent to this study. Mr. Storm also prepared the folding map of Fort Lernoult and Detroit.

Through the courtesy of the officers of the Historical Society of Pennsylvania, and of the former director, Dr. William Reitzel, I was able to use the papers of General Anthony Wayne bearing on the history of Detroit. The present director, Mr. R. Norris Williams, has assisted me by answering questions and by providing photostats of some of these papers.

A number of persons in various Government agencies in Washington contributed information and helpful suggestions: Dr. Clarence E. Carter, editor of *The Territorial Papers of the United States;* Dr. P. J. Hamer and Dr. Vernon L. Setser of the National Archives; Dr. St. George L. Sioussat, chief of the

Division of Manuscripts in the Library of Congress; and Lieutenant Colonel R. B. Hough, librarian, War College Library.

Mr. G. Lanctot, of the Public Archives of Canada, Ottawa, and Miss Rose Demorest, of the Carnegie Library, Pittsburgh, provided photostats of materials in their institutions.

In my search for details about the religious life of Detroit I had the cordial coöperation of the late Most Reverend Michael J. Curley, Archbishop of Baltimore and Washington; the Reverend Edward J. Hickey, chancellor of the Archdiocese of Detroit; the Reverend Thomas T. McAvoy, archivist of Notre Dame University; and the Reverend B. Desrochers, assistant chancellor of the Archbishopric of Quebec.

I am grateful also to Miss M. Agnes Burton, Dr. Norman E. Clarke, Mr. W. E. Davey, and Mr. Victor Gnau of Detroit; Mr. Harry Emerson Wildes of Valley Forge, Pennsylvania; the Reverend John Duggan and the Reverend John B. Leibfred of Baltimore, Maryland; Colonel Thomas M. Spaulding of Washington, D.C.; and Mrs. Elvert M. Davis of Tallahassee, Florida, for their assistance in locating sources of information about the history of Detroit.

Mr. Calvin Goodrich, of Hendersonville, North Carolina, read the first draft of the manuscript and made many helpful suggestions.

To Dr. Lewis G. Vander Velde, who has previously been mentioned, I owe a special debt of gratitude for his painstaking reading and rereading of my manuscript and for his searching but kindly criticism.

It is a pleasure to express my thanks to the University of Michigan Press for undertaking the publication of this book and to Dr. Eugene S. McCartney, the editor, for his unremitting labor on the manuscript.

Finally, the services of my wife as critic and typist were of inestimable value. Without her assistance and encouragement this book would never have been completed.

F. CLEVER BALD

ANN ARBOR, 1948

TABLE OF CONTENTS

CHAPTER		PAGE
	Preface	v
I.	Uneasy Tenure	1
II.	Under the American Flag	16
III.	Composite Community	29
IV.	General Wayne Arrives	42
V.	Civil and Military Administration	55
VI.	The Fur Trade	73
VII.	Culture in the Wilderness	88
VIII.	Rumors of War	105
IX.	Yankee Arrivals	122
X.	Experiment in Democracy	137
XI.	Controversy and Coöperation	151
XII.	The First Regiment Returns	165
XIII.	An Incorporated Town	180
XIV.	John Williams Fights a Duel	191
XV.	In Indiana Territory	207
XVI.	End of the Cuyahoga Dream	221
XVII.	Hope for Better Days	235
	Bibliographical Essay	250
	Index	259

ILLUSTRATIONS

General Anthony Wayne. By Henri Elouis, 1796. From the original in the possession of the Historical Society of Pennsylvania . . . . *Frontispiece*

FACING PAGE

Detroit in 1796. From a photostat in the Clements Library, University of Michigan, from the original in the Ministry of War Archives, Paris. 18

James May. From a photograph, in the Burton Historical Collection, Detroit Public Library, of an old portrait. . . . 32

Commodore Alexander Grant. From a photograph, in the Burton Historical Collection, of the portrait in Glenmoriston House, Inverness-shire, Scotland 33

Rev. Gabriel Richard. From the original in Ste Anne's Church, Detroit. Photograph by S. Lucas 132

Solomon Sibley. From the original in the possession of Miss Frances W. Sibley, Detroit 133

Frederick Bates. From the original in the possession of the Missouri Historical Society, St. Louis. 192

Governor William Hull. By Gilbert Stuart. From a photograph in the Burton Historical Collection. 193

Tomb of Colonel John Francis Hamtramck in Mt. Elliott Cemetery, Detroit. Photograph by Frederick E. Moncrieff 208

"A View of Detroit and the Straits, taken from the Huron Church June 22nd 1804." By Dr. Edward Walsh. From the original in the Clements Library. 209

Part of "Plan of the Settlements at Detroit in 1796." By Patrick McNiff. From the original in the Clements Library.
End paper

Fort Lernoult and Detroit in 1796. By Major John Jacob Ulrich Rivardi. From the original in the Clements Library. Street names and a few other designations have been added. . . . . *In pocket at end of book*

CHAPTER I
UNEASY TENURE

IN THE spring of 1796 Detroit was in the hands of the British. Although the Treaty of Paris, formally terminating the Revolutionary War, had established a boundary which placed the town on American soil, British magistrates still administered the law, and a garrison of redcoats occupied Fort Lernoult. Repeated demands by the United States Government for transfer to its jurisdiction had been of no avail. Alleging failure of the Americans to fulfill certain treaty obligations, Great Britain continued to hold all the western forts. Only in the fall of 1794 did the British Government promise to deliver the posts on or before June 1, 1796.

The commandant of Fort Lernoult, which dominated Detroit from its position on higher ground behind the town, was Lieutenant Colonel Richard England. A man of gigantic stature, standing six feet six inches tall, the Colonel was a very capable officer, with more than thirty years of service to his credit. During the Revolutionary War he had served in Sir Guy Carleton's regiment; now he was in command of the Twenty-fourth Infantry. Jacob Lindley, an American Quaker who visited Detroit in 1793, described him as "a cheerful, open countenanced, masculine soldier, who received us like a gentleman, and kindly offered civilities to us." The Colonel told Lindley that he had procured the release of more than fifty Americans from the Indians, at great expense, clothed them, and sent them home.[1] Many, he added, had shown little sense of gratitude.

In anticipation of the evacuation of Detroit Colonel England, during the spring of 1796, directed the building of a new

[1] One of them was Oliver M. Spencer, a twelve-year old boy who had been captured by the Indians on the Ohio River. He was brought to Detroit in 1793 and released to Colonel England. Spencer characterized the Commandant thus: "... being both a gentleman and a man of great humanity he received me with much kindness and, regarding my wretched appearance with sympathy for my condition, followed only the generous impulse of his nature in ministering to my relief and comfort." M. M. Quaife (ed.), *The Indian Captivity of O. M. Spencer* (Chicago, 1917), p. 139.

British post near the mouth of the Detroit River, on the Canadian side. This was the beginning of Fort Malden at Amherstburg. Sheds for the storage of supplies which would be removed from Detroit were erected, and the construction of blockhouses was begun. After he was certain that the project was proceeding in a satisfactory manner, there was nothing further for the Colonel to do but await orders to deliver Fort Lernoult to the Americans.

June 1, the date set for the American occupation, came and passed; but neither orders nor Americans appeared. On June 5, however, Captain Bartholomew Shaumburgh arrived bearing a rather pompous note from General James Wilkinson asking when the Fort would be evacuated. Colonel England answered politely that he would inform the American general as soon as he received his orders.

It was not until the evening of June 30 that the order to evacuate, issued on the first day of the month, arrived at Detroit. On the same ship that brought it came Captain Henry De Butts, aide to General Anthony Wayne.

Colonel England immediately wrote to inform General Wilkinson that he was preparing to withdraw, and that he had directed vessels to sail for Fort Miamis at the foot of the rapids of the Maumee River, a few miles above the present city of Toledo, Ohio, to remove the garrison there under the command of Captain Shortt. He mentioned the arrival of Captain De Butts and added: "I shall have much pleasure in affording him every assistance in my power, in hiring or procuring Vessels to bring your Troops here."[2] This letter and De Butts' of the same date to General Wayne, who was on his way to Detroit to take command, were sent off by Colonel England's own courier.

Captain De Butts, in his letter, promised to "dispatch three vessels to the Miamis immediately; all that I can possibly procure at this place."[3] On July 2 he chartered from James May, of Detroit, the schooner *Swan* for £140 a month, the owner promising to provide the crew and all necessary supplies. De Butts also hired the schooner *Weazell* from John Askin, and purchased the sloop *Detroit* from Meldrum and Park.

[2] England to Wilkinson, July 1, 1796, Anthony Wayne Papers, 44, 87, Historical Society of Pennsylvania, Philadelphia.
[3] De Butts to Wayne, July 1, 1796, *ibid.*, 44, 88.

At this time Lieutenant Colonel John Francis Hamtramck was at Camp Deposit on the Maumee River, a short distance above Fort Miamis and not far from the present town of Waterville, Ohio. There he had arrived on June 6, with his command of about five hundred American soldiers—infantry, riflemen, artillery, and light dragoons—ready to advance when the British should retire from Fort Miamis and Detroit.

2

The order for the evacuation of Detroit, which Colonel England received, directed him to make a detailed report in duplicate of the condition of the public works. He could expect an American officer to arrive a day earlier than the occupying force to examine the works and sign a copy of the report, which would be delivered to the headquarters in Quebec. The order required that only a captain, two subalterns, and fifty men remain in the Fort until the Americans arrived.

Colonel England might have set out with his family for Lower Canada, leaving a subordinate to deliver the post. Nevertheless, he remained to perform that duty himself. While he awaited the arrival of the Americans, he may well have reviewed in retrospect the three years he had spent at Detroit. If he did, he must have recalled many pleasant memories. He was fortunate to have his family with him at this distant outpost. Here his son Richard had been born in 1793. And then there were friends, especially John Askin, one of the influential merchants of the town. Their families were often together, and neither of them would forget the pleasant companionship of the years in Detroit.

There had also been dinners, and dances to the music of French fiddles, and sleighing parties on the frozen river. The people in this isolated frontier town, who had to provide their own amusements and recreations, managed very well.

It was during the final period of waiting that an incident occurred which must have warmed the soldier's heart. On July 6 an address was presented to him, signed by forty of the townspeople, expressing their regret at his departure and appreciation of his services.

"The merchants and inhabitants of the town of Detroit,"

it began, "impressed with a lively sense of your zealous and indefatigable exertions towards the promotion of their general welfare during a period of four years, beg leave to offer some testimony of their approbation, and to thank you for the encouragement and security which your command has conferred, as well on the commercial as the general interests of this settlement."[4]

There was much more in the same vein, with praise for the officers and men of Colonel England's regiment, the Twenty-fourth Infantry, and for the artillerymen and engineers stationed at the Fort. In closing, the inhabitants returned to the personal note in expressing the wish "that yourself and family may be blessed with all the comforts of domestic happiness." The Commandant replied to this address with a graceful note of thanks.

There were also memories that were not so pleasant. Some of the annoyances were to be expected and had to be accepted as acts of God. Of this kind was malarial fever, which incapacitated many of his soldiers every year. In the summer of 1794, for example, Colonel England informed Lieutenant Governor Simcoe that "we have at present a hundred & twenty on our sick list." But the civilians also were stricken, and there was little that could be done about it.

Probably in the same category was the gradual decay of the Fort and the stockade under the continuous barrage of their only active enemies, time and weather. The condition was chronic. Officers of the Royal Engineers surveyed the defenses at various times and invariably found some parts in a ruinous state. In the fall of 1793 Colonel England reported a long list of damages that required attention. A later report by the Commandant shows that some repairs were made during the spring and summer of 1794.

Another source of irritation was the Indian Department. The officers were often overzealous in their desire to aid the savages. There were several reasons for this attitude. One was that officials like Alexander McKee, Matthew Elliot, and Simon Girty, loyalists who had fled from persecution at the

[4] *The Baltimore Federal Gazette & Daily Advertiser*, Friday, September 16, 1796. Copied from the *Quebec Gazette*, August 25, 1796.

time of the Revolutionary War, were able, by assisting the Indians, to satisfy in some measure their hatred for the Americans. This bitterness made them willing to believe their former fellow countrymen capable of the basest kind of treachery toward the natives. Writing in 1796 to the Secretary of Indian Affairs at Montreal, Colonel McKee declared: "A great proportion of the Chiefs who attended that meeting [Wayne's conference at Greenville], have died very suddenly and were probably poisoned by some of their own people who disapproved of the Treaty, tho' it is generally said they were poisoned at Fort Greenville where the treaty was held."

A few months later McKee expressed the fear that "small Pox may be introduced among the Indians, soon after the evacuation of the Posts." There was no foundation whatever for his suspicion. It is true that smallpox had once been considered as a means of exterminating the Indians, but it was not an American who made the suggestion. It was the British commander in chief, Lord Jeffrey Amherst, who had inquired of Colonel Henry Bouquet at Fort Pitt, in 1763, whether they could be inoculated with the disease. Bouquet had answered that infected blankets sent to the Indians might accomplish the desired result, but the project was not carried out.[5]

McKee's "fear" in this case was entirely the result of prejudice. Although there were many frontiersmen who regarded the Indian only as dangerous vermin which should be destroyed, General Wayne and the responsible officials of the Government at Philadelphia would never have sanctioned such a scheme.

There were also, undoubtedly, in the zeal of the agents to protect the savages, a genuine friendship for them and resentment engendered by their misfortunes. These men had lived among the natives so long that they had come to identify the interests of the red men with their own. And, indeed, they had much in common. The officers of the Indian Department were usually engaged in trade. Their positions gave them special advantages with the natives, but attacks by the Americans were often ruinous. In August, 1794, for instance, McKee's store on the Maumee was destroyed by Wayne's army. Furthermore, some of the agents had Indian wives or mistresses,

---

[5] Francis Parkman, *Conspiracy of Pontiac* (Boston, 1890), II, 39–40.

and their very jobs depended upon their ability to make the Government realize the importance of their services.[6]

The Indian officers believed also that the Commandant should grant their requests for provisions and presents for their wards to any amount. Although Colonel England was usually able to maintain good relations with these men, his attempt to exercise strict economy, according to orders, involved him in controversies with McKee, Elliot, and Prideaux Selby, assistant secretary of Indian Affairs at Detroit. Apparently, the only way to live comfortably with these officials was to let them do as they pleased.

3

All these troubles of Colonel England, however, were of little moment compared with those brought upon him by General Wayne. Nicknamed "Mad Anthony" because of his impetuous daring in the Revolutionary War, Wayne found that his appointment by President Washington to command the army intended to crush the Indian menace in the West caused some hostile criticism. The President, however, embittered by the defeat of General Josiah Harmar in 1790, and the rout of General Arthur St. Clair in 1791, at the hands of the savages, chose the only man he thought capable of retrieving these disasters; and the results proved that his confidence was not misplaced.

Contrary to his earlier reputation, this time Wayne was extremely patient. Taking command of an undisciplined force at Pittsburgh in June, 1792, he advanced with impressive deliberation down the Ohio River to Cincinnati, then north through the present state of Ohio, building forts, drilling his men, and literally whipping them into a first-class fighting machine. Penalties of twenty-five, fifty, or one hundred lashes on the bare back for breaches of discipline are numerous in the court-martial proceedings recorded in his order book.

---

[6] Captain Hector McLean to Major James Green, August 27, 1799, *Michigan Pioneer and Historical Society Collections* (Lansing, 1888—), XII, 305. McLean wrote that Elliot and Prideaux Selby were trying "to impose a belief on Government that the Service of the former and his influence among the Indians may be supposed of too much consequence to be dispensed with." Also: "The whole of the officers of the Indian Department are indeed in some shape connected with this tribe [Shawnee] either by marriage or Concubinage...."

By the winter of 1793, he had reached a point eighty miles north of Cincinnati, where he built Fort Greenville[7] to serve as quarters for his army. Here he remained during the winter and into the summer of 1794, while supplies were being collected, waiting for mounted riflemen from Kentucky to join him.

The Indians, elated by the prediction on February 10, 1794, of Lord Dorchester, governor general of Canada, that Great Britain would soon be at war with the United States as the result of the westward advance of American settlers, assembled to resist General Wayne's advance. Colonel McKee and other officials of the British Indian Department obtained arms for them and directed raiding parties into the region occupied by the invading army.

Fearing that Wayne was aiming at Detroit as his principal objective, Dorchester authorized Lieutenant Governor Simcoe to build a fort on the Maumee River. Although Henry Dundas, British Secretary of State for War, disapproved of this action as a dangerous provocation to a war which his government was anxious to avoid, Fort Miamis was constructed during the spring and summer of 1794 and garrisoned with troops from Detroit. The Indian agents told the Indians that it was a token of their British "Father's" interest in their welfare. These officials knew that the savages had been discouraged by Wayne's relentless march through their country, and that concrete evidence of British support was required to retain their allegiance.

Colonel McKee and his aides mustered a force of more than fifteen hundred Ottawa, Chippewa, Potawatomi, Wyandot, Miami, Shawnee, and Delaware braves near Fort Miamis to block the advance of the Americans. In addition, there were seventy militiamen from Detroit and the vicinity commanded by Captain William Caldwell.

On August 20, 1794, General Wayne with about three thousand men attacked this force, which had taken up a position among a tangle of tornado-felled trees at the foot of the rapids of the Maumee. His infantry and cavalry routed the savages

---

[7] Wayne named the fort for the late General Nathanael Greene. Wayne always spelled it "Greeneville." Others, however, usually omitted the *e*; and the name of the town now occupying the site is spelled without it.

from their lair, driving them back to Fort Miamis and beyond, in the decisive battle of Fallen Timbers. In obedience to orders Major William Campbell, commander of the fort, sent no aid, nor did he open its gates to the fleeing tribesmen; and when the Americans ranged over the immediate vicinity, destroying storehouses and Indian crops, he remained steadfastly behind his palisade. McKee, Elliot, and Girty "were in the field, but at a respectful distance, and near the river," according to Antoine Lasselle, a captured volunteer from Detroit. On that day these men, who had labored so earnestly to keep the Indians on the warpath, saw all their work undone. The refusal of Major Campbell to support the savages, or even to give them shelter from the victorious Americans, taught them that their faith in the British had been futile.

To Detroit fled the surviving militiamen and swarms of Indians with news of the defeat. Colonel England expected Wayne to continue his advance. The situation was serious. The Commandant knew the mercurial nature of the savages and of his French Canadians as well. Besides, the defenses were not in first-class condition, in spite of repairs that had been made during the summer, one hundred and twenty of his soldiers were ill, and the militia was mutinous.

This latter condition simply reflected the general attitude of the people, who apparently preferred American rule to a bloody war. For example, when Colonel England charged Jean Baptiste Chapoton with encouraging disaffection among the militia, and had him prosecuted by the attorney general before Judge William Dummer Powell for sedition, the jury promptly found Chapoton not guilty.

4

This, however, was only the first of a host of troubles which descended upon Colonel England like a plague of locusts. A short while after Wayne's victory rumors of an impending evacuation of Detroit began to circulate. The merchants in the town were worried by warnings from their London and their Montreal correspondents that the troops would soon be withdrawn.

The principal reason for holding Detroit and the other frontier posts on American soil had been the desire to aid the powerful Montreal fur traders and their London agents, who had asked for at least enough time to reorganize their business there, and they were vigorously supported by the officers of the Indian Department.

In spite of pleas to hold on, the British Government finally decided to evacuate. Several important factors united to force this decision. Among them were the declining price of furs, the expense of maintaining garrisons, the necessity of concentrating all resources for the prosecution of the war against revolutionary France, and the victorious march of General Wayne, which showed that the United States was now capable of taking the posts by force. Consequently, when John Jay negotiated a commercial treaty with the British Government in 1794, he had no difficulty in securing an article that provided for the evacuation of the posts.

The rumors of evacuation made Colonel England's position more difficult than ever. Although he had no direct notice of the relinquishment, he could be certain that it would occur. In the meantime he must maintain his authority in Detroit and in the surrounding country. This was a disheartening task, for disaffection seemed to have overrun the whole region.

At the River Raisin settlement, now Monroe, Michigan, there arrived in 1794 the Reverend Edmund Burke, Catholic vicar-general of Upper Canada and political emissary of the British Government to the Canadians and the Indians. He found that his ability to influence either was very slight. In letter after letter to the authorities he attacked individuals for disloyalty. Probably the priest was overzealous, and his charges were extreme; but Colonel England also bitterly accused some of the leading subjects of secret correspondence with the enemy.[8]

[8] The correspondence of Father Burke and Colonel England about the activities of the disaffected subjects is printed in E. A. Cruikshank (ed.), *The Correspondence of Lieutenant-Governor John Graves Simcoe* (Toronto, 1926), IV, 26, 27, 44, 62, 63, and 72. *Mich. Pio. and Hist. Soc. Colls.*, XII, 160, 162, 166, 169, and 171, contain further correspondence on the same subject.

Father Burke was sent by Bishop Jean François Hubert at the request of Lord Dorchester to counteract the influence of Father Thomas Le Dru, a Dominican who had been a missionary in the Illinois country. In the spring of 1794, he appeared on the River Raisin and urged the people to support the American cause. Obeying an order of Lord Dorchester, Colonel England arrested the priest, and he was deported to the United States. Cruikshank, *op. cit.*, II, 292, 361, 416; III, 90, 96, 140; IV, 20.

In August, 1795, Father Burke wrote that "the few seemingly good subjects veered about with the wind on the first surmise of the evacuation of their Posts." This was, of course, an exaggeration; but there was enough truth in it to suggest the difficult position of the harassed Commandant. For fur traders such as François Navarre, George McDougall, and Antoine Lasselle; petty Government officials such as Patrick McNiff, until recently deputy-surveyor, and John Askwith, clerk of the district court; and even William Macomb, a member of the assembly of Upper Canada and owner of Belle Isle, Grosse Ile, and a great deal of other property in and about Detroit, now showed an unmistakable desire to appease the Americans.

Against these men the angry priest made specific charges, some of which are supported by other evidence. George McDougall, he asserted, had hired a brace of Indians to murder Matthew Elliot, Indian agent, and Adam Brown, a white chief of the Wyandots. He said he had seen Brown, "his rifle in his hand and his Tomahawk under his belt standing on his defence least he should be surprised by the Assassin. Whilst McDougall swaggered away in Detroit amongst his friends threatening to prosecute according to law any man who would dare to defame him." The magistrates, Burke insisted, were in league with the Yankees, and he urged that Colonel England declare martial law to protect the loyal subjects. According to the priest, when the Wyandots had forced the hired assassins to confess, they pursued McDougall "in almost every direction," and he fled to the American fort at Greenville for protection.

William Macomb was stigmatized as "a staunch friend to Congress" by the embittered priest. On him was cast the blame for interfering with an Indian council that otherwise would have favored Great Britain.

Burke also attacked François Navarre, McDougall's cousin, who lived at the River Raisin settlement. He charged him with leading the Indians away from British control and with favoring the Americans; "that peasant's impudence deprives me of all patience," he wrote, during the spring of 1795. There was also a group of lesser persons who plagued the priest, the Indian agents, and the Commandant with their activities among the savages.

After his victory of Fallen Timbers General Wayne retired

to Greenville, confident that he had broken the military power of the Indians. But he was anxious to complete his work in the West by negotiating a comprehensive treaty with all the tribes of the region. His problem was to engage men who could persuade the chiefs to go to a conference; and it was among the French Canadians in the vicinity of Detroit that he found some of his emissaries.

Antoine Lasselle, who, disguised as an Indian, had been captured at the battle of Fallen Timbers and sentenced to be shot as a spy, owed his life to a plea by Colonel Hamtramck. Now he repaid his captors for their mercy by taking Jean Baptiste Romain *dit* Sans Crainte and François Pepin to Wayne. Sans Crainte, some time later, after a few drinks, boasted in Detroit that he was being paid two dollars a day to induce the Indians to attend a council in June. He even showed Alexander McKenzie, an interpreter in the Indian Department, the speech which Wayne had entrusted to him. Lasselle also enlisted his nephew, Jacques, in the service of the Americans. Jacques, whose wife was a daughter of Blue Jacket, brought that powerful Shawnee chief to Wayne's assistance. His influence, which reached far beyond the villages of his own people, induced many chiefs to go and treat with Wayne.

There were others involved in this traffic; so many, apparently, that McKee wrote: "The Canadians are not at present to be relied on, and their busy interference, as well as that of some natural born subjects, with the Indians, presents to my mind nothing but confusion and trouble." But McDougall, Navarre, Macomb, François La Fontaine, the Lasselles, Sans Crainte, and Pepin seem to have been most active. The last two especially irritated the Reverend Edmund Burke when they intercepted a letter he had written to the Potawatomi and appended a postscript declaring him to be "neither a Frenchman nor a Priest but a rascal who is chosen by the English to deceive you & blind you as McKee has always done." Gaining possession of the note somehow or other, Burke, in a rage, sent a copy of it to Colonel McKee as an example of how the Canadians defamed loyal servants of the King.

5

Colonel England was in a very difficult position. Responsible to his government for the safety of his post, he could do nothing effective to prevent the increase of disloyalty. He could not control the civil authorities, some of whom were reported to be in league with the Yankees, and his superiors would hardly have sanctioned a resort to martial law.

The Commandant must have reflected bitterly on the inconstancy of man: his soldiers were deserting, the militia was worse than useless, civil officers were faithless to their King, and even his personal friends, among many others, were so eager to add to their land holdings that they were sending emissaries to General Wayne to beg that huge grants recently acquired from the Indians be confirmed.

Under British rule lands could be purchased from the savages only by the inspector general of Indian affairs, by his deputy, or by someone else especially commissioned by the commander in chief. Although the leading merchants in Detroit were undoubtedly acquainted with this regulation, perhaps they felt themselves released from its restrictions during the present interregnum. There was also an American statute which forbade the purchase of land by individuals; but British subjects may well have been ignorant of its existence.

However that may have been, the traffic in Indian land assumed gigantic proportions during the years 1795 and 1796. John Askin, John Dodemead, Patrick McNiff, Robert McNiff, John Kinzie, William Forsyth, Jr., and John Askwith "obtained the Indian cession of a million acres of land on the Maumee River, embracing the site of the present city of Toledo."[9] About this transaction and the intention of Patrick McNiff and John Askwith to go to Greenville to treat with General Wayne, Colonel England wrote angrily to Lieutenant Governor Simcoe in June, 1795. He was especially irritated by the attitude of these two envoys of the group; but he withheld the name of his good friend John Askin, not even mentioning him as one of the speculators.

This attempted coup, however, was only the beginning. The principals in this affair, with several other men, secured from the natives title to that part of northern Ohio lying between the present city of Cleveland and Sandusky Bay. This was known as the Cuyahoga Purchase.[10]

[9] M. M. Quaife, "Detroit Biographies: John Askwith," *Burton Historical Collection Leaflet*, VII, 53.

[10] The original grant of the Cuyahoga tract is in the Burton Historical Collection.

A still more audacious scheme was the attempt, in 1795, to purchase the entire Lower Peninsula of Michigan for half a million dollars before the United States took possession. John Askin and several associates agreed with Ebenezer Allen and Charles Whitney of Vermont, and Robert Randall of Pennsylvania, to acquire the land from the Indians. The Americans attempted to bribe members of Congress to pass a bill legalizing the enterprise. When the proposals of these men were denounced by a Representative who had been approached, the whole scheme fell through. Whitney and Randall were arrested; but no blame in the affair was imputed to Askin and the other Detroiters.

Among the white men from Detroit who accompanied the Indians to Greenville was John Askin, Jr., who went at the request of the Ottawa and Chippewa to protect their interests. His father advised him in a letter to take care that the Indians were not induced to relinquish control of their lands. These, he wrote, would be "a future Source of wealth for these poor people." Besides, recognition of their ownership would insure the confirmation of grants already made and leave with them resources which they could later use to "reward such others as have been their friends."

This letter, which John Askin, Sr., entrusted to George McDougall for delivery to his son, never reached him. On the way to the conference he was overtaken and passed by McDougall, who had previously threatened to inform the Americans that Askin had fought against them at the battle of Fallen Timbers. Making no mention of the letter he carried, McDougall hastened on to Greenville, where he handed it to General Wayne. The latter ordered young Askin to headquarters, confronted him with the letter, and then had him confined in Fort Jefferson for the duration of the negotiations. Consequently he could do nothing for the Indians or for his associates.

Patrick McNiff, John Askwith, and Israel Ruland, three of the speculators, set out for Greenville to have the Cuyahoga Purchase confirmed. Colonel Hamtramck stopped them at Fort Wayne. Although McNiff insisted that he was eager to serve General Wayne, and displayed surveys of the water communications from the Maumee River to Lake Huron and of Fort Lernoult and the town of Detroit which he intended to present to the Commander in Chief, Hamtramck was suspicious of the ex-surveyor who had turned against the government which had removed him from office. The Colonel charged that "the privation of fifteen shillings Halifax money per day has induced him to Change his Coat," and asserted that "this is the total amount of the patriotism of that Gentleman," but added an underlined qualification, *that is, if we have a right to draw Conclusions from Circumstances.*"

General Wayne, nevertheless, received McNiff and accepted the proffered maps.[11] McNiff gave the General an alphabet of cabalistic characters representing such names as England, Detroit, McKee, Elliot, and Simcoe to be used in secret correspondence. In spite of his eagerness to be of service to the Americans, McNiff was unable to obtain a confirmation of the Cuyahoga Purchase. He and his two companions wrote to Alexander Henry of their failure and named him attorney for the whole group to bring the matter before Congress.

Henry was likewise unsuccessful. He then asked Alexander Hamilton for his opinion as a lawyer. It was, in brief, that the Indian deeds were invalid because, by a statute of the United States, no private person could acquire land from the savages either as a gift or by purchase. "We have lost a fortune of at least one Million of Dollars," wrote the disappointed speculator to his partners.

6

The emissaries of Wayne from Detroit and the vicinity—Lasselle, Sans Crainte, Pepin, and the rest—had their way with the Indians. During the fall and winter of 1794-95 tribe after tribe sent delegations to Greenville, where they agreed to assemble for a treaty the following summer. As late as the middle of June, 1795, Hamtramck wrote that McKee was still trying

---

[11] Wayne sent the map of Fort Lernoult and Detroit to Secretary of War James McHenry. He ordered the Quartermaster General to pay McNiff $100 for these or other maps in November, 1796. The order and the receipt are in the William L. Clements Library, University of Michigan.

A large map showing the farms on the American side of the Detroit River with the names of the owners, which McNiff drew in the fall of 1796, by order of General Wayne, was sold at public auction in May, 1944, with some James McHenry papers, among which it had been found. It was later purchased by the William L. Clements Library and published in 1946 under the title *Patrick McNiff's Plan of the Settlements at Detroit, 1796.*

to keep the Indians from the council; but as the American Colonel aptly phrased it, "the Bayonet of the 20th of August last Embarrasses him." During June and July chiefs and warriors straggled into the fort, and protracted negotiations ensued.

The Treaty of Greenville, August 3, 1795, was signed by General Wayne and other officers on behalf of the United States, and by chiefs of the Wyandots, Delawares, Shawnee, Ottawa, Chippewa, Potawatomi, Miami, and Wea— the tribes that had been warring against the American Government. They agreed to return all prisoners and to cede to the United States most of the present state of Ohio, and part of southeastern Indiana, with a number of enclaves including "The post of Detroit and all the land to the north, the west and the south of it, of which the Indian title has been extinguished by gifts or grants to the French or English governments. . . ." As compensation they received on the spot goods worth $20,000 and the promise of an annual distribution of goods to the value of $9,500, "forever."

This treaty "brought to an end forty years of warfare in the valley of the Ohio, during which it is estimated five thousand whites were killed or captured. For three years past the war had cost the Government of the United States over a million dollars a year. The peace which Wayne brought to the frontier endured for fifteen years. . . ."[12]

The men who had made the initial arrangements with the Indians for concluding the treaty participated in the final act. Among the names signed to the document appear those of the Lasselles, Sans Crainte, and Pepin. Others from Detroit and the vicinity who also signed were: François Navarre, François La Fontaine, Jean Baptiste Beaubien, and Louis Beaufait.

[12] M. M. Quaife, *Chicago and the Old Northwest, 1763-1835* (Chicago, 1913), p. 125.

CHAPTER II

UNDER THE AMERICAN FLAG

FROM June 6 to July 7, 1796, Colonel Hamtramck remained in his camp on the left bank of the Maumee River, awaiting orders to advance to Detroit and means to transport his expeditionary force. The delay this time was the fault of the Government of the United States. In spite of the tension along the border the British Government in London and its agents in Canada and in the United States had coöperated cordially with the Americans in arranging for the abandonment of the posts. In May Lord Dorchester had offered to order an immediate evacuation. Captain Lewis, however, who had gone to Quebec to receive the documents which the American officers commanding the occupying forces were to present to the British commandants, asked him for time to permit the United States troops to prepare for the advance. Further delay was caused by the failure of James McHenry, Secretary of War, to forward these papers at once. It was not until June 28 that he sent them "by express" from Philadelphia.

Finally, on July 7, two small ships from Detroit arrived at the camp on the Maumee. They were the schooners which Captain De Butts had chartered: the *Weazell*, Captain Louis Derineau, master, and the *Swan*, under the command of Captain Joseph May, brother of the owner. The first was a ship of sixteen tons burden and carried a crew of three. The other was probably of about the same size, for she also carried three men.

On these two schooners Colonel Hamtramck embarked sixty-five men commanded by Captain Moses Porter of the artillery, an officer who had served during the War for Independence, from the battle of Bunker Hill to the end of the conflict. Now he would have the honor of leading the first American troops into Fort Lernoult.

Carrying ammunition and cannon for arming the fort, the little vessels sailed down the Maumee River past Fort Miamis, still occupied by Captain Shortt and his British regulars, out into Lake Erie and northward toward their destination, a two days' sail, if wind and weather favored.

A short while after they had entered the mouth of the Detroit River a number of wooded islands loomed ahead as if to block their passage. The most notable were Grosse Ile, reaching far up the river, and, by its side, the smaller Bois Blanc. On the eastern bank of the river stood a few traders' houses, the beginning of the present town of Amherstburg. A little way above, a blockhouse appeared, with red-coated guards on duty. Soldiers were still engaged in erecting ramparts and other works of Fort Malden.

On Bois Blanc Island, popularly known today as Bob-Lo, there were a small blockhouse and a detachment of British troops. Suspicious of the Yankees to the end, Lieutenant Governor Simcoe had warned Lord Dorchester that they might seize this island on their passage. The Commander in Chief expressed the opinion that the United States would carry out the terms of the Jay Treaty in good faith. Nevertheless, to humor Simcoe he ordered a sergeant and eight men stationed there as a guard.

The *Weazell* and the *Swan* sailed ever northward between low-lying meadows rank with rushes and marsh grass. Gradually the river banks began to rise, and houses appeared. On both sides of the stream they became more and more numerous and stood so close together that now it seemed as if the stream were bordered by two continuous villages.

To the American soldiers this was a strange new world into which they were silently intruding. Everything looked different from the scenes to which they were accustomed. The houses, built of wood, had steeply sloping roofs into which one or two dormer windows were set. All of them faced upon the river and each had a picket fence in front.

Behind the houses there were orchards of peach and apple trees, and the narrow fields of nearly ripened wheat or of half-grown Indian corn stretched back to the virgin forest beyond. These slender French farms, often only four or five hundred feet in width, each with its front on the river bank, or rather, just back of the river road, were unlike the isolated clearings in the woods with which the Americans were familiar. In Ohio, or Kentucky, or in western Pennsylvania the nearest neighbors might be miles away. Here they fairly touched elbows.

There were other strange sights, too. Here and there along the shore appeared windmills, the base of stone, the upper part of wood surmounted by a conical shingled roof, their long gaunt spars with white flapping sails revolving slowly in the breeze to turn the stone that ground the grain. Sometimes, when the ships edged in near shore, a wayside shrine was visible—a tall weather-beaten cross by the side of the road, or a gaunt crucifix.

And now, on the left, the Americans could see the banner of Great Britain waving above the ramparts of Fort Lernoult, which overlooked the close-ranged roof tops of the town below. The western wall of palisades reaching from the southwest angle of the Fort, the blockhouse over the open West Gate, the long Government wharf, the shorter merchants' wharf with the water blockhouse between, and ships at anchor in front of the town—all were now plainly spread before their curious eyes.

2

When Captain Porter landed at Detroit on July 11, 1796, he carried no copy of Lord Dorchester's order for the evacuation; for the one sent by Secretary McHenry was still on the way. In fact, it reached General Wayne at Greenville only on July 16.[1] Colonel England, apparently, felt that it was not necessary. Undoubtedly Captain De Butts had already inspected the Fort and the other public works and had signed the required report.

Since Colonel England had long been awaiting the arrival of the Americans, he needed little time to arrange for the embarkation of his troops, and when they marched down to their transports, Captain Porter's little army of occupation was ready to enter Fort Lernoult.

Captain De Butts, who witnessed the transfer of sovereignty, described it simply: "... on the 11th inst. about noon,

[1] Wayne to McHenry, July 22, Wayne Papers, 45, 23, Hist. Soc. of Pa., Phila.

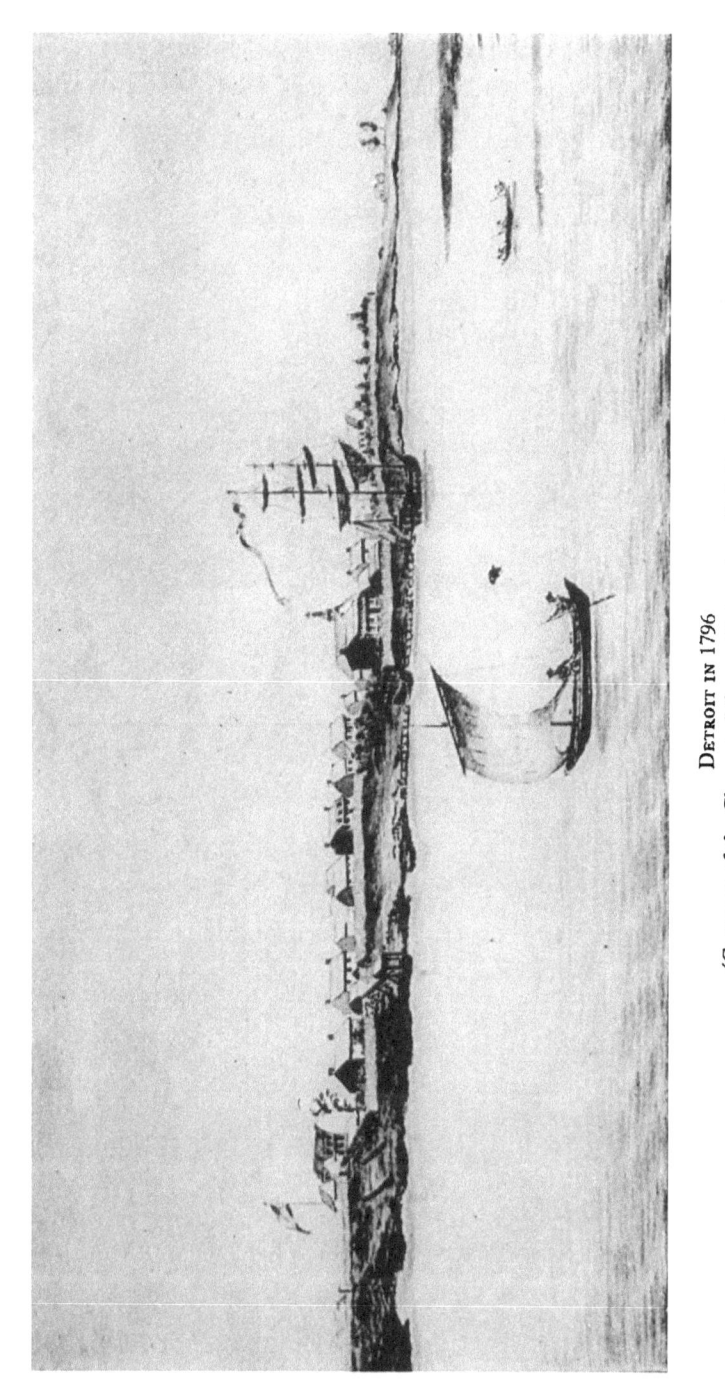

DETROIT IN 1796
(Courtesy of the Clements Library, University of Michigan)

the flag of the United States was displayed on the ramparts of Detroit, a few minutes after the works were evacuated by Col. England and the British troops under his command, and with additional satisfaction I inform you that the exchange was effected with much propriety and harmony by both parties."[2] He reported that "every attention was paid by the British and inhabitants to our troops."[3]

3

On Wednesday, July 13, Colonel John Francis Hamtramck arrived with the remainder of his force. The sloop *Detroit*, commanded by Captain Peter Curry, had reached Swan Creek on the Maumee on July 9; and two days later the British evacuated Fort Miamis. Leaving a garrison there of fifty-nine soldiers under Captain Andrew Marschalk, Colonel Hamtramck embarked his men and supplies on eleven bateaux and the sloop, and sailed for Detroit.

The arrival of the Colonel with the main body of troops now gave the post a respectable force of about four hundred men. They were housed in the barracks of the Fort and of the Citadel, and the Commandant established his headquarters within the latter enclosure. Unlike Colonel England, his predecessor, he had no family with him. His wife had died less than two months before, while she was traveling from Fort Wayne to visit her parents at Vincennes. Two small daughters, Julienne, not yet four years old, and a younger one named Henriette, were left to the care of their father, but they did not accompany him.

The inhabitants of Detroit must have been surprised at the appearance of the new commandant. Accustomed to the huge

[2] Extract of a letter from De Butts to Secretary McHenry, July 14, 1796, in *The Gazette of the United States, & Philadelphia Daily Advertiser*, August 12, 1796.

[3] *Kentucky Gazette*, August 27, 1796.

Captain De Butts' statement is supported by General Wayne's letter to Secretary McHenry, September 29, 1796. Wayne Papers, 46, 86, Hist. Soc. of Pa., Phila. (See below, p. 49.) Nevertheless, most of the histories of Michigan and of Detroit contain an account of the destruction of public property by the British before they left.

The story first appeared in James H. Lanman, *History of Michigan* (New York, 1839), p. 167. The author wrote: "The posts of Mackinaw and Detroit were evacuated after the wells of the latter station had been filled with stones, the windows broken, the gates of the fort locked, and the keys deposited with an aged negro, in whose possession they were afterwards found."

bulk of Colonel England, they were probably disappointed by the diminutive figure of the man who now replaced him at the Fort.[4] Colonel Hamtramck was only five feet five inches tall, but, to compensate for his slight stature, he had vigor and years of experience. A peppery temper and an imperious manner kept his subordinates attentive to their duties. Severe in discipline but ready to recognize merit, he was loyally supported by his officers.

Born in Quebec in 1756, Hamtramck was the son of a native of Luxemburg who had emigrated to Canada in 1749. When the Revolutionary War began, John Francis left his native land and espoused the cause of the Americans. He joined Montgomery's army in the fall of 1775, and he was a captain in the Fifth New York Regiment in November, 1776. After having fought throughout the war, he became one of the officers of the tiny army which was maintained after the Treaty of Paris.

Hamtramck was promoted to the rank of major on October 20, 1786. Serving under General Josiah Harmar in the Ohio country, he built Fort Knox at Vincennes in 1787. There he married Marie Edeline Perrot, widow of the late Nicholas Perrot, a merchant of the town. On February 18, 1793, he was commissioned lieutenant colonel and given command of the First Sub-legion. General Wayne cited Hamtramck for personal bravery and for inspiring his men in action at the battle of Fallen Timbers. During the autumn of 1794 he built Fort Wayne and was in charge there until May, 1796, when he advanced to take possession of the posts about to be evacuated by the British. Canadian by birth and Roman Catholic in faith, Hamtramck was well qualified to command at Detroit.

4

The Citadel, in which the Colonel established his headquarters, was an area enclosed by palisades of oak posts ten or eleven feet high. The southern line of pickets ran along the north side of Ste Anne Street from Lernoult Street to the western wall of the town, which formed a side of the enclosure. The eastern line of pickets extended along Lernoult Street north

---

[4] Hamtramck was nicknamed *Le Crapaud à cheval* ("The Frog on Horseback") because of "his singular appearance when riding." Louise Rau, manuscript biographical sketch of Hamtramck (1933), p. 11, Burton Hist. Coll., Detroit.

to Savoyard Creek. Within these palisades there were two-story barracks for officers and soldiers, a guardhouse, the hospital, and the commissary provision store surrounding an open square which served as a parade ground. As the two western bastions of the town were within this area, troops were always at hand to man them in case of attack.

Colonel Hamtramck inspected the defenses of his new post at the first opportunity. The Fort, of course, was of primary importance. To reach it from his quarters in the Citadel he took Lernoult Street and, proceeding north, crossed Savoyard Creek by a bridge, skirting the Grand Parade to his right. Before him bristled the abattis—felled trees with the sharpened branches pointing outward—protruding from the earthen bank of the glacis, the most advanced defensive work. Both the abattis and the glacis were in great need of repair because of neglect, and damage caused by the weather.

Through an opening in the glacis the Colonel reached the ditch before the rampart. Rains had washed earth into it from the inner face of the glacis and from the outer face of the rampart, so that it was too shallow to be of much service for defense. In the middle of the ditch stood a palisade of logs about nine feet high. These were badly decayed, and some of them had fallen from their places. Beyond rose the rampart, which faced toward the river. Halfway up the slope was a fraise of pointed stakes driven horizontally into the earth. At the top the parapet was notched with embrasures, from which the muzzles of newly planted cannon grimly surveyed the river and the town. Hamtramck crossed the ditch on a bridge and entered the Fort through the main gate, which was surmounted by a blockhouse.

Within there were wooden barracks for officers and men, and shops for the armorer, the baker, and the carpenter. By means of a ladder Hamtramck ascended the inside slope of the south rampart to the banquette behind the parapet. From this point of vantage he could look across the river and follow its course for some distance in both directions; and the village lay just below in perfect detail.

The Commandant must have been impressed by the view. What he thought of the town and its surrounding country is nowhere recorded; but others had described the settlement and its environs in glowing terms. Father Pierre Jean de Bonnecamps, who was there in 1749 with Céloron, wrote: "... its situation appeared to me charming. A beautiful river runs at the foot of the fort; vast plains, which only ask to be cultivated extend beyond the sight." Nearly forty years later Major Robert Matthews, lieutenant governor at Detroit, thus expressed his aversion to abandoning the place: "Had Mr. Oswald, or even Lord Lansdane [Lord Shelburne, Marquis of Landsdowne] seen this delightful settlement, they surely never could have signed away the right of the nation to it. In point of climate, soil, situation & the beauties of nature, nothing can exceed it."[5]

The gazetteers of the period were unanimous in asserting that "Its situation is delightful, and in the centre of a pleasant and fruitful country." This was also the first impression of Dr. Charles Brown, surgeon of the regiment of artillerists and engineers, who arrived with the first American troops. To a friend in Philadelphia he wrote that "the country is beautiful & healthy."

Looking out from his position on the south rampart of the Fort, Colonel Hamtramck surveyed the panorama that lay before him. On the Canadian shore directly opposite, narrow French farms reached back to the woods. On the river all sorts of craft—sloops, schooners, bateaux, pirogues, and canoes—lay quietly at anchor or passed up and down. Just below was the town encircled by its defenses, which appeared as an irregular hexagon, the palisade along the river bank forming the longest side. It was pierced by two gates leading to the wharves, which were guarded by the water blockhouse between them. At each extremity of the palisade, raised above the pickets, a water battery completed the defensive works of the river front.

The shortest side of the hexagon was the south rampart of the Fort. From the salient angles at its extremities the east wall and the west wall of palisades reached away in a southeasterly and a southwesterly direction respectively; then, to form the fifth and sixth sides of the hexagon, each, with a dog's-

---

[5] Oswald was the British agent who negotiated the Treaty of 1783; Shelburne was Prime Minister.
This quotation is from a letter to General Frederick Haldimand, August 3, 1787, *Mich. Pio. and Hist. Soc. Colls.*, 26, 287. Haldimand was governor general of Quebec.

leg angle, turned south to meet the ends of the river wall at the water batteries. Two blockhouses guarded each of these long lines of pickets between the Fort and the river; and cannon mounted on the parapet commanded the river, the town, and the adjacent countryside.

Beyond the palisades, to the east, Isle aux Cochons (Belle Isle) with its dense forest stood in the strait, dividing its waters in two. Along the shore the River Road stretched away past the Côte du Nord-Est[6] and the Grand Marais to Grosse Pointe. About a mile and a half from the Fort, Hamtramck could see Parent's Creek spanned by Bloody Bridge, the site of Captain Dalyell's disastrous encounter with Pontiac's braves in the early morning of July 31, 1763. Behind the road the ribbon farms, enclosed by high picket fences, stood side by side, the farmhouses nestling in their gardens and orchards seeming to form half of a village street. Between the nearest farm and the eastern palisade an open space extended from the woods to the river. This was the Common; and at the foot of it, on the river bank, were the shipyard with its sail loft and the artificers' yard surrounded by a line of pickets.

To the west the River Road, between the edge of the high bank and the close-set farmhouses, led from the gate of the town along the Côte du Sud-Ouest toward the settlements at River Rouge and the River Raisin. Just outside the wall a narrow wagon track branched off to the left and sidled down the steep slope to the beach at the water's edge.

From his point of vantage Colonel Hamtramck could look down upon the roof tops of the village entrusted to his care. Lying cramped within the circuit of the palisades on three sides and Savoyard Creek on the fourth, its houses—there were fewer than a hundred of them[7]— along with stores, sheds, stables, warehouses, and some public buildings, appeared as groups of rectangular masses set off by unequally spaced streets. Ste Anne Street was the principal thoroughfare. It was a contin-

[6] This was the name given by the *habitants* to the region east of the town. The region west of the town was called the Côte du Sud-Ouest.

[7] The number of houses in Detroit was said by various writers to be 100, 150, or 300. A report drawn up by Patrick McNiff on August 19, 1796, for Acting Governor Winthrop Sargent, however, gives the number of dwelling houses as 72. He also listed 77 stores and gave the total number of privately owned buildings as 149. Winthrop Sargent Papers, August 19, 1796, Ohio State Archaeological and Historical Society, Columbus.

uation of the River Road, which entered at the West Gate and continued through the Pontiac Gate in the eastern palisade. Within the walls there were buildings on both sides instead of on only one. It was only about twenty feet wide; the other streets were narrower. South of Ste Anne, St. Louis ran parallel with it; and to the north St. Jacques and St. Joseph completed the tale of east and west streets.

Leading north from the water blockhouse, St. Honoré Street cut through the center of the town and reached the Savoyard, where a bridge connected it with a path that angled to the left and led to the Fort. To the east Campau Alley, or St. Antoine Street, ran north from the merchants' wharf to the creek; and to the west Lernoult Street stretched from the Government wharf north to the Savoyard, where a bridge across the stream joined it with a road along the west side of the Esplanade that reached to the Fort. Between St. Honoré and Lernoult streets, and parallel to them, McDougall Alley extended from the river wall to St. Jacques Street. Just within the circuit of the palisades an open space called Le Chemin du Ronde gave room for defending troops to move from point to point inside the walls and served as a terminal communication for the several streets.

Among the buildings of the town Ste Anne's Church was the most conspicuous. Not far inside the Pontiac Gate and on the north side of Ste Anne Street, it stood almost surrounded by the cemetery. Just beyond and across the street was the commanding officer's garden, with tree-lined walks and formal garden beds. A vacant space in it marked the site of the governor's house, which had been destroyed by fire. In the southwest corner of this area, in the angle formed by Campau Alley and Le Chemin du Ronde, stood the Indian council house and the officers' mess.

At the other end of Ste Anne Street the buildings of the Citadel dominated the scene. North of it and across the creek was the barrack master's garden, laid out as a parallelogram with diagonal walks meeting in a circle at the center. Next to the garden, and closer to the Fort, was the squat powder magazine of stone, its "arch turned by good English masons," connected by a subterranean passage with the ditch between the glacis and the rampart of the Fort. The Esplanade or parade ground north of the creek occupied a central position; and on the east the officers' mess garden, with its tree-lined paths, filled in the space between the east and the west walls above the town.

5

The Commandant was, of course, interested principally in the defenses and the public buildings entrusted to his charge. There were also, however, private residences, stores and taverns in the town, which, for a time at least, were his responsibility; and there were civilian residents with whom he would become more or less intimately acquainted.

As he rode through the narrow streets of the village to inspect the public buildings and to survey the exterior defense works, Colonel Hamtramck noticed many interesting details. The houses were "generally from One story to two stories & a half high—many of them well finished."[8] Some were "Frame buildings."[9] Others were "Built of Loggs & Covered with Boards of ab.ᵗ an Inch Thick, Cut at a Saw Mill."[10] The Commandant could not but be impressed by the superiority of these Detroit houses to those of the French at Vincennes, where he had formerly been stationed. There the walls were of hewn logs standing "erect with one end set well in the ground."[11] The first buildings in Detroit had been constructed in the same manner.

Many of the houses had porches that encroached on the narrow streets. The front doors were made in two sections, so that the upper half could be left open in warm weather, while the lower part kept out vagrant animals and prevented small children from straying. The windows were glazed with tiny panes of glass, and every house had an enormous chimney or two built of stone, or brick, or simply of sticks and clay.

The streets were dusty in dry weather. After a heavy rain

---

[8] Wayne to McHenry, Detroit, September 29, 1796, Wayne Papers, 46, 86, Hist. Soc. of Pa., Phila.

[9] *Ibid.*

[10] Beverley W. Bond, Jr. (ed.), "The Captivity of Charles Stuart, 1755-57," *Mississippi Valley Historical Review*, 13 (1926), 77.

Stuart, who thus described the houses, was in Detroit from April 27, 1756, to April 13, 1757.

[11] John Cleves Symmes to Robert Morris, June 22, 1790, Beverley W. Bond, Jr. (ed.), *The Correspondence of John Cleves Symmes* (New York, 1926), p. 287. Symmes was a judge in the Northwest Territory.

they were seas of mud. Then the half-wild horses of the *habitants* needed all their energy to draw a loaded cart into town. At the sides of most of the streets there were footways "of square logs, laid transversely close to each other."[12] Stables, open drains, the slaughterhouse at the water's edge just outside the western line of palisades, packs of raw furs, John Askin's tan yard operated by Jacob Clemens, and offal which had been carelessly thrown into the streets—all contributed to the racy odor of the summer air.[13] These smells were probably not noticed by the inhabitants, who were used to them; and they likewise accepted mosquitoes, flies, fleas, and other insects as pests which could not be escaped.[14]

The town was well supplied with hostelries where travelers might lodge and where convivial Detroiters could quench their thirst. Thomas Smith, James Donaldson, George Sharp, Matthew Dolson, and John Dodemead were tavern keepers. There were several large stores, most of them on Ste Anne Street, kept by Angus Mackintosh, George McDougall, Meldrum and Park, James Abbott, John Askin, William Robertson, and Joseph Campau. Sometimes the living quarters for the family were in the same buildings, at the back, or upstairs. These merchants dealt in a bewildering variety of commodities, for which they were more likely to be paid in skins and produce than in coin.

The people whom the Commandant passed on the streets were dressed like those he had known in Vincennes. It was the costume brought by the French from Lower Canada. The men wore brightly colored shirts, trousers supported by a

[12] Isaac Weld, Jr., *Travels through the States of North America, and the Provinces of Upper and Lower Canada, during the years 1795, 1796 and 1797* (London, 1807), II, 183.

[13] This condition was not peculiar to Detroit. The *Columbian Centinel*, Boston, August 20, 1796, contains a letter to the editor from "Amicus," who complains that "my nose and eyes are offended with the filth which is wantonly thrown into the streets.... Dead cats, dogs, hogs, old potatoes, & & rotting in the streets, undoubtedly generate more or less diseases...." New York at this time was badly paved, undrained, and foul. Conditions in Philadelphia, however, were better. Henry Adams, *History of the United States of America* (New York, 1921), I, 24. 25, 28.

[14] Jacob Lindley complained in 1793 of the flies by day and the fleas and bugs by night, in his "Account of a Journey to Attend the Indian Treaty, Proposed to be held at Sandusky in the Year 1793," in John and Isaac Comly (eds.), *Friends' Miscellany* (Philadelphia, 1832), II, 110.

leather belt or a cloth sash, and straw hats or colored handkerchiefs on their heads. Some wore moccasins instead of shoes, and many enjoyed the luxury of bare feet. The women wore short gowns reaching only to their knees, with petticoats to their ankles. Broad-brimmed straw hats protected their heads and faces from the sun. The important merchants and other gentry wore brocaded waistcoats, lace jabots, long-tailed coats, and breeches with buckles at the knee. Their hair was powdered and done up in a queue, or clubbed at the back. Ladies dressed in the style of London, a little late, perhaps, but authentic nevertheless.[15]

The population of Detroit at this time was probably about five hundred. As the figures given by men who were in the town in 1796 vary widely, it is impossible to know just how many there were. Whatever the exact number may have been, Detroit was only a village.[16] Nevertheless, it was cosmopolitan. There was not the narrow provincialism which usually characterized a frontier settlement. Established by express sanction of Louis XIV, it had always been an important post. The commandant, an officer of the King's army, maintained his miniature court; and the traders, through their agents, were in communication with Montreal, Quebec, and even Paris. Officials of Church or State visiting the place, or pausing on their journeys to more distant posts, brought with them some of the glamor of the Old World.

After the British occupation the military element was still of consequence; and Scottish merchants, vigorously pursuing their vocation, imported their own culture as well as merchandise. War and commerce attracted all sorts of people to

[15] Archange Meredith, daughter of John Askin, and the wife of a British army officer in England, included in her letters to her family details of the current London fashions. October 5, 1795; September 5, 1796; February 1, 1797, Askin Papers, Burton Hist. Coll., Detroit.

[16] Isaac Weld reported that Detroit contained "at least twelve hundred people." *Op. cit.*, II, 103. This figure probably included the farmers in the neighborhood.

Winthrop Sargent reported to General Anthony Wayne that there were only 290 men, women, and children in the town. Wayne Papers, 46, 95, Hist. Soc. of Pa., Phila. This figure seems to be too small. In a letter to the Secretary of State, Sargent wrote that more than 100 persons absent on "Voyages in Trade" were not included in his census. Clarence E. Carter (ed.), *The Territorial Papers of the United States* (Washington, 1936), III, 459.

Detroit. As Joseph Moore, a Quaker visitor from Philadelphia in 1793, remarked: "The inhabitants of the town are as great a mixture, I think, as ever I knew in any one place. English, Scotch, Irish, Dutch, French, Americans from different states, with black and yellow, and seldom clear of Indians of different tribes in the daytime." This statement was not an exaggeration. The author could easily have pointed out representatives of every nation and race which he mentioned.

CHAPTER III
COMPOSITE COMMUNITY

IN THE heterogeneous population of Detroit the British element was the most influential. Following the troops in 1760, or shortly afterwards, they had soon made themselves masters of the country. More aggressive and painstaking than the French, who had been there since Cadillac built his stockade on the high bank above the river in 1701, they had become officials, owners of great tracts of land, merchants, and fur traders. Government contracts, grants of land from the Indians and from the Crown, the importing of goods from Europe, and the exporting of furs from Detroit provided rich fields for exploitation.

Dr. Charles Brown, shortly after his arrival in 1796, including this whole group in one broad generalization, wrote of "the merchants who are all Scotch & as great torys as ever you knew." They were not all Scots, nor were they all hostile to the new régime, but they were vexed by the change in authority and uncertain of the future. One of these merchants, William Park, writing to his partner, George Meldrum, at Mackinac, only two days after Hamtramck's arrival, probably expressed the feeling of his class when he explained that "everything has a new face... nothing is changed in business, but the New Appearance is not very agreeable to Many who has long breathed under the British Government." Both of these men were residents of long standing, Meldrum having been in Detroit as early as 1768. He had married Marie Catherine Angélique Chapoton, and thus allied himself with the French element.[1] Park, besides being a merchant, was a justice of the peace. His wife, Thérèse Gouin, was French.

[1] The sources of the genealogical and biographical information in this chapter were Father Christian Denissen's manuscript compilation of Detroit genealogies, in the Burton Historical Collection, and Milo M. Quaife (ed.), *Burton Historical Records*, I: *The John Askin Papers* (Detroit, 1931). Two volumes.

On the other hand, John Askin, as British as any native of old Albion, although he was born in Ireland and had migrated from there, could find no fault with the new régime after two weeks of living under the American flag. To his old friend, Colonel England, he wrote: "... I cannot say since the Arrival of Lt. Colonel Hamtramck that he has given any Cause of dislike." Askin had extensive interests in trade, ships, and land. In 1793, Jacob Lindley, a companion of Joseph Moore, called him "one of the most respectable merchants of this place." Under British rule he was a member of the Land Board, a local magistrate, and captain of militia. Although he had earlier been established at Mackinac, he had visited Detroit frequently on business, and it was there that he had married Marie Archange Barthe in 1772. Askin moved to Detroit in the summer of 1780.

Another one of this group was Angus Mackintosh, justice of the peace, merchant, and factor of the North West Company, which dominated the fur trade in the region. Although he had probably come to America as a result of the declining fortunes of his clan after the defeat of Bonnie Prince Charlie, he remained a staunch Briton. Like the others, he had married a French woman of the neighborhood, Marie Archange Baudry.

These men were not happy to see the Americans take over; but there were others who were not greatly disturbed; and some had helped to prepare the way for them. First among this group was George McDougall. A native of Detroit born in 1766, his father was Lieutenant George McDougall, of the Royal American Regiment, and his mother, Marie Françoise Navarre. He had prospered as a trader, in part at least, because of his French connections. How he assisted General Wayne through his influence with the French and the Indians has already been told (see pages 10–11).

Another merchant who espoused the cause of the young republic was William Macomb. Coming to Detroit about the year 1770 he and his brother Alexander had joined with William Edgar in the firm of Macomb, Edgar, and Macomb to furnish supplies to the British army. After the Revolutionary War Alexander went to New York City, where he soon became a successful businessman.

Perhaps it was his brother's influence that caused William Macomb to coöperate with McDougall and the others in aiding the Americans. Although he had labored successfully in their favor, fate prevented him from enjoying the satisfaction of living under their rule, for he died on April 16, 1796, leaving a widow, Sarah Dring Macomb, three sons, and five daughters. At the time of his death he was probably the wealthiest man in Detroit.[2]

On his farm, which was the first one west of the town, besides the "Mansion House," there were a barn, a sheephouse, a cider press, a root cellar, and a bakehouse. The improved land included an orchard, a garden, and a "yard," each enclosed by pickets. Fences extended along the borders of the farm into the woods, where they were connected by a cross fence. Besides these enclosures and the cultivated fields, there was also the "Deer Park" with its "Look out house."[3]

James May was one of the middle group of British merchants. Although he seems to have had no correspondence with the Americans before their arrival, he apparently did not resent their presence. He leased his ship to the United States, and charges for goods purchased by the newcomers appear in his journal immediately after their arrival. May was a very large man, energetic, and engaged in widely diverse activities. He held a commission as justice of the peace, owned at least one ship, dealt in all sorts of merchandise, operated a boardinghouse, and had extensive land holdings. A native of Birmingham, England, in 1778 he had come to Detroit, where he married Rose St. Cosme.

Another important merchant was James Abbott. Only he and Macomb, of all the British merchants in Detroit, had found helpmates outside the community. His wife was Mary Barkle, of Philadelphia. Six children were born to them, three sons and three daughters. Engaged in trade under the firm name of James Abbott and Sons, the father, with Robert and James,

---

[2] Alexander Macomb went to Detroit in August, 1796, and took his brother's widow and her children to New York to live. General Wayne ordered the commanding officers at Niagara and Oswego to assist them on their journey. Wayne Papers, 45, 89, Hist. Soc. of Pa., Phila.

[3] Report of Matthew Ernest and Jonathan Schieffelin, August 26, 1803. Solomon Sibley Papers, Burton Hist. Coll.

Although this report was written seven years after the American occupation, it deals with improvements made by the late William Macomb before the Americans arrived.

The Macomb farm later became the Cass farm.

had an extensive business in Detroit and throughout the Indian country. Colonel Hamtramck opened an account with them two days after his arrival, and by the next April he owed the company £182 13s. 2d.

An influential British subject who must be included here was Alexander Grant. The "Commodore," as he was generally known, was in command of the Royal Navy of the Upper Lakes. Born in Scotland and trained for naval service, he had enlisted in the army and come to America, where he fought in the French and Indian War. From 1759 to 1763 he had command of the ships on Lake Champlain; then, until 1778, he was commander of the British navy on all the Lakes. In the latter year he was given charge of the ships on Lakes Erie, Huron, and Michigan. At Detroit he married Thérèse Barthe, a sister of John Askin's wife, and acquired an estate at Grosse Pointe. There he was living in his "Castle" when the Americans took over. Although he had informed Askin in December, 1795, that he and his wife were "upon the figets" at the prospect of the change of government and were planning to cross the river, he remained where he was.

Some of the other residents of British origin when Detroit changed hands in 1796 were James Fraser, George Knaggs, William Robertson, and his brother David, merchants; George Sharp, John Dodemead, and James Donaldson, tavern keepers; Matthew Donovan and John Burrell, schoolmasters; Walter Roe, lawyer; Robert Nichol, clerk; Captain Joseph May, master of his brother's ship, the *Swan;* and Thomas Smith, surveyor. Some of them moved across the river after the American occupation, but many remained. A few became citizens of the United States; the majority, however, elected to retain their British nationality.

2

Most of the people of Detroit were French. Antoine de la Mothe Cadillac and his successors had granted lots within the palisades, and farms above and below the town along the strait. These lands were held by feudal tenure on conditions prescribed in the Custom of Paris. All grants were *en roture*, similar to those made by seigniors in Lower Canada; but at Detroit, where the King was overlord, feudal dues were paid to a govern-

JAMES MAY
(Courtesy of the Burton Historical Collection,
Detroit Public Library)

COMMODORE ALEXANDER GRANT
(Courtesy of the Burton Historical Collection)

ment official instead of to a seignior. In order that every grantee might have access to the river the farms were narrow, varying in width from one to five *arpents*.[4] The depth was usually forty or eighty *arpents*, a mile and a half or three miles.

Some of the French had come to Detroit as soldiers and remained as settlers. Others had been attracted by the lure of the fur trade; and still others had established themselves as farmers or skilled artisans.

Volatile, generous, hospitable, and sociable to a fault, these French men and women enjoyed life to the full. They were never too busy for a feast or a frolic. Intensely loyal to their church, they gladly celebrated the numerous days of fête without worrying about the consequent neglect of their own affairs. Taking advantage of the opportunity which offered, the more practical British traders had easily gained control of the business of the community.

There was, however, no sharp division between the governors and the governed. The former had married French wives, and thus had united, in some measure, the two nationalities; and, in spite of the fact that most of the French were simple peasants—*habitants* they called themselves in the New World—or *engagés*[5] of the influential merchants, some were officials, and others were successful in trade.

There were families in Detroit which had their roots in the very foundations of the settlement. Such a one was that of Jean Baptiste Marsac, whose grandfather, Sergeant Jacob Marsac, had come as a soldier with Cadillac in 1701. The grandson was now a farmer at Grosse Pointe.

Another was the family of St. Aubin. Jean Casse was a corporal in the garrison of Fort Pontchartrain, Detroit, in 1707. At some time or other he had been nicknamed St. Aubin because he was a native of that town in France. Consequently he was known as Jean Casse *dit* St. Aubin, the *dit* meaning "called." As years passed the family name was discarded, and only the designation St. Aubin remained to be passed on to children and grandchildren.

The conferring of nicknames was a common custom among the French of Canada. As families were usually large, it served

[4] A lineal *arpent* was equal to 192.25 feet.
[5] This word is derived from *engagement*, a contract which stated the terms of employment.

to distinguish one branch from another. The origins of these appellations were various. Sometimes it was the name of the town from which a man came. Again, it might be the result of chance. Nicholas Campau *dit* Niagara was so called because he was born at the portage while his parents were on their way to Detroit. Or, perhaps the nickname was descriptive, as in Jean Baptiste Romain *dit* Sans Crainte ("the Fearless"). The designation frequently became permanent, and the original surname was lost.

The system of land tenure in Canada provided another source of second names. Seigniories were granted by the King to persons of influence. Adopting the practice of nobles in France, they gave names to these estates and, by adding them to their surnames, they achieved a quasi-noble form of appellation. Thus plain Julius Trotier had a number of sons who obtained seigniories and so became Trotier de l'Isle Perrot, Trotier de la Rivière de Loup, Trotier de Bellecour, Trotier des Ruisseaux, and Trotier de Beaubien.

Two Detroit families were descended from Julius Trotier, but neither was known by his name. François X. Trotier *dit* Bellecour, who came to Detroit in 1770, was a descendant of Antoine Trotier des Ruisseaux. He signed his name "Francis D^x Bellecour," thus using the name of his father's estate as his surname and that of his earlier ancestor for the middle name. During the 1790's he was a notary.

The other branch of the Trotier family that settled in Detroit was the de Beaubien. The origin of this name, which has figured largely in local history and which is perpetuated in the name of a street, is interesting enough to deserve a few paragraphs.

At Batiscan in Lower Canada Marie Catherine Trotier de Beaubien, daughter of Antoine Trotier de Beaubien, in 1696 became the wife of Jean Cuillerier. The husband died before 1712, and the widow married François Marie Picoté de Belestre in 1714. He was ordered to Detroit, where he served as an officer in the garrison until his death in 1729. Marie Catherine went there to join him and brought their children. One of them, bearing the same name as his father, was commandant of Fort Pontchartrain when Major Robert Rogers arrived with orders for its surrender in 1760.

Madame de Belestre's two sons by her first marriage, Antoine and Jean Baptiste Cuillerier, also went to Detroit. To their father's name they added "*dit* Beaubien," and in time Beaubien replaced Cuillerier as the family name.

The Beaubien farm was the second one east of the town along the River Road. It adjoined John Askin's, which was next to the Common. Antoine was the leader of the Frenchmen who favored the Indians during the Pontiac War—"the old Canadian, named Quilleriez," of Parkman's *Conspiracy of Pontiac*. The author describes him as a conceited fellow who expected to become commandant of the Fort if the British were expelled. His daughter Angélique was the fiancée of James Sterling, a merchant in the town. It was she, some believe, who warned Major Gladwin of Pontiac's intended treachery. If these stories are true, the father's position is not difficult to understand—François Marie Picoté de Belestre, the last commandant of Detroit, was his half-brother; and the daughter's desire to save her lover from the impending massacre was reason enough for an act, which, if her father had known of it, would have appeared treasonable to him.

One of the French merchants of Detroit when Hamtramck came was Joseph Campau. Sixth in a family of twelve children, he was the great grandson of Jacques Campau, who came to Detroit in 1708. Twenty-seven years old when the Americans occupied Detroit, Joseph had a trading house on Ste Anne Street, just opposite the church.

A notable resident of Detroit at this time was François de Joncaire de Chabert. His father and his grandfather had ably served the King of France for many years as agents among the Iroquois. After the fall of New France his father went to Detroit as a trader. François was as loyal to King George as his father had been to King Louis. Serving as a captain in the local militia during the Revolutionary War, he accompanied Lieutenant Governor Hamilton in 1778 on his expedition against Vincennes. Captured there by George Rogers Clark along with the rest, he was released on parole and returned to Detroit. Shortly afterwards he married Marie Josette Chêne, daughter of Captain Isidore Chêne, the interpreter, who also had been with Hamilton. Chabert, who had been born under the French flag and had later become a British subject, was now to become an American citizen.

The most distinguished family in Detroit, so far as ancestry was concerned, was that of Navarre. Claiming descent from Anthony of Bourbon, Duke of Vendôme and King of Navarre, the first of the name to come to America was Robert, who was sent to Detroit in 1729 by Louis XV as subintendant and royal notary of Fort Pontchartrain. He served also as magistrate, surveyor, collector, and subdelegate until 1760. After the British occupation in that year he was made notary by the new government because of his intimate knowledge of the French language and customs.

On February 10, 1734, he married Marie Lootman *dit* Barrois; and in 1747 he received a grant of land on the Côte du Sud-Ouest, where he lived after 1762. Robert died in 1791; his wife, in 1799. One of their daughters, Marie Françoise, became the mother of George McDougall. A son, Robert, was granted land by the Potawatomi near where the Detroit approach to the Ambassador Bridge now stands. His wife was Louise Marsac. One of their fifteen children was François, who settled at the River Raisin, and who coöperated with his cousin George McDougall to facilitate the advent of the Americans.

The French families which have been mentioned were only a few of those which were in Detroit or in the vicinity in 1796. It would not be possible to include here a complete list; but some of the others were the Chapoton, descendants of Dr. Jean Chapoton, physician to the troops during the early part of the French régime; the St. Onge *dit* Chêne; the Peltier; the Parent; the Godfroy; the Meloche; the Beaufait; the Piquette; the Berthelet; the Girardin; the Labadie; the Cicotte; and the Voyer.

Some of the people of Detroit were half-bloods, offspring of Indian women and white men, usually French. Although the late Father Christian Denissen, authority on local genealogy, asserts that "The French of Detroit and vicinity never intermarried with the Indians to any great extent," he does record some such marriages in his compilation of local family lines. For example, Jacques Godfroy married an Indian woman, Frances L'Eveille. After her death he took for his wife Louise

Clotilda Chapoton, who died in 1762. Sometime later a Miami chief gave him his favorite daughter as a mark of friendship.

Jacques was the "Canadian Godefroy" mentioned by Parkman in his *Conspiracy of Pontiac,* who had been threatened with death by Colonel John Bradstreet at Detroit in 1764 because of his aid to Pontiac during the siege. Godfroy, however, purged himself of his treason by faithfully guiding Captain Thomas Morris, who had been sent on an embassy to Pontiac. At an Indian town on the Maumee River he saved the Captain's life by protecting him from drink- and hate-frenzied savages.

Having an Indian squaw in the woods, usually without benefit of clergy, was a rather common practice on the frontier, where young men served as *engagés* in the fur trade. Later, after returning to settle down more or less permanently, a man would marry a French girl. No stigma was attached either to the parent or to the offspring of these forest unions. If the children were brought back to civilization by their fathers, they were accepted as members of his family. John Askin, for example, had three children by an Indian woman before he married his French wife. The eldest, a son, was known as John Askin, Junior. He and his half-Indian sisters made marriages in the best circles of the community.

3

Moore's list of nationalities included Dutch but no Germans. Perhaps he intended to include both within the single term, for there were few Dutchmen in Detroit in 1793. Only four can be definitely identified. John Visger came to Detroit, probably from Schenectady, before the Revolutionary War. His partner in business was Gerrit Graverat, a Dutchman from Albany. Jacob Visger arrived at Detroit from Albany in 1788 with William Groesbeck. Visger married Agatha Cicotte; Groesbeck, Teresa Beaufait. All of these Dutchmen were merchants.

The Germans were slightly more numerous. The names of Jonathan Schieffelin, merchant; Israel Ruland, silversmith; Conrad Seek, tailor; George Jacob Rudhart, Conrad Showalter, Joseph Gruenist, Dr. Hermann Melchior Eberts, and the numerous children of Michel Yax appear in various records.[6]

---

[6] John A. Russell, *The Germanic Influence in the Making of Michigan* (Detroit, 1927), pp. 42–50.

Schieffelin and Ruland have already been mentioned among those who were engaged in large land speculations. Dr. Eberts had come to America during the Revolution as surgeon in a Hessian regiment. He reached Detroit in 1791 and practiced medicine in the community, where, when the Americans came, he was the only physician in town.

Yax and his wife, the first German settlers in Michigan, had arrived in Detroit as Indian captives. He had originally settled in Pennsylvania; then, like many of his compatriots, he had moved south and west into Kentucky, where he and his wife were captured by Ottawa Indians in 1747 and carried to Detroit. Ransomed by sympathetic townspeople, they acquired a farm and spent the remainder of their lives in the neighborhood.

4

The Americans at Detroit to whom Moore referred must have been Tory refugees from the East. Alexander McKee, Simon Girty, and Matthew Elliot have already been mentioned. Another was John Little, who also had fled from Pennsylvania during the Revolution. Although the others crossed the river before the arrival of Captain Porter, Little continued to live on his farm at Grosse Pointe.

American citizens were not wanted at Detroit. In 1784 General Frederick Haldimand ordered Lieutenant Governor Jehu Hay to investigate carefully any would-be settlers from Virginia and Maryland. Only those who were loyal to the King were to be admitted, and even they would have to take a special oath swearing to defend to the utmost the authority of King and Parliament.

The Indians hated Americans, and the British commandant rounded them up and sent them to the authorities in Lower Canada. Jacob Lindley tells how he and his companions were menaced by a band of Chippewa in 1793 when the savages learned that they were from the United States; and in the same year Colonel England shipped William Irvine (or Irwin), variously described as an American deserter and as a spy, down the Lakes to Lieutenant Governor Simcoe. The next year he sent Dr. James C. Freeman, and two Americans who had been captured by Indians. In an accompanying letter he wrote:

"There are a few more in the settlement who by degrees I will discover and send away." This was the routine practice. Consequently, when Detroit became American, all the inhabitants were foreigners.

5

Besides the various nationalities of white men at Detroit there were Indians and Negroes. The former, of course, were the more numerous. Those who were more or less permanently located in the vicinity belonged to the Potawatomi, Ottawa, and Huron nations. Others, especially Chippewa, Shawnee, and Miami, came to trade or to receive presents from the commandant.

At certain seasons, particularly in the early summer, when they came in from the woods with their winter's catch of furs, the red men outnumbered the whites. Camping along the river bank, they slept under their overturned canoes, or in dome-shaped wigwams made of saplings covered with bark or with mats woven from reeds. Frequently they camped on the farms of the *habitants*, with whom they were on the best of terms. Isaac Weld noticed that if an Indian was ill or wanted protection from a storm, he always applied at the house of a Frenchman.

Although the British Government had long since adopted the policy of supporting the Indians and giving them presents, Englishmen and Scots could never abandon the belief that the natives belonged to an inferior race. The Indians resented their attitude and never became warmly attached to them.

The Americans viewed the natives with even less regard than did the British. Although the United States Government tried to deal fairly with the red men, the people, hungry for land, could not see why the claim of lazy savages to vast areas should be used as an excuse to exclude white men who wanted farms. As a result Americans were very impatient and even brutal in their insistence that the natives should be dispossessed.

When Hamtramck arrived, there were many Indians about the town. The new commandant informed Wayne that a "large number" were awaiting with great anxiety the arrival of the commander in chief. Dr. Charles Brown also observed that "the Indians are numberous & civil having in memory the

20th August 1794." Some were there to trade; others had come to see the Americans and to ask for presents. Since they were there, they had to be fed. Wayne estimated that Hamtramck would need rations for at least five hundred Indians "who from principles of Humanity as well as good policy we must feed for the present."[7]

During the day they thronged the streets of the town. In their hands or on their backs the Indians carried pelts, mococks[8] of maple sugar, moccasins, and mats of woven reeds which they had made. They spent their time bargaining with the merchants, visiting their friends, drinking, quarreling with each other, and begging food from officials or inhabitants. At sundown they withdrew from the village, and the gates were closed behind them.

Some of the Indians at Detroit were slaves.[9] They were captives who had been taken in wars between hostile tribes and sold to the whites. These people were known as Panis, a phonetic spelling of Pawnee, a tribe considered by more warlike savages to be degraded and fit only for servants. Visitors to Detroit reported that there were none better.

When slaves were mentioned, both Panis and Negroes were included in the term unless a qualifying word was used. Consequently it is impossible to say which were the more numerous. Perhaps there were more Panis than Negroes; but there must have been a considerable number of the latter, many of them having been carried captive from Kentucky by raiding parties from Detroit. The names of the twenty-six slaves owned by

[7] Wayne to James McHenry, July 22, 1796, Wayne Papers, 45, 23, Hist. Soc. of Pa., Phila.

[8] Mocock—a box or carton made of birch bark.

[9] Slavery continued to exist in Michigan after the American occupation, in spite of the prohibition contained in the Ordinance of 1787. Legally, however, the right to own slaves was limited. Judge A. B. Woodward ruled on October 23, 1807, that "a right of property in the human species cannot exist in this Territory, excepting as to persons in the actual possession of British settlers within this Territory on the 11th June [July], 1796." *Mich. Pio. and Hist. Soc. Colls.*, 12, 521.

The exception, as the judge wrote in another opinion (*ibid.*, p. 518), was based on a law of Upper Canada which continued in slavery all persons who were slaves on May 31, 1793, but which limited to a term of twenty-five years the servitude of children born of slave women after that date.

Judge Woodward ruled that British subjects living in Michigan at the time of the American occupation might legally retain their slaves under the provisions of Jay's Treaty, which protected their property.

William Macomb would indicate that most of them were probably black.

Some of the Negroes were free. William Lee is so designated in a list of those indebted to Macomb's estate, and a colored woman, Black Betty, must have been free, too. She seems to have been a peripatetic servant who was engaged from time to time by the merchants. Contemporary account books contain entries showing that she was paid for her services as a cook by John Askin, by George Meldrum, and by William Park.

CHAPTER IV

GENERAL WAYNE ARRIVES

BRITISHERS, Frenchmen, Dutchmen, Germans, Indians, and Negroes—these were the people whom Colonel Hamtramck found in the community which had been placed under his command. Villagers and farmers, as well as soldiers, were in his charge, for, although Detroit was now in the Northwest Territory, no civil government was yet established in the region recently evacuated by the British.

As one of his first acts the Commandant issued a proclamation addressed to his "Friends and fellowcitizens." In it he expressed the wish that there be "a perfect good understanding between the Citizens of the place, and the Soldiery." In order to attain this end, he requested "a strict obedience to all regulations that may be established." Until civil government could be provided, he expected "that the Citizens of the place will cheerfully comply with his orders, which will always be consonant to the Laws that have been made for the Government of the Territory North West of the River Ohio."

The first orders were that liquor must not be sold to soldiers without a permit, or to Indians; and that arms, ammunition, and clothing must not be bought from soldiers. These mandates were probably received with mixed emotions by the townspeople. John Askin, writing to Colonel England, mentioned the restriction on the sale of liquor and commented: "I am happy at this on Account of some rum Sellers who shewed much Ingratitude for the Indulgences they rec'd in that way under your command." Others must have resented the edict, for the feud between commandants at the Fort and "some rum Sellers" was perennial.

The Colonel, in one of his early orders, promulgated a comprehensive plan for the protection of the Fort, the Citadel, and the town. Each day guard-mount was held on the Esplanade with one piece of artillery in attendance and "all the music."

After the ceremony the detachment was marched to its stations, the main guard, consisting of a subaltern, a sergeant, a corporal, a drummer, and fifteen privates, being posted at the guardhouse just inside the Pontiac Gate. Every fifteen minutes the sentinel there cried out "All is well." The call was repeated by the sentry in the first bastion on the east wall and passed along to the Fort and from there around the town. In case of an alarm the drummer would beat the call to arms. Another large unit was based on the guardhouse in the Citadel, with one sentinel stationed at the Colonel's quarters there.

The order required that the large gates of the Fort and of the Citadel be shut at retreat and the wickets at tattoo. The latter were opened at reveille; the former at "troop-beating." The gates of the town were closed at retreat and opened at reveille; but before they were opened a sergeant and four men from the main guard went out and around the town "to examine if any uncommon event has taken place."

Before Colonel Hamtramck arrived at Detroit he was worried about his food supply, especially in view of the numerous Indians who demanded provisions. He took with him from Fort Miamis only 38,000 pounds of flour and ninety cattle. To General Wilkinson he wrote that "money for the Quarter Master's Department is absolutely necessary—a Soldier cannot boil his kettle without first purchasing the wood."

Upon his arrival at Detroit the Colonel found means of obtaining supplies without money. Captain De Butts borrowed from the merchants as much flour as he required on condition that it be later replaced by a like quantity, and Hamtramck received fifty barrels of salt pork as a loan from the British at Malden.

This transaction was made possible by the courtesy of Lieutenant Governor Simcoe. When James O'Hara, who had a contract to provide the American army with food, applied to Simcoe for a loan of pork on the ground that without it a detachment could not be sent to relieve the British garrison at Mackinac, the Lieutenant Governor immediately agreed to the proposal and requested Colonel England, who had just arrived at York, to give orders that fifty barrels be lent from the stores either at Malden or at Mackinac. Colonel England forwarded the order to Captain George Salmon, commandant at Malden, who shipped the meat to Detroit—ten thousand four hundred pounds.

Unfortunately, the relations between the commanders of the forces on opposite sides of the river were not always so amicable. On the night of July 18 Charles Mulholland, a private in the Queen's Rangers stationed at Malden, and David Robertson, a merchant of Detroit, were arrested and charged with attempting to bribe an American soldier to desert. At a court of inquiry held the next day testimony showed that Private Angus Shaw of the First Sub-legion, a deserter from the British army, had been approached by Mulholland, who showed him a pardon signed by Captain William Mayne and urged him to return to his regiment. Robertson, a British subject who had shown his dislike for the new régime by excluding American soldiers from his store, had offered Shaw money as an extra inducement.

Both Robertson and Mulholland pleaded not guilty, the latter protesting that he was simply obeying the orders of his captain.[1] Nevertheless, they were imprisoned and held in confinement for at least a month. Captain Mayne appealed to General Wayne, who declared Mulholland's arrest a mistake and ordered him released. The British captain insisted that he wanted to be friendly and suggested that Wayne send soldiers to Canada to arrest American deserters. The General, on his part, asserted that he had given positive orders forbidding the enlistment of British deserters in the American Army.

Thus the affair promised to lead to more friendly relations; but Captain Mayne's policy was roundly condemned by his superiors. Major David Shank, commanding the troops of Upper Canada, wrote that the Commander in Chief was displeased at Mulholland's conduct. He added: "It is Major Shank's most positive order that an entire stop be put to all communication with the Troops of the United States and His Majesty's Troops under His command." Since these men might be ordered to face each other in battle, it was not expedient to permit them to become friends.

Desertion was frequent from both posts. Captain Mayne was troubled by his losses; and Colonel Hamtramck complained that thirty men had slipped away in less than three weeks.

[1] Certified copy of the Proceedings of a Court of Inquiry, Detroit, July 19, 1796, Wayne Papers, 45, 84, Hist. Soc. of Pa., Phila.

The responsibility, he declared, lay with some citizens who, "more swayed by their own Interest than a just regard to the Laws of their Country," sold liquor to soldiers, who, fearing punishment for drunkenness, fled to the other side of the river, where they were conducted to the British garrison. Both commanders, it seems, were glad to accept experienced men without asking embarrassing questions. Besides, both armies offered a bounty to recruits. On the American side it was set by statute at fourteen dollars; on the British, the amount varied with the difficulty of obtaining soldiers.

The punishment that Hamtramck mentioned was brutal enough to frighten even the most hardy. For practically every offense—petty thievery, drunkenness, sleeping on post, and desertion—it consisted of lashing a man upon the bare back. The number of lashes ranged from fifty to one hundred "effectually applied," and occasionally the sentence prescribed the use of "wired cats"—whips made of cords wrapped, at intervals, with wire. The extent of the penalty was fixed by a court-martial, subject to review by the commandant, who might remit the whole or a part of it. Sometimes hanging was decreed by the court for desertion. All punishments were inflicted before the whole garrison drawn up on parade.

The pay of a private in the United States army was four dollars a month. Because of the bounty paid to recruits men frequently deserted and enlisted in another regiment. At this time British soldiers were paid at the rate of eight shillings a day, but deductions for food and clothing reduced their cash payments to eighteen shillings ten and one-half pence a year. Hamtramck, however, called Wayne's attention to the fact that British privates were paid for extra fatigues. He wisely urged that the best way to reduce desertion was to place American soldiers "upon an equal, if not a better footing, than that on which the British Soldiers now stand." Wayne accepted the suggestion, ordering that wages be paid men who were ordered out to cut and haul firewood.

2

While the Commandant and the swarm of Indians in and about Detroit were impatiently awaiting the arrival of the

Commander in Chief, the troops were drilled in preparation for maneuvers and a parade to be held in his honor. The band of the First Sub-legion, Colonel Hamtramck's regiment, provided the music for these rehearsals and for the review that was held every Sunday on the Esplanade.[2] Under the impression that Wayne would make the journey from Fort Miamis to Detroit on horseback, Hamtramck sent a detachment to build a bridge over the Huron River, and dispatched the *Swan* to bring up his baggage.

General Wayne was at Fort Washington, Cincinnati, when he received Captain De Butts' letter of July 1, announcing the latter's arrival at Detroit to arrange for the evacuation. On July 10 Wayne wrote: "The friendly & polite manner in which the Abandonment takes place is worthy of British Officers, & does honor to them & the Magnanimous Nation to which they belong. I therefore pray you present my best & kindest wishes to Colo. England & the Officers under his Command—which I hope to reiterate in person in the course of a few days, but shou'd eventual circumstances deprive me of that pleasure, may happiness, life & Laurels attend them."[3] Unfortunately, this gracious message from one military gentleman to another was never delivered. For on the day after it was written the British commander departed with his troops to Lower Canada, whence he returned to England.

From Pittsburgh to Cincinnati Wayne had sailed down the Ohio River. Then he set out on horseback to retrace the route of his campaign of 1793 and 1794. Traveling by way of Fort Hamilton, Fort St. Clair, and Fort Jefferson, he arrived on July 16 at Fort Greenville, where Colonel David Strong was in command.

At Greenville Wayne met General James Wilkinson, who had been commanding in the West during his absence. Their relations were only official and formal, for Wilkinson had filed charges with the War Department in 1794 against his superior and urged that he be court-martialed. Wayne knew that

[2] A manuscript subscription paper signed by the officers of the regiment states that the instruments were purchased from General Wilkinson, June 28, 1796. The band was "always to be stationed at the Head Quarters of the Regiment." J. F. Hamtramck Papers, Burton Hist. Coll.

[3] Wayne to De Butts, July 10, 1796, Wayne Papers, 44, 115, Hist. Soc. of Pa., Phila.

Wilkinson was jealous of him, and he suspected that his subordinate was meditating treasonable designs in the West against the Government. Wilkinson with his wife left Greenville, July 24, bound for Philadelphia, where he intended to press his charges in person. A few days after they had gone a private letter arrived from James McHenry, Secretary of War, advising Wayne that Wilkinson had preferred new charges against him.

The Commander in Chief thanked the Secretary for his "friendly hint," and asserted that Wilkinson's motive was a desire to get him out of the way. "The fact is, my presence with the Army is very inconvenient to the nefarious Machinations of the Enemies of Government & may eventually prevent them from dissolving the Union." He stigmatized Wilkinson as "that worst of all bad men, to whom I feel myself as much superior in every Virtue as Heaven is to Hell."

Although Wayne was eager to push on to Detroit, an attack of gout and pain from an old wound kept him in camp. Besides, he was expecting Winthrop Sargent, secretary of the Territory North West of the River Ohio, whom he had invited to accompany him to Detroit to establish civil government there.[4] Because Governor Arthur St. Clair was absent from the territory, Sargent was acting governor. A feud had existed between Wayne and St. Clair since the time of the Revolutionary War. Consequently, the Secretary would be a more congenial traveling companion than the Governor would have been. Sargent arrived on July 27; but because Wayne was not ready and was "a little indisposed,"[5] it was not until July 30 that the cavalcade began to advance.

Besides Wayne and Sargent, there were in the party John Wilkins, Jr., quartermaster general of the United States Army, and Peter Audrain, a Frenchman who had emigrated to America and was on his way to Detroit. Escorted by a detachment of dragoons, and traveling almost due north, the troop reached Fort Defiance on August 3. After resting there two days they sent their horses ahead overland, and embarked in boats to sail down the Maumee River to the Rapids.

On the night of August 6 they encamped about a mile above

[4] Wayne to McHenry, July 22, 1796, *ibid.*, 45, 23.
[5] Peter Audrain's manuscript Journal, p. 6, Burton Hist. Coll.

Fort Deposit. The next day, having mounted their horses again, they rode down beside the river, and soon reached the field of Fallen Timbers. The sight of this familiar ground recalled to Wayne memories of his momentous victory two years before. Here his companions had a rare treat: "Gen'l Wayne described every position of his army, every movement, and all the particulars of the action."[6]

The party soon reached Fort Miamis, where they camped. Since the *Swan* had come and gone, and since a Frenchman and a soldier came in to report that the road was bad and that a bridge could not be built across the Huron River, the General decided to use in the journey to Detroit the boats he already had. Some of them, however, were so badly damaged by the rocks over which they had been dragged on the voyage down the Maumee that they required extensive repairs, and it was not until the afternoon of August 10 that they set sail on the last leg of their journey.

3

It was on Saturday, August 13, that the fleet of small boats bearing General Wayne, his companions, and the military escort landed at Spring Wells, about three miles below Detroit. Mounting their horses, the travelers set out along the River Road toward the Fort. Shortly before they reached the village, they heard the sound of a scattering fusillade. A moment later a straggling horde of savages appeared running toward them, leaping, shouting, and firing into the air as they ran. General Wayne was pleased and flattered by the "repeated Volleys delivered from their Rifles and ear piercing Yells," which he understood were simply "demonstrations of joy agreeable to the Custom & usage of those brave & hardy sons of the wilderness of the West."[7] Wayne had a paternal regard for the savages; he gladly received their "friendly shakes by the hand," and he was proud to hear them call him "Father."

Little Turtle, the Miami chieftain, was among the first to greet the "Chief-who-never-sleeps," as he had dubbed his conqueror; and Blue Jacket, chief of the Shawnee, who had com-

---

[6] *Ibid.*, p. 7.
[7] Wayne to his son Isaac, September 10, 1796, Wayne Papers, 46, 47, Hist. Soc. cf Pa., Phila. Wayne informed his son that 1200 Indians were awaiting his arrival.

manded the braves at Fallen Timbers, also shook his hand. The Indians admired this soldier who had defeated them in battle, and who had dealt fairly with them in council. The Miami had nicknamed him "Blacksnake" because of his deceptive advance through the forests north of the Ohio; and the Potawatomi, remembering the impetuosity of his charge at Fallen Timbers, called him "Tornado."

Wayne was "flatteringly received by the Garrison and Inhabitants of Detroit." There was music by the band of the First Sub-legion, and "a federal salute of artillery" welcomed him to the Fort. As soon as the military formalities had been completed, Colonel Hamtramck escorted the General to the house of Walter Roe, British attorney who had moved across the river. Situated on the north side of Ste Anne Street in the first block east of the citadel, this was the home of General Wayne while he lived in Detroit.[8]

The Commander in chief no doubt felt a peculiar satisfaction in establishing his headquarters at Detroit. This act was the culmination of his western campaign begun in 1792. He could smile now as he thought of the opposition in certain quarters to his appointment, and of the dire predictions that Washington's policy was leading straight to war with Great Britain. Here was the proof that they had been wrong. A little later he expressed this conviction in a letter to the Secretary of War:

> ... the posts have all been surrender'd up to the Troops of the United States, by the respective British Commandants, in the most polite, friendly & accommodating manner, without any injury or damage—other than what time has made, An event that must naturally afford the highest pleasure & satisfaction to every friend of Order & good Government; & I trust will produce a conviction to the World that the measures adopted & pursued by that great & first of men the President of the United States, were founded in wisdom, & that the best interests of his country have been secured by that Unshaken Patriotism & Virtue, for which he is so universally & justly celebrated (a few *Demon* crats excepted—& even they in their hearts must acknowledge his worth).

General Wayne undoubtedly took the earliest opportunity to visit the military works and to view the town. Of the Fort he wrote to McHenry:

> ... the pickets & Fraise, with which the Earthen work is surrounded, & part of the Platform are in a perfect state of ruin; hence it is indispensibly necessary that these at

---

[8] Winthrop Sargent Papers, August 19, 1796, Ohio State Archaeological and Historical Society, Columbus.

all events should be immediately replaced & repair'd least we should eventually experience an unpleasant disaster.

I shall therefore give immediate orders for procuring the proper Materials—both for the Fort & Magazine & wait your Orders for those for the Citadel & Town.

The Commander in Chief had Captain Porter prepare an estimate of the timbers and pickets "necessary to put the Works of the Town, Citadel, and Fort Lernoult in A State of Defence." He found that several thousand feet of timbers and planks, and nearly twelve thousand pickets would be required.

Wayne was delighted with the location of the town. To his son he wrote: "Detroit is beautifully situate upon the West bank of the river of the same Name...." The water-borne traffic of the strait astonished him. Although he was accustomed to seeing ships on the Delaware River at Philadelphia, he could not refrain from expressing his surprise at the sight of them so far from the seaboard. "Here in the Center of a Wilderness," he wrote, "you see Ships or large Vessels of War & Merchantmen laying at the Wharf or sailing up & down a pleasant river of About One Mile wide as if passing & repassing to & from the Ocean."

He was equally pleased with the town and the people. Of the houses he wrote: "... they are generally from One story to two stories & a half high—many of them well finished & furnished, & inhabited by people from almost all nations, among whom are a number of wealthy & well informed Merchants & Gentlemen & fashionable well bred Women."

Some of the leading citizens of Detroit entertained General Wayne at dinner, as was their custom with visiting celebrities.[9] When or where the dinner was served is not known; but it was undoubtedly a sumptuous feast. Jacob Burnet, a Cincinnati lawyer who came to Detroit from time to time during the early years of the American occupation to practice his profession, was astonished at the great profusion of food and drink, and the good taste of the hosts. Each of the leading merchants tried to outdo the others in the quality and the quantity of the provisions. According to this observer, it was a mark of distinction to serve the best wines and to have at one's party the greatest number of intoxicated guests. Burnet describes such

[9] James May's Day Book contains an entry of charges for a "dinner given to the officers of Fort Lernoult," August 29, 1796, Burton Hist. Coll.

a dinner which he attended at the house of Angus Mackintosh: "... the bottom of every wine glass on the table had been broken off, to prevent what were called heel-taps; and during the evening, many toasts were given which the company were required to drink in bumpers."

At some time during the day of August 14 an extraordinary document was found in Wayne's quarters. An address to the General from his soldiers who begged "leave to welcome our beloved Chief in Command," it contained a recital of the sufferings of the troops, especially the lack of sufficient food, ever since December 15, 1795, when he had left them to go to Philadelphia. The men complained that, in his absence, their condition had been worse "than we experienced during the time we were honored with your presence on the Western Waters." Requesting him to see that their wrongs were righted, they signed the paper simply but eloquently in a bold, round hand: "The American Army."

It was characteristic of Wayne's soldiers that they awaited his return to present their grievances. They knew that he was a strict disciplinarian, and that he never spared his men when there was need for action; but they knew, too, that he never spared himself; that he shirked no labor and feared no danger. They knew that he would as readily fight Congress to win their rights as he would attack an enemy to defend his country's honor. During the Revolutionary War he had been the idol of the Pennsylvania Line. At Valley Forge he had shared their sufferings and had fought the politicians to obtain food and clothing for them. His soldiers now placed their petition in his hands, confident that he would not fail them.

4

When General Wayne arrived at Detroit, Ste Anne's Church was without a pastor. The transfer of sovereignty had placed the parish outside the jurisdiction of Bishop Jean F. Hubert of Quebec and within that of Bishop John Carroll of Baltimore. In anticipation of the arrival of the Americans Father Pierre Frechette, the village priest, had left for Quebec on July 6, 1796.[10]

[10] Father F. X. Dufaux to Bishop Jean F. Hubert, July 6, 1796, Archives of the Archbishopric of Quebec, E. U. 122. Father John Carroll was the first Roman Catholic bishop in the United States.

A little after nine o'clock on the night of August 14 a ship from Mackinac tied up at the wharf. It carried, among others, Father Michel Levadoux, vicar-general of the western country. Formerly director of the Sulpician seminary at Limoges, he had left France with a number of priests of his order because of restraints laid upon ecclesiastics by the National Assembly. In 1791 they had sailed for America and landed at Baltimore, where they established St. Mary's Seminary. Since there were soon more emigré priests than enough to man the infant institution, he had been sent by Bishop Carroll with several others, in 1792, to minister to the French communities in the Illinois country. With the evacuation of the Lake posts imminent, the Bishop had ordered him to make a tour of the western parishes and to visit Detroit. He was to decide for himself whether to remain there or to return to his own parish.

Since his departure from Cahokia, where he had left his good friend and confrere, Father Gabriel Richard, Father Levadoux had been two months on the way. He had traveled up the Illinois River to Lake Michigan, where he found a village called "chicagou." From there he had sailed to Mackinac Island, where Major William Doyle of the British army was still in command. After a sojourn of three weeks the priest embarked for Detroit.

As the gates were closed when he landed, Father Levadoux had to find lodging for the night outside the town. Early in the morning, however, he ordered the bells of Ste Anne's rung to make known his arrival. There was great rejoicing at the news, for it was a holy day, the feast of the Assumption, and the priest announced that he would officiate in the church.

As soon as it was possible Father Levadoux sought Colonel Hamtramck at his quarters. He had known the Commandant when both were stationed at Vincennes. Hamtramck received the priest kindly and, at his request, introduced him to General Wayne. The Commander in Chief welcomed him to Detroit. Father Levadoux proposed that after vespers he would sing a "Te Deum," in the presence of all his parishioners, to thank God for his goodness in permitting them to be fellow citizens of the Americans, and to ask Heaven to preserve the life of the hero who was presiding with so much wisdom over the United States, and also of the hero who, by his victories, had delivered them from the hands of a savage people.

Wayne, for all his proud spirit, must have been surprised by this frank eulogy of himself delivered to his face. Nevertheless, he was probably pleased by the naïve sincerity of the priest, and he gladly gave his consent. Accordingly, the "Te Deum" was sung in Ste Anne's where, for the first time, were heard the words Washington, Wayne, and the United States. The reverend Father thus began at once to try to make loyal Americans of his *habitants*. Most of them were willing to accept his guidance; but in asking the Bishop to express his approval of this *démarche*, Father Levadoux admitted that it had not been well received by some of his people.

Unlike Wayne, the priest could see nothing attractive in Detroit. The town itself, he wrote, "is of little consequence." It was the extent of his parish up and down the river—twelve leagues in each direction from the village—that impressed and appalled him. Still, he found something good to write about. "The people in this region," he reported, "are very much better instructed and much more religious than those of the Illinois." He praised their good manners and informed Bishop Carroll that they had charged him to express their gratitude for his having sent them a priest.[11]

Father Levadoux decided at once to remain in Detroit. Immediately after the service on August 15 he read to the congregation Bishop Carroll's letter authorizing him to take charge of the parish. He then informed his parishioners that he would call another meeting to decide how they would pay his salary.

Father François Xavier Dufaux, of Sandwich, was happy at the arrival of the new incumbent at Ste Anne's. He described him in a letter to Bishop Hubert as "a small, dignified priest, worthy of respect," and added, "he appears greatly attached and devoted to the American government."[12] To support this observation, the pastor of L'Assumption Parish mentioned Father Levadoux's special service of thanksgiving for the occupation of the western posts. In spite of their separate loyalties, Father Dufaux felt sure that he would be able to live on friendly terms with his confrere; but he was surprised at some differences of practice which he learned were

[11] Father Michel Levadoux to Bishop Carroll, September 10, 1796, Letters to Bishop Carroll, 4Y5, Archives of the Archbishopric of Baltimore and Washington, Archbishop's House, Baltimore.
[12] Dufaux to Hubert, Archives of the Archbishopric of Quebec, E. U., 124.

prevalent in the United States. For instance, he reported that the priests no longer intoned "God save the King," but "God save the People"; and that the clergy, even the Bishop, wore secular clothing.

Father Dufaux informed Bishop Hubert that he had visited Colonel Hamtramck, who, accompanied by seven officers, had returned his visit. Soon after Wayne arrived, Father Levadoux introduced the Canadian priest to the General, who invited them to dine with him. After dinner Wayne proposed a toast and requested Father Dufaux to do the same. The latter responded with the sentiment "Universal peace," and the toast was drunk in bumpers.

According to Father Dufaux, there appeared to be no cause for discord between the Americans and the British if the Reverend Edmund Burke remained in Lower Canada. The priest asserted that General Wayne and his officers detested the former vicar-general on account of the Indian atrocities for which they held him responsible, and he advised the Bishop to keep Father Burke out of the vicinity of Detroit.

CHAPTER V
CIVIL AND MILITARY ADMINISTRATION

DETROIT had never before witnessed so important a succession of activities as those that occurred only a month after the American occupation. On August 13 General Wayne arrived and established the headquarters of the army of the United States; the next day Father Levadoux, vicar-general representing the sole Catholic bishop in the nation, came to the town; and on the third day Winthrop Sargent, acting governor of the Territory Northwest of the River Ohio, erected the county of Wayne. His proclamation, dated August 15, drew the boundaries with a generous hand. Within them lay all of the present state of Michigan, except the northwestern extremity of the Upper Peninsula, with the addition of northern Ohio and Indiana, and a strip of eastern Illinois and Wisconsin bordering on Lake Michigan.

Sargent's authority to act as chief executive was limited to the periods during which Governor Arthur St. Clair was absent from the Territory. There was no doubt about his absence when the Secretary accepted Wayne's invitation to accompany him to Detroit. Sargent had made the journey in good faith, believing that civil government should be established at once, even though the return of the Governor, of which he could have no immediate news, would cancel his power. The Secretary was conscious of this possibility, for he had already been prosecuted for acting as governor "when unluckily his Excellency had been at the Muskingum a few days."[1] In spite of the risk, the urgency of the occasion and, perhaps, the opportunity to wield authority caused him to complete the organization.

Sargent's next step was to appoint officers to govern the new county. This was a difficult task. There was no American at Detroit except Peter Audrain, the naturalized Frenchman,

---

[1] Sargent to the Secretary of State, September 30, 1796, Carter, *Territorial Papers of the United States*, III, 456.

who had just arrived, and the Englishmen, many of whom had held office under the British Crown, were for the most part too strongly attached to their former government to accept positions under the United States. According to Article II of Jay's Treaty, the inhabitants who desired to remain British subjects had to make a formal declaration to that effect within a year of the evacuation of the posts. Although this action had not yet been taken, men like Askin, Mackintosh, and Park let it be known that they intended to retain their allegiance.

The inhabitants of French descent, Sargent found, were more favorable to the new régime. Unfortunately, many of them were not able to read or write; a majority of those who could knew only French; and, on the whole, there was little enthusiasm among them for self-government. In fact, the acting governor reported that they would be perfectly content to be treated as colonists of the United States. Some of them, however, had held office under the British Government, and thus were experienced.

The acting governor's intention was to observe "the Utmost Impartiality" in all his appointments. Consequently he distributed the offices among both British and French. His first establishment was the Court of General Quarter Sessions. To serve as justices of the peace he named Robert Navarre, James Abbott, Louis Beaufait, James May, Joseph Voyer, François Navarre, and Nathan Williams. Of these, Beaufait, Williams, and May had been justices under British rule, and Robert Navarre had been a notary. Sitting together they composed the court. Sessions were to be "holden and kept four Times in every year at the Town of Detroit," on the first Tuesday of December, March, June, and September. Sargent appointed Peter Audrain clerk of the court, George McDougall sheriff of the county, and Dr. Hermann Eberts coroner.

It was not until September 29 that Sargent completed the organization of the civil government. On that day he established the Court of Common Pleas with Louis Beaufait, James May, Patrick McNiff, Charles Girardin, and Nathan Williams as judges. Every one of these men had been a justice of the peace before the Americans arrived. Audrain was made prothonotary of this court. He was also named judge of Probate because of "The Difficulties of finding Suitable

Characters to fill the civil offices of the County." On the same day Sargent appointed François Chabert county treasurer, François Bellecour notary public, and Patrick McNiff surveyor.

The duplications in civil offices show clearly the shortage of men able or willing to serve the new régime; and some of the magistrates held militia commissions besides. In the roster of officers of the county militia, issued by Sargent on August 19, appear the names of François Chabert, lieutenant colonel, and James May, George McDougall, and François Navarre, captains. In the whole list of officers it is notable that, of twenty-nine, twenty-four were French. This was, of course, a wise choice, since they spoke the language of the men whom they would command.

In the plurality of offices held by one man at Detroit Peter Audrain outdid all the rest; but there was still another appointment for him. Sargent had been impressed by the uncertainty of land titles in the region, especially since the records had been carried across the river. In order to remedy the condition he issued a proclamation directing those who had claims to lots in Wayne County to file exact statements of them with the recorder; and it was upon Audrain that he conferred this title. Now Audrain's quota was full: clerk of the Court of Quarter Sessions, judge of Probate, prothonotary of the Court of Common Pleas, and recorder. As events proved, this factotum of the county of Wayne had a hand for many a year in all the legal business of the little community. Although he was seventy years old in 1796, Audrain continued to hold public office until 1819, when he was removed because of his advanced age. He died on October 6, 1820.

Two letters from Governor St. Clair were delivered to Sargent late in September. The first informed him that the Governor would be in the Territory on August 14. He was sorry to hear that the Secretary had gone with Wayne, especially since Congress had failed to act on the President's recommendation that civil government be extended to the recently acquired posts, and he reminded his errant subordinate that, if both of them performed the duties of governor at the same time, "of course, the acts of one must be void."[2]

In the second letter St. Clair wrote that he was coming to

[2] William H. Smith (ed.), *The St. Clair Papers* (Cincinnati, 1882), II, 404.

Detroit himself, so that whatever was done there would be properly done. He was irritated because Sargent had taken the territorial seal with him and had thus deprived the Governor of its use.

These letters infuriated Sargent. Quick to take offense, he felt that they contained a severe censure on his conduct. He answered that he was willing to stand trial if he had done wrong, but, he asserted hotly, "no man under Heaven has over me the right of reprimand." Fortunately, perhaps, for the newly fledged county of Wayne, St. Clair changed his mind about coming to Detroit; but the letter which announced this decision contained the information that he had been unable to find the territorial records. "I cannot conceive," he wrote, not quite frankly, one suspects, "that you have had them transported to Detroit."[3] Sargent replied: "The records of the Territory are indeed with me at Detroit." He explained that he intended to bring them up to date during his journey; besides, since he was responsible for them, he would not entrust them to anyone else.

Personal antagonisms had a great part in the staging of this comedy of errors, but the lack of any satisfactory means of communication was largely responsible. For even though Sargent had been too eager, perhaps, to play the part of governor, it was true, as he maintained, that without occult powers he could not be expected to know the whereabouts of St. Clair, who frequently retired to Pennsylvania because of ill health or on Government business. Since St. Clair never found occasion to visit Wayne County, Sargent's work proved to be of first importance; and, although every one of his acts performed after August 16 was illegal, if the letter of the law had been observed, the irregularity was overlooked, and the county which he had proclaimed was permitted to function.

2

While the county bearing his name was being organized, General Wayne had not been idle. Detroit was now the head-

---

[3] *Ibid.*, 406.

On August 28, 1796, St. Clair wrote to Sargent informing him that he had returned to the Territory on August 17, i.e., two days after the erection of Wayne County. In a letter of September 6, 1796, St. Clair announced his decision not to go to Detroit. Winthrop Sargent Papers, Ohio State Archaeological and Historical Society, Columbus.

quarters of the United States Army, and all administrative details passed through his hands. The old posts had to be regulated and the newly occupied ones put in a state of defense. Mounted couriers—"expresses" they were called—galloped up the River Road to the Citadel with dispatches from Philadelphia, Pittsburgh, Cincinnati, Fort Defiance, Fort Wayne, or Fort Miamis, and, mounting fresh horses, set out again carrying in their saddlebags orders from the Commander in Chief.

The necessity of occupying Mackinac was pressing. There alone, of all the forts in the Northwest, a British garrison remained. The problem of providing food for the relieving force having been solved by the loan of pork from Fort Malden, troops and supplies were put aboard the sloop *Detroit* for the voyage up the Lakes. Major Henry Burbeck was chosen to command the post, and Winthrop Sargent accompanied him. On August 19 the ship set sail bearing officers and one hundred and ten soldiers who would remain in garrison, and the acting governor, who would return in about a month. Because of "the accommodating politeness of the British," Wayne directed that their guard, consisting of a subaltern and twenty men of the Twenty-fourth Infantry left at Mackinac, be transported on the *Detroit*, on its return trip, to Fort Malden.

Now that the necessary measures had been taken for occupying the last of the posts, Wayne turned to the problem of desertion. He issued a proclamation in English and in French offering a reward of eighteen dollars to be paid to any citizen, soldier, or Indian who delivered a deserter, or to anyone giving information with proof about the intention of a soldier to desert, or about emissaries tampering with the troops. There were immediate results. On the day after the notice was posted Toussaint Chêne brought in a deserter and collected his reward.

Drastic punishment was meted out to offenders. A court-martial on September 2 found John Voss, an artilleryman, guilty of deserting, but, since he had a pass, "they only sentence him to receive one hundred lashes at 5 different times with *wired Catts.*" Stephen McConnell, a soldier in the Second Sub-legion, at the same session was ordered to be given one hundred lashes in four installments, to be branded on the forehead with the letter *D*, and to be drummed out of camp with a halter about his neck. Another soldier of the same regiment,

Henry Sevey, convicted of deserting his post, was sentenced to be shot. General Wayne approved all these decisions of the court and, as was his custom when the death penalty was to be inflicted, addressed a solemn injunction to the condemned man: "The Commander-in-Chief impressed with the purest feelings of Humanity—calls upon the unhappy prisoner to prepare for that tremendous (*sic*) and awful change—which, as certain as there is an all powerful and Just God—he will shortly experience."[4] He added the general warning that mercy would no longer be extended to any "degenerate soldier" who deserted the colors of the United States.

Quarrels among officers increased Wayne's difficulties. Captain Joseph Brock brought a formidable array of charges against Lieutenant John Bowyer, including conduct unbecoming an officer and gentleman, mutinous conduct, and disobedience to the orders of the commandant. Testimony revealed that the officers had been quarreling over a woman. The court found the Lieutenant not guilty, and the Commander in Chief expressed his regret "that Gentlemen cannot *devise* some other mode to accomodate their private disputes, than that of a General Court Martial." If this was intended as a hint that dueling would be a more honorable method of settling their quarrels, the officers failed to take it; for a few days later Lieutenant Aaron Gregg was acquitted of charges preferred by Captain Zebulon Pike; and when Captain Hamilton Armstrong was released from arrest after Lieutenant Jacob Kremer had withdrawn a complaint he had filed against him, Wayne wearily repeated his lament, adding that the practice did not "tend to the benefit of the Service."

The Commander in Chief was fortunate in having a capable quartermaster general. John Wilkins, Jr., was meticulous in his attention to duty and as careful in the expenditure of public funds as if they had been his own. For instance, he balked at paying $2.50 a cord for firewood delivered on the wharf. Consequently he requisitioned from Colonel Hamtramck twenty-four men to cut it and to carry it by boat, since "the

---

[4] Wayne's Order Book, Wayne Papers, 50, 99, Hist. Soc. of Pa., Phila. Sevey was held a prisoner to await the decision of the President on his case. See below, pp. 111–112.

wood about here is generally cut off, & leaves us no choice but that of cutting it at a considerable distance." He urged that the soldiers be paid for this service, which would save the government money.

General Wilkins was responsible for providing all the supplies of the army except food. He had to secure horses and oxen, wagons, and equipment of various kinds; pay for the sloop and the schooners Captain De Butts had engaged, and for materials to repair the barracks, storehouses, and stables at Detroit. The salaries of interpreters, pilots, packhorsemen, and Captain Curry of the *Detroit* were also paid from his funds.

His work was the more difficult because of inadequate and uncertain means of communication and transportation. There were three routes by which supplies reached Detroit. The first was by way of the St. Lawrence River, Lake Ontario, and Lake Erie. It had been followed by *coureurs de bois*, explorers, and missionaries long before Cadillac founded his post, and it was still used by the merchants of Detroit to bring in their trade goods and to send out their furs. A branch of this route led from New York up the Hudson and the Mohawk to Oneida Lake and Lake Ontario. This branch was used by Americans to some extent, but the army employed two other routes. One followed the Ohio past Fort Washington at Cincinnati to the mouth of the Great Miami, which was navigable as far as Lorimer's (Piqua, Ohio), where there was a portage to the headwaters of the St. Marys River. Loaded boats floated down this stream to Fort Wayne, where the St. Joseph River from the north united with the St. Marys to form the Maumee, or the Miami of the Lakes, as it was then called. From there the way was clear for boats to Fort Defiance and, with some difficulty at the Rapids, to Fort Miamis and Lake Erie. This route was especially useful for sending supplies which were to be distributed to the various forts in the West, for it either passed or lay near all of them. Expresses also usually followed approximately this course on horseback, with dispatches for the posts, where fresh mounts were kept for them.

Besides the water route there were two roads or, rather, trails from Fort Miamis to Detroit. The "upper" road, the one farther away from the water, was said to be the better.

Even so it was not fit for hauling supplies. Captain De Butts warned Wayne that, if he came that way, he should have guides, "and a few axes may prove useful."

The other army route ran north from Pittsburgh by way of the Allegheny River and its tributary, French Creek, to Fort Le Boeuf. There goods were loaded on oxcarts, which carried them to Presqu' Isle (Erie, Pennsylvania), where schooners, sloops, or bateaux took them aboard for Detroit and its dependent posts. Heavy equipment, such as ship's rigging, cannon, or other manufactured goods including whisky, usually took this course. Both routes were subject to interruption by floods and droughts in spring or summer, and by ice in winter.

Captain Henry De Butts was assistant quartermaster at Detroit. He was also the agent of James O'Hara, who had signed a contract with Oliver Wolcott, Jr., Secretary of the Treasury, to furnish commissary supplies to the western posts. These included food, whisky, candles, and soap.[5] Some of the provisions could be obtained at Detroit. Wilkins, finding that the wheat harvest had been abundant, sent quantities of grain from there to Fort Defiance and even to Presqu' Isle. Wayne believed that Mackinac and Fort Miamis, as well as Detroit, could be supplied with flour and some meat by the farmers on both sides of the river, but "at a very extravagant price."

Nevertheless, great quantities of supplies had to be moved long distances by water and across portages. O'Hara was nearly frantic sometimes because of the seeming impossibility of fulfilling his contract. In October French Creek was so low that he could not transport whisky to Lake Erie. There was an unparalleled drought, he explained, throughout the whole country, and the proximity of freezing weather made his position very uncomfortable.

Wayne reported in September that there were three hundred head of cattle at Detroit, sufficient for the needs of the army, but that it was too early in the season to slaughter them and salt down the meat. Consequently, it was again necessary to appeal to the British for a loan of pork. When Captain De Butts went to Fort Malden and requested Captain William Mayne to lend the United States fifty barrels, the British com-

[5] A copy of the articles of agreement, with prices to be charged for each article at the various posts, is in the Solomon Sibley Papers, Burton Hist. Coll.

mander sent them at once. General Wayne thanked him in a gracious note: "Permit me to assure you, Sir, that it will afford me singular pleasure to have an opportunity in turn of accommodating any of His British Majesty's Garrisons in Canada with such supplies as they may occasionally want and Particularly that under your charge."

It is unfortunate that again the attempt of one military gentleman to assist another was to result in a reprimand from headquarters. A complaint lodged at British headquarters by officers of the Indian Department brought Captain Mayne a sharp rebuke from the Commander in Chief. Admitting that the loan was contrary to regulations, the Captain explained simply: "I thought it incumbent on me as the servant of a liberal Nation to make the loan at the time & in the manner I did."

3

General Wayne knew the importance of gifts for winning and holding the friendship of the savages. He must have heartily approved the dictum of Hamtramck that "speaking to an Indian without presents is like Consulting a lawyer without a fee." He therefore distributed gifts to them on his arrival; but they were not satisfied. Difficulties of transport retarded the bringing up of the goods required for the regular payment of annuities provided for in the Treaty of Greenville; and so he had to put them off with promises. According to Isaac Weld, Jr., this delay produced a new nickname for Wayne. The Indians called him "General Wabang," that is, "General Tomorrow."

The discontent of the Indians was aggravated by the British on the other side of the river. Winthrop Sargent charged that Colonel Alexander McKee was especially active, telling the natives that the United States was their "Step Father" and urging them to cross to the territory of their "Father." In order to counteract this hostile influence and to keep a promise made to them at the Treaty of Greenville, Wayne sent a delegation of chiefs to Philadelphia to visit their Great Father, President Washington, believing that the trip would impress the Indians with the power of the United States and hoping that it would "also afford us time to secure ourselves in our new possessions, without experiencing a second *Pontiac* business—whilst we have so many Great men hostages for the good Conduct of their subjects during their absence."

Two chiefs were to represent each nation. The most famous of them were Blue Jacket, representing the Shawnee, and Little Turtle, the Miami. Mash-i-pi-nash-i-wish, the principal chief of the Chippewa and "a firm friend of the United States," was unable to go because he was suddenly taken ill. Captain John Heath was the conductor of the delegation, and three capable interpreters accompanied them: Whittmore Knaggs for the Ottawa, Chippewa, and Potawatomi; Christopher Miller for the Shawnee; and Captain William Wells for the Miami. They left Detroit October 4 on the schooner *Swan*, with directions to travel to Philadelphia either by way of Presqu' Isle and Pittsburgh or by way of Niagara, Oswego, Albany, and New York.

Before the chiefs left Detroit the local "land-jobbers" provided the wherewithal for a party. The Cuyahoga Associates gave them some cash to purchase liquor, so that they would not forget their friends while they were being entertained by the Americans.[6]

4

Toward the end of September the French philosopher and traveler Constantin François Volney visited Detroit. In the book that he wrote on his return to France he declared that General Wayne gave him a most flattering reception.[7] The fact is that when he arrived on the evening of September 23 he went directly to Wayne and asked for quarters. Wayne was embarrassed by Volney's sudden appearance. He had been introduced to him at the home of George Clymer in Philadelphia, where both of them were dinner guests. The Frenchman had been entertained as a scientist and a philosopher, and Wayne had met him frequently "in the first circles" of the

---

[6] "The Cuyahoga Purchase Dr. To cash gave the Chiefs who are going to Philadelphia to drink tonight with their Friends £1-4." Askin's Journal, September 30, 1796, *ibid*.

[7] C.-F. Volney, *Tableau du climat et du sol des États-Unis d'Amérique* (Paris, 1803), p. 411.

capital city. Now, however, the Commander in Chief had good reason to suspect that Volney was engaged in a plot with Victor Collot, Thomas Power, and other French and Spanish emissaries to foment rebellion in the western states and territories. In fact, when Major Caleb Swan arrived a few days later he informed Wayne that Volney had been intimate with Power at Cincinnati. Nevertheless, the General gave him a room in the house occupied by Captain De Butts, and made a place for him at his own table.

Another suspicious circumstance was the sudden departure of the Frenchman from the quarters assigned to him by Wayne. Without a word to the Commander in Chief he went to live with Colonel Hamtramck. This action apparently caused Wayne to doubt the latter's fidelity, perhaps on account of the Colonel's Canadian origin; for Volney had confided to De Butts the information that France intended to unite Canada with Louisiana. In that case the territory of the United States would surely have been invaded. Under the circumstances Wayne kept Volney under close surveillance during the remainder of his visit.[8]

The Frenchman had little time for spying in Detroit, if that was his purpose, for he suffered a severe attack of malaria. His illness also gave him slight opportunity to gather material for his book. In it, however, he did report that most of the French were talking of removing to British territory in order to escape the burdensome American system of self-government. Volney himself said that the French were great talkers; in this instance, probably, the majority satisfied their distaste for the new régime simply by talking about moving; for most of them remained on the American side of the river.

Another foreign visitor was Isaac Weld, Jr., a young Irishman who arrived in October. He also wrote a book. A typical British traveler, he found fault with people and customs which were unfamiliar to him. The French were ignorant and superstitious, and their houses smelled bad. American soldiers were

[8] Wayne to McHenry, September 30, 1796, Wayne Papers, 46, 89, Hist. Soc. of Pa., Phila. Wayne seemed suspicious also of Major Henry Burbeck at Mackinac. The reason is not clear, for Burbeck had been born in Massachusetts and had served in the army since 1775. Francis B. Heitman, *Historical Register and Dictionary of the United States Army* (Washington, 1903).

undisciplined, and their officers were coarse and quarrelsome. "The belles of the town are quite *au desespoir*," he wrote, "at the late departure of the British troops...." The Americans assured them, according to Weld, that they were superior to the British. "Three months, however, have not altered the first opinion of the ladies,"[9] he concluded smugly.

The British element on both sides of the river, with which Weld spent most of his time, seems to have met with his approval. He reported that some had moved to Canada from the American shore, but the "majority of them stay at Detroit." He was glad to learn, however, that only a few intended to become citizens of the United States. Some of them, resenting the fact that they were called to "serve in the militia and to perform duties, from which, as British subjects they were exempted by the articles of the treaty," held a meeting and drew up a memorial which Weld carried "to the British minister at Philadelphia." This project must have been managed very quietly, for no hint of such active discontent is contained in the correspondence of American officials.

Weld was enthusiastic in his praise of the country and its produce. He asserted that the soil was rich, providing large crops of wheat and corn, and that the orchards produced some of the finest apples and peaches he had ever eaten. The Quakers, Lindley and Moore, also had been impressed by the "luxuriant orchards" of apples, peaches, pears, and cherries. Detroit apples and cider were exported. A Connecticut newspaper of the day informed its readers that "the French at Detroit have fine orchards, from which Niagara is at present supplied with cyder and apples." General Wayne must have found the cider satisfactory, for he bought a half barrel of it from J. B. Beaubien in October.

Weld was astonished at the business activity in Detroit. He wrote that twelve trading vessels belonged to it: brigs, sloops, and schooners of from fifty to one hundred tons each; and that the stores in the town were well furnished with "fine cloth, linen, &c. and every article of wearing apparel, as good in their kind and nearly on as reasonable terms, as you can purchase them at New York or Philadelphia."

[9] Isaac Weld, Jr., *Travels Through the States of North America*, II, 184.

5

Another traveler reached Detroit two days after Volney arrived—the Reverend David Jones, chaplain to the United States Army. A Baptist preacher and an ardent patriot, he had first become a chaplain in 1777. During the Revolutionary War he had served with Wayne, and they had become fast friends. Consequently, when Wayne was given command of the troops for the western campaign, he had secured the appointment of Dr. Jones as chaplain to the Legion. On his arrival at Detroit he learned that the General was angry because he suspected the Chaplain of having given information to General Wilkinson which he should have kept to himself; as a result, no quarters had been prepared for him. He soon found lodging with James Abbott, and on Sunday, October 2, he delivered a sermon in the Citadel "from the Piazza of the Commandant's Quarters."

This was probably the first Protestant service held in Detroit since the Quakers had left in the summer of 1793. It is likely that the Abbotts and some of the other townspeople attended; but on the whole the Detroiters who were Protestants, at least nominally, seem not to have been greatly disturbed by the lack of organized religious activities. The pious Quaker Joseph Moore had described the place as "a small garrison town, with a variety of inhabitants. Here is much of the sound of drums and trumpets, but not much religion." To him it was "sorrowful to behold the power and influence that satan has too generally amongst the inhabitants of these parts." Nevertheless, he reported that "The people here ... were very respectful to us ...." In order to counteract the machinations of the Evil One, Moore and his companions had held meetings every Sunday in the sail loft in the shipyard. His comment on the meeting of July 23 is typical: " ... had a considerable gathering of the town's people, and a few soldiers, who behaved quietly. The meeting held about two hours and a half, and, I believe, ended well."

Dr. Jones remained in Detroit until November 3, preaching every Sunday except on October 16, when he made this entry in his journal: "Was very rainy. I preached none." He soon met General Wayne and, not without some difficulty, convinced him of his loyalty. On November 2 the Chaplain collected $230 from Major Caleb Swan, paymaster general of the army, and the next day left Detroit on board the *Saguinah*.

Father Levadoux, of course, was celebrating mass every Sunday, and also on holy days, of which there were very many. According to Jacob Lindley, one of Joseph Moore's companions, the *habitants* went to church "more than two hundred days in the year." This visitor had not been impressed by the degree of piety among the French; in fact, their ideas of religious observance were shocking to him. He was astonished that they would come eight or ten miles on a Sunday just to step in the church, "rhyme over their paternoster," dip their fingers in the font, cross themselves, and go out again to drink and frolic. He declared that he had even seen them "horse racing in the road passing the worship house, or, as it were, at the very door, the remaining part of the day, to their reproach."

The grave Quakers and the Puritans, too, observed Sunday as the Lord's Day, a day of quiet contemplation and long, solemn meetings for communion with their Maker. During the remainder of the week they applied themselves assiduously to their secular affairs, for time was a gift from God, and it must not be frittered away in any foolish fashion. Consequently, they prospered marvelously in business.

To the Frenchman this regimen was not sensible. He attended Mass on Sunday, met his friends from near and far, listened to the sacristan read notices of auctions, or bits of news from the steps of the church, went to market, and amused himself during the rest of the day. On the other six days as well, even if there was no *jour de fête*, the *habitant* rarely took his work very seriously. Edmé Rameau de Saint-Père, contrasting the French Canadians with the Americans, expressed very well the point of view of the former:

> They understand how to live very much better than their neighbors [the Americans], whose dismal Sundays, with their doleful aspect, have been one of the fundamental causes of the American moroseness, which is very wearisome without being, in fact, any more virtuous than our extravagant gaiety.
> . . . .
> But Puritanism, joined to the lust for gain, has spoiled the natural instincts of Americans.
> The French colonist has ordered his life in a much better fashion, and he has retained a much more pleasing disposition. If you maintain that he has thus wasted a great deal of time which the Americans have put to better use, we shall answer that even

a century is not a long enough time on which to base a forecast of the future of a people.... [10]

On September 11 Father Levadoux called a congregational meeting to determine his salary. The assembly unanimously decided that every farmer should contribute one twenty-sixth of all the grain he harvested, and that others should make an annual subscription, each according to his means. In addition, members would continue to pay the customary fees.

Father Xavier Dufaux, curé of L'Assomption Church across the river, died on the same day this meeting was held. Since the pastor of Ste Anne's felt that he should minister to those parishioners also, he urged that a priest be sent to assist him. He was anxious to have a Sulpician, and he especially requested Bishop Carroll to send Father Gabriel Richard. The usual seasonal epidemic of ague or malaria was taking its toll of the *habitants* and increasing the labors of Father Levadoux. "I have scarcely time to breathe," he wrote, toward the end of September. "Sickness is so frequent that I bury as many as four persons at a time."

General Wayne probably witnessed the passing of many funeral corteges along Ste Anne Street. The tolling of the church bell informed the community of the ceremony. First came the sexton bearing a large cross; he was followed by Father Levadoux, who was attended by male chanters and by two small boys with lighted candles. All of them wore black gowns, with white surplices reaching to the knee. The casket was carried by pallbearers. From time to time, as the procession moved slowly toward the church, the priest opened his missal and intoned a prayer for the deceased. The mourners, on foot, followed in the rear.[11]

The army did not escape the ravages of the malaria epidemic. General Wayne himself was ill, and Dr. Charles Brown informed him, on September 12, that "upwards of fifty non-commissioned officers & privates, & six commissioned officers are at this time afflicted with that disease." He reported that he had no "peruvian bark [quinine], opium, wine, brandy, nor rum" in the hospital to administer to the sick. The store-

[10] Edmé Rameau de Saint Père, *La France aux colonies* (Paris, 1859), p. 107.
[11] Jacob Lindley, "Account of a Journey," *Friends' Miscellany*, II, 108, 125, gives detailed descriptions of two such processions.

keeper at Greenville had been unable to fill his requisition for these and other medicines, and they could be bought in Detroit only "at an extravagant price." Dr. Brown expressed the opinion, that "many will die if bark is not administered."[12]

6

As the days became shorter there was frost in the air. Sumac bushes turned a fiery red, and the leaves of the maples changed from green to pink or yellow. Autumn is a beautiful season in Detroit, and General Wayne must have enjoyed it as a respite from the oppressive heats of August and early September. Nevertheless, he was eager to be back home in Waynesborough. His thoughts must have turned often to the sturdy old stone house, near Paoli, built by his grandfather, and to the broad acres of rolling land that surrounded it. His son Isaac was living there now, and his daughter Margaretta, with her husband, Will Atlee, was not far away. Perhaps he thought too of the little stone church, St. David's, Radnor, where his father and his grandfather slept beneath the great gray slabs in the churchyard and where his wife Polly had been buried in 1793, while he was campaigning in the West.

In addition to the natural desire to return to familiar scenes, General Wayne had other reasons for wanting to leave. Wilkinson was still in the East and, by insinuation and intrigue, was pressing his campaign to ruin the Commander in Chief. Once at home, Wayne could easily meet the rascal face to face and demand amends. Besides, if he tarried too long in Detroit, the storms and ice of winter might make traveling impossible.

There was, however, one more task for the General to perform before he could leave Detroit. The army of the United States was to be reorganized, and the change had to be completed before November 1. By a law of May 30, 1796, Congress provided that the Legion of the United States, with its four sub-legions, which had been established in 1792, was to be abolished and the sub-legions replaced by four regiments of infantry. The Corps of Artillerists and Engineers, organized

---

[12] Fevers and ague were common in the western part of the country. Volney wrote: "In the autumn of 1796, during a journey of more than three hundred leagues, I have not found, I dare say, twenty houses which were entirely free of it . . . ." Volney, *op. cit.*, p. 309.

in 1794, was to remain; and there would be also two companies of light dragoons.

President Washington's orders, dated at Philadelphia, August 27, 1796, reached Wayne at Detroit. The officers of each organization were named, from the commander in chief to ensigns of infantry and cornets of dragoons. James Wilkinson was retained as the only brigadier general, second in command to Wayne, and Hamtramck was named lieutenant colonel commanding the First Regiment. Wayne issued these orders on October 26. After the reorganization was complete, he granted the requests of four of his officers for furloughs. Captain Moses Porter, Artillery; Captain Joseph Brock and Ensign Henry Bowyer, Fourth Infantry; and Ensign Meriwether Lewis, First Infantry, were each given four months' leave.

In spite of his manifold duties the General did not overlook small details. Because they had no overcoats, soldiers walking their posts as sentries tied blankets about themselves to keep warm. The sight of them hurt Wayne's sense of military propriety. They appeared, he complained, "more like Indians than anything else." Consequently he ordered that the practice be stopped after the end of November, but he suggested that the men have overcoats made of their blankets.

On November 13 the Commander in Chief was preparing for his departure. In the absence of Colonel Hamtramck, who had gone to Fort Wayne, perhaps in connection with the reorganization of the army, the General wrote a letter of instruction for him. He confirmed his appointment as commandant at Detroit, and directed him to hasten the repair of the defenses. He ordered him to take care of the health and the comfort of the troops, to pay attention to their military appearance, to drill them in the manual of arms, and to perfect them in adroitness of maneuver.

His final word of advice dealt with the treatment of the Indians. He warned the Commandant that he must be sparing in his issues of provisions to the natives, and that he must keep them under close observation; but the Commander in Chief added that Hamtramck must "evince to them the justice and regard of the United States."[13]

[13] Wayne to Hamtramck, November 13, 1796, Wayne Papers, 47, 82, Hist. Soc. of Pa., Phila.

On Monday, November 14, a farewell message was delivered to General Wayne. This document bore the title:

"Address of the Curé & Inhabitants of Detroit to-gether with the Officers, Civil & Military of the County of Wayne in the Territory of the United States north west of the River Ohio.—

"To his Excellency Anthony Wayne Esqr. Major General & Commander-in-Chief of the Army of the United States."

The signers expressed their gratitude for all the favors they had received at his hands; thanked him for his kindness in permitting their county to bear his name; assured him of their loyalty to the United States and of their "joy in becoming united to *Citizens Free and Generous*"; begged him to speak favorably of them to the President; wished him a fair passage across the Lake; hoped that he would receive from the Government rewards commensurate with his great services; and prayed that God might "grant us the favour of seeing you here again to compleat the happiness of us all."

The address was signed by Michel Levadoux, curé; François Chabert, colonel of militia; James May, justice of the peace; Jean Baptiste Cicotte, major of militia; François Navarre, justice of the peace; Charles François Girardin, judge of the Court of Common Pleas; and Joseph Voyer, justice of the peace.

The General wrote with his own hand a gracious reply. He thanked the officials and the inhabitants for their flattering expressions of esteem, praised them for their loyalty to the new government, and promised to inform the President of it. In conclusion, he wrote: "I cannot permit myself to depart from hence without assuring you, that I shall always take a peculiar interest in whatever may contribute to promote the happiness & prosperity of this County, to which my name has the honor to be attached."

Now that the last duty had been completed, there was no further reason to remain. The next day General Wayne and his aide, Captain De Butts, boarded the *Detroit*, which cast off and set sail down the river for Presqu' Isle, whence they intended to proceed to Pittsburgh and Philadelphia.

CHAPTER VI
THE FUR TRADE

TOWARD the end of October, 1796, the streets of Detroit had begun to stir with brisk activity; and before General Wayne sailed away the whole village had been aroused from its summer lethargy. Everyone was busy preparing for the annual departure to the hunting grounds. Each day saw the arrival of new bands of Indians seeking merchants who would provide equipment and supplies for the winter hunt. *Voyageurs* in moccasins, leggings, and hunting shirts girdled with gaudy sashes swaggered noisily from store to store, drinking, quarreling, and soliciting employment to carry merchandise to the traders' outposts. Young men of the neighborhood who, a few weeks ago, had nothing better to do than to loaf about the town, now were exceedingly industrious making ready to winter in the wilderness. The merchants bustled about their stores assembling outfits to send to their wintering partners in the woods, hiring *voyageurs*, directing the work of their *engagés*, and negotiating with importunate savages.

At the docks ships were moored unloading trade goods from London and Montreal and loading stores for the trading posts. During this busy season the ships of the Detroit merchants were constantly in service: the sloop *Saguinah*, John Fearson, master, owned by Meldrum and Park, and John Askin; Askin's schooner *Weazell*, Louis Derineau, master, and his sloop *Annette*, commanded by Captain Timothy Grummond; the North West Company's sloops *Athabasca* and *Beaver*, the latter under Jonathan Nelson, master; James May's schooner *Swan*, captained by his brother Joseph; the schooner *Thames* under Captain William Gilkinson; the schooner *Charlotte*, owned by Angus Mackintosh and the North West Company, under Captain William Baker; the sloop *Russell*, Captain John White, and the schooner *Nancy*, commanded by Captain William Mills. These ships carried cargoes for the United

States Army and for the lesser merchants as well as for their owners. The captains signed the invoices, agreeing to deliver the merchandise safely at its destination, "the danger of the Lake excepted." Despite the hazards involved, neither ships nor cargoes were insured.[1]

From the very beginning of its existence Detroit had been principally a fur-trading post. Although Cadillac in his petition to Louis XIV had stressed the importance of a fort on the strait as a check to the advance of the British, it was their fur traders who were to be excluded; and Cadillac himself was eager to manage the trading at the post. The founder's quarrels with the Jesuits, with the officials at Quebec, and with the Company of the Colony grew out of the commerce in furs; and succeeding commandants also were usually more interested in returns from the trade than in the welfare of the *habitants*.

The early arrival of British traders after Major Robert Rogers occupied the fort in 1760 indicated that they understood the value of Detroit as a trading center. Lying between Lake Erie and the lakes farther north, it served as a convenient base for operations in both directions. Furs from Saginaw and from Sandusky gravitated to its warehouses; packs from Mackinac were frequently unloaded at its wharves for whipping and pressing into bales; and trade goods from England, liquor from various sources, and flour, meat, and corn produced in the neighborhood were taken aboard ships bound for the northern posts. The rivers, also, were highways for canoes and bateaux laden with furs. From the valleys of the Maumee and the Wabash came the richest cargoes for the merchants at Detroit.

After the Revolutionary War the fur trade had been unprofitable. Too much merchandise was sent out from Montreal, the Indians north of the Ohio River were restless because of the advance of American settlers, and there were too many merchants engaged in the business. In order to overcome the evils of unbridled competition six firms and individuals in Detroit organized the Miamis Company, probably in 1786. The Company, composed of Leith and Shepherd, Sharp and Wallace, Meldrum and Park, James Abbott, Angus Mackin-

---

[1] At this time the British Government maintained the following ships on the Upper Lakes: Sloops—*Felicity* and *Francis*; schooners—*Dunmore*, *Maria*, and *Miamis*; and snows—*Chippewa* and *Ottawa*. The sloop *Detroit*, Captain Peter Curry, master, was the only United States ship on the Upper Lakes.

tosh, and John Askin, furnished outfits to smaller traders and carried on some trade of its own by hired clerks. In spite of this attempt to control prices conditions did not improve, and the Company vanished after a few years.

The other local traders probably shared the misfortunes of John Askin. In the summer of 1793 he wrote to William Robertson in London: "I have been Uncommonly unlucky in my Returns from ye Ind^n Country this Year & those who made many packs paid too much for them."[2] He had recently received a letter from Robertson warning him that rumors of an impending war with France had already reduced the price of furs in England. Another letter, written in London on April 10, reported that the war had begun and spoke dolefully of bankruptcies in Great Britain, of furs returned from China, and of a further fall in price. Robertson predicted that the next year raccoon skins would be worth only one half or even one sixth of their former value.

Isaac Todd, of the Montreal firm of Todd and McGill, which handled Askin's business, also wrote from London that "there will be a Loss on your furrs, and your Son's, and ... the prospect for Next year is so bad thers no saying what price they May bring...." He added the surprising news that forty thousand raccoon skins had been shipped from London to New York and Philadelphia. Early in 1794 James McGill wrote that Askin's remittances fell far short of the value of the goods which the firm had sent to Askin in 1793. Because of an even greater adverse balance for the previous year Askin now owed the partners nearly £4,000. McGill was anxious not to hurt his friend's feelings, but he urged him to try to reduce his debt. This Askin was able to do only by transferring to Todd and McGill from time to time some of his holdings of land, which, for friendship's sake, they accepted "at valuations far in excess of anything ever realized from them."[3]

The fundamental difficulty was that the fur trade was

[2] William Robertson, however, became very wealthy during the same period. He was in Detroit from 1782 to 1790, when he returned to England, leaving his business in the hands of his younger brother David. William returned to Detroit in 1795, dissolved the partnership with David, and left Detroit in 1796. Most of the rest of his life was spent in England.

Perhaps Robertson thought there was slight opportunity for profit in the business while the war in Europe continued.

[3] Milo M. Quaife (ed.), *The John Askin Papers*, I, Introduction, p. 9.

simply a gamble. It could not be otherwise, considering the methods of doing business. The merchants in Montreal dominated the industry. They imported goods from England, usually on a commission basis, and shipped them to the merchants at Detroit and other posts at an advance on the sterling cost. These consignments were sent at the expense of the consignee, who also had to accept the risk of loss during transportation.

The trade goods consisted of guns, powder, lead, gunflints, fishhooks, horn or ivory combs, jew's-harps, laced hats, blankets, cloth of various kinds, knives, hatchets, axes, pipes, tobacco, firesteels, mirrors, nests of tin, brass, and copper kettles, vermilion, ribbons, and silver ornaments in the form of crosses, brooches, and earbobs.[4]

There were several methods of distributing these goods. The merchant at Detroit might send them to wintering partners or *hivernants* who remained in the woods. John Anderson served in this capacity for John Askin on the Maumee River. These men gave supplies to Indians on credit. The natives went off to hunt, promising to bring back the pelts they took during the winter.

Another practice was to send out a stock of goods in charge of a trusted clerk, who would make the arrangements with the Indians. James Melvin went out in charge of George McDougall's "Miamis Adventure" to the Au Glaize River. Perhaps he would follow the hunters to prevent their selling their furs to an independent trader; or he might arrange to meet them in the spring.

For both methods of trade men had to be hired to row the *bateaux*, to paddle the canoes, and to carry the goods across the portages. These were the *voyageurs*, drunken, noisy nuisances in the settlements, but indispensable to the trade. Jacob Lindley characterized them as "quite as hardy, and almost as savage as the Indians themselves." They could drive a loaded

---

[4] There were a number of silversmiths in Detroit during the first decade of the American régime. Making ornaments for the Indian trade was an important part of their work. The names of the following silversmiths occur in merchants' records of the period: Peter Desnoyers, Israel Ruland, George Smart, James Brown, Isaac Brunson, Paul Malcher, and Antoine O'Neal.

canoe[5] over lake or river with the tirelessness of a machine, timing the strokes of their paddles to the meter of a rollicking song. At the numerous portages they took canoe and bales of furs or merchandise upon their backs and trotted patiently along the trail until the transfer from one stream to another had been made. If they remained in the woods during the winter, they lived on hominy and bear's grease, which they cooked together into a kind of porridge.

These veterans were contemptuous of the *mangeurs de lard*, tenderfeet not yet hardened to the Spartan fare, who ate salt pork and hardtack. All the men who remained in the woods throughout the winter, whether traders, clerks, or *voyageurs*, endured the same hardships. So great they seemed to Joseph Moore that he declared no one but the Canadian French could bear them. His companion, Jacob Lindley, marveled at the privations these people accepted as a matter of course. Writing at Detroit, he observed: "In short, the young men hereaway, think themselves no more accomplished for company or conversation, not having taken this journey, than our young gentlemen, not having taken the tour of Europe."

A third method of trade was more direct. Indians came to Detroit in the fall and made their bargains with the merchant himself. If all went well, they returned in the spring with furs sufficient to pay for the supplies they had received. If the hunting was poor, the Indian accepted no obligation to pay the amount owing to the merchant. It was not his fault if animals were scarce; and so he simply shrugged off the loss to his creditor. The merchant at Detroit, however, could not so easily satisfy his creditors at Montreal. They entered the deficit in their books and charged him interest on it. If his debt became too great, he would find his credit cut off; no Montreal merchant would sell him goods.

These middlemen in Lower Canada protected themselves by acting simply as agents. They ordered the goods in England and shipped them to the western posts. Later they received

---

[5] The largest canoes were of birch bark, thirty-three feet long and four and one-half feet wide. They could carry a load of four tons, including the weight of eight paddlemen. M. M. Quaife (ed.), *Alexander Henry's Travels* (Chicago, 1921), pp. 15-16.

the furs and sold them either in Montreal or in London for what they would bring. Their risk was not great if they avoided granting too much credit. It is notable that, while men like Askin were sinking more deeply into debt, James McGill was becoming the wealthiest man in Canada.

The great length of time required for a turnover of merchandise was another cause of uncertainty. Goods sent from England in 1794 might not be exchanged for furs until 1795; and the furs might not reach London until 1796 because of the distances to be traversed and the long winters that closed the water communications. During this period a change in the price of merchandise, a decrease in the demand for furs, disturbances in the Indian country, or adverse weather conditions that reduced the size of the catch might bring ruin to the traders.

As in all games of chance, despite present failure there was always the lure of a lucky strike in the future. Besides, some other sources of profit were available to prevent complete disaster. There were government contracts, land speculation, and trade with the great North West Company. This organization operated out of Montreal into the farthest reaches of the known West, its greatest trade being carried on north and west of Lake Superior. Some of its furs passed through Detroit, where Angus Mackintosh was the company's agent. John Askin sold hominy and flour to feed its employes in the North; and many others profited in one way or another by this business.

Establishing a policy for the management of the fur trade was one of the early tasks that faced the young government of the United States. The French and the British had found the regulation of the trade practically impossible. One writer summed up their experience thus:

> France attempted to place this traffic in peltries in the hands of a few, a fur-trading aristocracy, and piled decree upon decree to hold it there, control it, limit it, and preserve it; the result was, illegal trade on every hand and defiance of the laws and decrees which men considered unjust. England made it free to all for the mere asking [licenses were required]; a policy which ended in disaster, because men unwilling to control their greed for the precious pelts waged bitter war on one another, each bent on obtaining the biggest share.[6]

---

[6] Ida A. Johnson, *The Michigan Fur Trade* (Lansing, 1919), pp. 66–67.

The British traders and the merchants in Montreal were at first fearful that the American occupation would completely ruin their business. Observation and reflection, however, gradually convinced them that they had slight cause for worry. A memoir drawn up by Isaac Todd and Simon McTavish, probably in 1794, pointed out that the cost of transportation from American ports to the Indian country was nearly double the cost by way of the St. Lawrence, and that heavy duties charged on articles of European manufacture by the United States raised the price of goods for Yankee traders. Besides, the Jay Treaty gave the British free navigation of the lakes and rivers; they would pay no higher duty on goods carried into the United States than would American citizens; and no duties would be laid on pelts carried by land or by inland waters. Although the British granted the same rights to Americans in Canada, the former had the advantages of long experience in the business and organization of the means of trade.

Besides, the British Government continued its policy of giving presents to Indians who came to the posts. At Fort Malden, on the other side of the Detroit River, the Indian Department was still actively engaged in caring for its wards. The traders, of course, reaped the benefits of the expenditures of the government for the Indians, which, in fact, served as a subsidy for the fur business. The French Government also had subsidized the traders by supporting troops at distant posts, by sending expeditions against hostile natives, and by a lavish distribution of presents. In this manner the taxpayer in the mother-country supported colonial adventures for the greater glory of His Majesty and the benefit of the fur merchants.

Faced with the necessity of winning the friendship of the Indians, the Government of the United States attempted to regulate the trade for the protection of the natives. Licenses issued by authority of the central government for the purpose of restraining the excesses of the traders had failed of their purpose. Consequently, in 1796, Congress passed a law authorizing the establishment of trading posts or "factories" under the immediate direction of the President. Agents were to be appointed to operate the posts where goods would be sold to Indians at low prices in the hope that this sort of competition would compel the traders to change their practices. For the present, however, this act was simply a threat. No store was established anywhere in the northern part of the country until 1802.

2

Besides their interest in the far-flung fur trade, which began in the forests in North America and terminated in London, Paris, St. Petersburg, or even Pekin, the merchants of Detroit also carried on a considerable local business. Visitors were astonished at the variety of goods offered for sale. The women of the town, when they went to shop at Askin's, or May's, or Abbott's, or Campau's, or Robertson's, could buy all sorts of food for their families. There were flour, bread, butter and bear oil, olive oil, cheese, olives, raisins, almonds, beef, veal, mutton, pork, venison, sometimes wildfowl, and, when a ship came in from the North, "St. Mary's whitefish"; of beverages there were coffee, tea, chocolate, Madeira, and Port; for sweetening and seasoning, loaf sugar, Indian sugar, mustard, pepper, salt, vinegar, cinnamon, and nutmegs. Housewives would find, too, a limited variety of home remedies: Anderson's Pills, Hooper's Pills, "Jesuit Bark" (quinine), sweet mercury, and Glauber's salts.

There were also soap and candles; cups, saucers, and plates of pewter or Queensware, and glass goblets; pots and pans for the kitchen; blankets or buffalo robes for the beds; and hats, stockings, shoes, moccasins, and slippers. For the seamstress there were many kinds of cloth: muslin, linen, cambric, molton, swanskin, and calico, with needles, thread, pins, scissors, and buttons for making them into clothes, and starch for the laundress. Toothbrushes, handkerchiefs, ribbons, and mirrors also were for sale. There were no ready-made dresses; but most of the women probably made their own for everyday wear, and Madame Persie, the dressmaker, could copy London styles for her patrons.

There were also articles enough for a man's necessities or for his pleasure: snuff, pipes, tobacco, and playing cards to while away a winter evening; wines, rum, spirits, and ale for the table or for convivial occasions; shoes and blacking, moccasins, beaver hats, silver knee buckles, and white or black silk stockings for a gentleman to wear with his small clothes; hair powder, horn or ivory combs, and perfumed pomatum for dressing his hair. There were also stocks of paper, ink powder, and quills for writing. In these same stores the Detroiter could purchase nails, paint, carpenter's tools, axes, fishlines, scalping knives, guns, powder and shot, beaver traps, and harness. He could order a load of hay, planks, timbers, bricks, or supplies of cordwood; and he might bargain for horses, cattle, oxen, sheep, goats, or hives of bees.

If a Detroiter was not pleased with the clothing displayed in the stores, Mrs. Grahames and Miss Campau could make fine shirts for him; and John Cain, Thomas McCrea, René Mettez, Pierre Descomps Labadie, or Robert Gouie could make him a suit. These people and many others sold their products through the merchants, who credited the account of the maker and charged the cost to the purchaser.

Since cash was scarce in Detroit, this was a convenient way of exchanging goods and services. As a matter of fact, customers frequently paid their debts by the delivery of goods or by working for the merchants. For example, Mme Charles Chêne earned £6 15s. by boiling forty-five bushels of corn in lye to make hominy for John Askin. He entered the credit in his journal, and then charged against it purchases to the same amount that Mme Chêne made in his store.

The employes or *engagés* of the merchants also received most of their wages in goods. Thus Joseph Bariau earned £13 2s. by cutting and hauling wood and making hominy for Askin at 6s. a day. Bariau lived with Ignatius Billet, another *engagé*, in Askin's "Red House on the Common," which rented for £20 a year. Askin charged him £9 9s. 4d. for eleven and a half months' rent; then added £2 4s. for his half of the cost of replacing forty-four windowpanes in the house. What had happened to the panes is not recorded in the Journal; but when the debit was subtracted from the credit, Bariau had little more than one pound due for all his labor.

Although the general practice of settling debts by making entries in the merchants' books reduced the need for money, a medium of exchange was necessary for some transactions.

Silver and gold coins of Great Britain, Spain, Portugal, and France came into the town in trade; and coins of various kinds and bank notes were put in circulation by the soldiers and the quartermaster's department.[7] Some of the silver was made into ornaments for the Indian trade; some of it was cut into fragments to serve as change; and most of the rest, along with the gold and the bank notes, was drawn off to pay debts due in Montreal. Consequently the Detroit merchants issued their own currency in the form of notes or due bills based on the value of the goods of the issuer and, of course, on his reputation. These notes could not circulate outside the community or, at least, beyond the region in which the signer was known. As they were brought in from time to time by customers, they were destroyed, and new ones were issued. There must have been some counterfeit notes in circulation, or some which the signer was not able to honor when they were presented; for Askin frequently recorded in his Journal, besides the destruction "of my Current Money," "Destroyed this day of Bad Money" so many pounds and shillings.

Sometimes accounts were kept in Halifax shillings, worth three fourths the sterling shilling. Usually, however, they were reckoned in New York, or, for short, York currency. In 1796 the York shilling was worth twelve and one-half cents, half the value of the sterling shilling, and eight York shillings were equivalent to one dollar. This was the Spanish milled dollar, which had for a long time served as a standard of value and which the United States used as the basis of its monetary system. Entries in the journals of Detroit merchants show that the current local ratio of dollars to pounds was based on the York shilling. For instance, on December 6, 1796, James May accepted six dollars and translated that amount into £2 8*s*.; and in April of the same year George McDougall turned over $984 in "American Bank Notes" to Forsyth, Richardson and Company and debited their account with £393 12*s*.

[7] Daniel Mayo to James Henry, April 9, 10, and 19, 1797, gives the information that $10,000 in silver, gold, and bank bills are being sent to Detroit. The number of pieces of British, Spanish, and French gold are listed. Sibley Papers, Burton Hist. Coll.

Foreign coins were used throughout the United States. Henry Adams, writing about money in 1802, asserted that "a gold or silver coin of the United States was still a rare sight." Henry Adams, *History of the United States*, I, 299.

At this time, as there was no bank in Detroit, the merchants acted as bankers for their customers. Thus on July 4, 1796, François Bellecour, the notary, apparently needed some cash. Askin gave him £1 12s. and entered that sum as a debit to Gabriel Hunot, for whom Bellecour had written an Indian deed.

Sometimes the transaction was exactly like cashing a check. On September 25, 1796, Askin wrote in his account book: "Thos. Smith Esq Dr To paid his order to the Bearer for £5." Two days earlier Askin had recorded a more complicated transaction: "Thos. Smith Esq to W^m. Robertson Dr for the formers Order on the latter to pay Mr. Innis £1." These services were provided for the convenience of customers, apparently gratis. Interest, however, was charged on debts at the rate of 6 per cent.

3

The Court of General Quarter Sessions which Acting Governor Sargent had established held its first session on October 10. This was a preliminary meeting attended only by the justices in Detroit. The clerk, Peter Audrain, wrote to François Navarre announcing the sitting of a "general court" on the first Tuesday of December and urging him, as one of the justices, to be present. At that session, Audrain explained, the court would divide the county into townships and appoint three county commissioners and a constable for each township. The clerk requested Navarre to recommend for commissioner a man from his neighborhood who would be acceptable to the people. He asked him also to name an honest man for constable. This officer, Audrain wrote, should be able to read and write, "s'il est possible."

In November Sheriff George McDougall was preparing to leave for his wintering camp at Sandusky, where he was accustomed to trade with the Indians. With the consent of the judges, he surrendered the duties of his office to Coroner Hermann Eberts, who agreed to act as sheriff, to pay one third of the profits of the office to McDougall, to account for all money received as sheriff, and to be responsible for all escapes of prisoners.

Dr. Eberts must have been acting for McDougall before

they made the agreement; for on October 11 he signed a petition as sheriff, along with Justices May and Williams, directed to General Wayne and asking for permission to confine prisoners in the Citadel. The reason for the request was that a prisoner, Nathaniel Chapman, sailor on the sloop *Beaver*, had escaped. The sheriff had arrested Chapman for nonpayment of a debt. Eberts took him home and placed him in the custody of his bailiff while he tried to find a house to rent for a jail. During the sheriff's absence Chapman assaulted the bailiff and escaped. Eberts offered eight dollars' reward for his capture. The petition informed the General that he had been taken by some soldiers and was confined in the guardhouse.

Apparently Eberts soon found a building to use as a prison; for a week later James May charged an order of nails, spikes, hinges, and five padlocks to the "Jail in Detroit."[8] This expenditure seems to have been in vain, as two months later, toward the end of December, Eberts protested to the Court of Common Pleas "against the Strength and the insufficiency of the Jail of the County." He petitioned the Court to indemnify him in case any prisoner escaped for lack of a proper prison. Perhaps by this time the physician-coroner-sheriff had reason to regret his bargain with George McDougall.

The records of the December sitting of the Court of General Quarter Sessions in Detroit have not been discovered; but Peter Audrain, in a letter written on Christmas Day, 1796, to Secretary Winthrop Sargent, reported that the judges had performed their administrative duties. They had divided Wayne County into four townships: St. Clair to the east, then Hamtramck on the Côte du Nord-Est, Detroit, and Sargent, the last beginning at the River Ecorce and extending to the mouth of the Maumee River.

In addition, the judges had appointed two constables for each township except Detroit, which they provided with three, two overseers of the poor, and two highway inspectors. As county commissioners they had chosen Antoine Dequindre, François D^x. Bellecour, and Robert Gouie.

[8] Sargent's request to the Secretary of State, in his letter of August 23, 1796 (C. E. Carter ed., *The Territorial Papers of the United States*, III, 452), that the county be permitted to erect a jail and a courthouse on the Domain belonging to the United States would indicate that both had to be improvised for the present.

On December 8 the Grand Jury made its presentment to the Court. This document contained a recommendation that regulations be made to prevent fires, and specifically mentioned Meldrum's and Roe's chimneys as having long been considered "insufficient." The jury also urged that the burying ground be removed to some spot outside the stockade and that the streets be cleared of filth and dirt. The attention of the Court was called to the necessity of adopting standard weights and measures, especially for flour, bread, and cordwood. The prevention of horses galloping through the streets or running at large was another matter which the Court was asked to consider. The jurors also urged that the judges appoint only citizens of the United States to public office. Finally, they reported, probably as the result of their own experience, that "the chimney of the present Court House appears to be as insufficient as those already presented."[9]

"Insufficient" chimneys had previously been a matter of concern to the British magistrates. Reports of inspectors show that many of the residents were lax in their observance of the fire regulations of the town. It is likely that the existing code remained in effect after the arrival of the Americans, and the duty of enforcing the rules now fell upon the justices of the Court of General Quarter Sessions, who were responsible also for maintaining the fire engine.[10]

The mere transfer of sovereignty certainly did nothing to correct the careless habits of the inhabitants in regard to fire hazards. Perhaps, too, the magistrates found themselves without sufficient power to enforce their orders. However that may have been, in the fall of 1798 seventy-three householders signed an agreement to obey faithfully a comprehensive code of fire regulations consisting of seventeen articles. They promised, among other things, to sweep their chimneys every two weeks, on Saturday; to fasten on the roof ladders reaching from

[9] The Court and the jury probably sat in a tavern or in a private house. In June, 1798, Audrain paid Charles Cabassier "une piastre et Cinquante Cents" for the rent of a courtroom. A. D. Fraser Papers, Burton Hist. Coll.

[10] At the June term, 1798, the clerk of the court read "in english & French, the account of the Engine." Gabriel Godfroy Papers, ibid.

This is the first official notice of a fire engine. In the William Macomb Estate Ledger (Burton Hist. Coll.), however, a fire engine is included in the inventory of Macomb's possessions in 1796. Perhaps this is the same engine.

the eaves to each chimney and to have another ladder by which they could climb to the roof; to keep a barrel filled with water where it would not freeze; to have on hand two three-gallon buckets; to turn out at an alarm to assist in fighting a fire; to form a line from the river to the fire to supply water under the direction of the magistrates; and to keep their carts, sleighs, and firewood out of the streets and lanes where they would obstruct the work of the fire fighters. A fine ranging from three to eight dollars was to be assessed upon any signer who failed to observe these regulations.

To man the fire engine Colonel Strong was to detail twelve soldiers from the Second Regiment, and civilians were to be designated to assist them under the command of John Askin, Jr., and Augustine Lafoy. Four men under the direction of Jacques Peltier were to attend each fire with good felling axes. In order to prevent serious explosions, no man was permitted to keep more than a keg of gunpowder in his house or store. The fine for noncompliance with this article was the highest of all—twenty-five dollars. Each signer of the agreement gave bond for the sum of twenty pounds, New York currency.

4

With the departure of the Commander in Chief, Detroit lost its temporary distinction of being army headquarters. The garrison settled down to routine military duties under the command of Colonel Hamtramck, drilling, engaging in maneuvers, and parading every Sunday.

Because winter was approaching, repairs to Fort and Citadel had to be hastened. Peter Audrain, assistant quartermaster general, ordered from James May 6,919 pickets ranging in length from nine to fourteen feet, and in diameter from six to eight inches, at a cost of $3,390. The shortest pickets were to be red cedar; the others, swamp ash or oak. He also agreed to pay Meldrum and Park $945.83 for planks and timbers.

To expedite the work on Fort and Citadel, Colonel Hamtramck on December 20, 1796, ordered all artificers to assist the quartermaster's department, and he put Major J. J. U. Rivardi in charge of the construction.[11]

---

[11] Rivardi was a Frenchman serving in the Corps of Artillerists and Engineers. He had been commissioned major, February 26, 1795, and came to Detroit in the fall of 1796.

Toward the end of November Thomas Swaine, agent at Detroit of James O'Hara, army contractor, began the slaughtering of hogs and cattle to provide the soldiers with meat. That this was a large-scale operation is indicated by a letter from O'Hara to Eli Curtis, who was directed to go to Detroit and superintend the salting of at least one thousand barrels of pork and beef. Curtis was instructed to board the *Swan* at Presqu' Isle. Fortunately for him, perhaps, he arrived there after the ship had landed the Indian chiefs and had sailed for Detroit with a cargo of supplies for the garrison; for during this voyage the schooner was lost. James May, the owner of the *Swan*, immediately arranged to have a new ship built at Harsen's Island.

CHAPTER VII
CULTURE IN THE WILDERNESS

THE report of Territorial Secretary Winthrop Sargent that very few men of "even common Education were to be found in the Country" and his request that the Government grant land for schools which would "tend to the Happiness of a Deserving people" seem to imply that no means of education were provided in the community. That, however, was not true. For those who could afford to pay there were schools, one of which was conducted by John Burrell. Among the pupils who attended his school for a number of years during this period were James and John Burnett, sons of William Burnett, an American who had settled in southwestern Michigan a few years after the Revolutionary War as an independent fur trader. Although Burnett had had some difficulties with the British authorities, he had established a post on the St. Joseph River, a mile and a half above the mouth. There his marriage to Kakima, daughter of the influential Potawatomi chief Aniquiba and sister of Topinabee, made his position secure.

When the two boys, the oldest of Burnett's seven children, were ready for school, their father sent them to live with his friend James May, whose Day Book contains entries of numerous items purchased for them: beaver hats, tailor-made clothing, shoes, books, writing paper, quills, and ink powder, along with payments to John Burrell for instruction, all charged to the account of William Burnett. Although their father paid for their board and lodging, May probably treated these half-Indian boys as members of his family; for sometimes in his accounts he set down their names as Jimmy and Johnny. During a part of 1795, at least, Betsey May attended Burrell's school with the Burnett boys.

These children, and probably many others, must have gone to school during the day. Burrell also conducted evening classes for people who were employed. One of his evening

pupils was a boy who became a distinguished citizen of Detroit
—John R. Williams. It was in November, 1796, that fourteen-year-old John Williams—he later inserted the initial to avoid confusion with another John Williams—wrote to his uncle Joseph Campau asking for a place in his store. John promised to do whatever was required of him if Campau would clothe him, give him board and lodging, and provide schooling for him in the evening "with a good schoolmaster."

The letter was written in French, the only language the boy knew; for although his father was Thomas Williams, English merchant and magistrate at Detroit, his mother was Marie Cecile Campau, Joseph's sister. After her husband's death in 1785 she had married Jacques Lauzon and moved to the Clinton River in the vicinity of the present city of Mt. Clemens. Consequently the boy had grown up in a French community.

Joseph Campau apparently accepted his nephew's terms of employment; for the boy came to work for him, and his education began on the last day of November.[1] The charge for tuition was sixteen shillings a month; besides, Campau had to pay for his nephew's "quantum of Fire Wood" to heat the schoolroom and for one paper of ink powder. The merchant also engaged Burrell to come to his house on Ste Anne Street to instruct him in English, beginning December 20.

Another schoolmaster in Detroit at this time was Matthew Donovan, who had been there for about two years. Previously he had taught in Kingston, Upper Canada, where he was known as an excellent Latin scholar. From July 19 to November 19, 1796, James and John Burnett attended his school; then they returned to Burrell's. During 1796 John Askin was paying Donovan at the rate of thirty pounds a year, although which of his numerous children was or were being instructed is not set down in his Journal.

Besides Burrell and Donovan, Joseph Rowe, Jean Baptiste Roucour and a man named Delisle were schoolmasters in Detroit in 1796. Rowe and Burrell seem to have been partners. If they conducted a school together, it must have been a

[1] In the records of the Wayne County Court of Common Pleas, December Term, 1796, there is a beautifully written bill of articles purchased by Jean Baptiste Campau from Joseph Campau. At the bottom of the sheet is the phrase "Par John Williams." Legal Research Building, University of Michigan.

larger enterprise than one would expect to find on the frontier at that early day.

Roucour was called "Director of the Christian School," which one writer has surmised may have been Ste Anne's parochial school.[2] It is more likely, however, that Roucour, who was also the *chantre*, assisting the priest in the services, simply instructed children in the catechism and in the ceremonies of the church.[3]

There was also a musician in the town who had pupils. John Houghton, during September and October, earned £3 4s. by "teaching Charley" Askin. What instrument he played and how apt the eleven-year-old pupil was are not mentioned in the record. The only musical instrument, aside from fiddles, seems to have been Dr. William Harffy's harpsichord. When the Doctor retired to Amherstburg with the British troops, he left it in Detroit, where it remained until October, 1799, when he had it sent across the river to his house.

There were also schoolmistresses in Detroit at this time. Mrs. Pattinson was conducting a school, of which John Askin and Commodore Alexander Grant were the patrons. According to Askin's ledger, he paid one third the cost, and his brother-in-law paid two thirds. Mrs. Pattinson took a large part of her salary in foodstuffs charged at Askin's store. Perhaps Adelaide Askin attended this school. In a letter to their mother in October, 1795, her older sister, Archange, who was in England with her husband, Captain David Meredith, thanked Adelaide for her "nice French letter." "I am glad to see that my little sister Adelaide writes so well," she added. At that time Adelaide was twelve years old.

Four of Commodore Grant's ten daughters attended this school. Whether his only son Alexander, who was five years old, was attending or not, is not certain.[4] Nevertheless, he was

[2] Sister Mary Rosalita, *Education in Detroit Prior to 1850* (Lansing, 1928), pp. 20-21.

[3] These duties were specifically assigned to Etienne Dubois, the *chantre*, who succeeded M. Roucour. Livre des Assemblees de la Paroisse Ste Anne, 1796-1887, August 2, 1802, p. 28, Manuscript copy, Burton Hist. Coll.

[4] The Grants had a foster son, Jean or John Grant, who at this time was about nineteen years old. They had bought him when he was a baby from "a Chippewa war party, returning from a raid upon the American frontier." Milo M. Quaife, (ed.), *The John Askin Papers*, II, 342.

receiving instruction somewhere, for Askin sold Grant a spelling book for him in August, 1796. In addition to Mrs. Pattinson, other schoolmistresses were a Miss Papineau, to whom George Meldrum sent his daughter Nancy, a Miss Adhemar, and Madame Bellecour.

From the sources available it is not possible to reconstruct the curricula of these schools. Probably all taught the fundamentals, while the Latinist Donovan perhaps went beyond and put his pupils through the classics. All the schools, of course, were private. The parents paid fees, and often the work must have been on a tutorial basis. That there was some sort of classification appears from the fact that both Burrell and Donovan charged a higher fee for instructing James Burnett than they charged for his younger brother. A study of the dates of payment leads to the conclusion that there were no regular vacations. Children probably attended school as long as their parents were willing to pay the fees.

2

Among the other evidences of culture in Detroit, in addition to schools, books probably took first place. It is impossible to say how many volumes there were in the town and its vicinity, but inventories of the property of some of the residents indicate that books were not a rarity. For instance, when the belongings of John Askwith were sold after his death in 1795, about one hundred and thirty volumes were knocked down to the highest bidder. Among them were Johnson's *English Dictionary* (two volumes), Simson's *"uclide,"* Rollins' *History* (thirteen volumes), *History of Holland*, a French and English dictionary, Atkins' *Navigation*, and "Mathew Matical works." There were also a French grammar, a geographical gazetteer, two globes, and a "parcel of maps." Besides his books, his personal property included a microscope, mathematical instruments, two "fidles," and five music books.

Another resident of Detroit, who left the town in 1796, also had a considerable number of books. This was Pierre Jean Baptiste Testard, Sieur de Montigny de Louvigny, who usually signed his name simply Louvigny Montigny. He was active in the service of the British Government and had fought against Wayne on the Maumee in 1794. Among his property left to be sold were eight volumes of French books valued at thirty-two pounds and "a collection of English books" worth forty pounds. He had also a globe, an atlas, and "historical and geographical maps." In addition, he had "une Lanterne magique," which he valued at six pounds, and "un Pendegraphe" (pantograph?) worth twenty pounds.

William Macomb also had had a large number of books. Shortly after his death in 1796 his widow sold nearly two hundred volumes to Richard Pollard of Sandwich. Among them were: Swift's *Works* (twenty-four volumes), Plutarch's *Lives* (six volumes), Chesterfield's *Letters* (four volumes), Fielding's *Works* (twelve volumes), Gibbon's *Roman Empire* (one volume), Hume's *Essays* (four volumes), Hume's *England* (eight volumes), Chambers *Dictionary* (four volumes), Smith's *Wealth of Nations* (two volumes), Robertson's *America* (two volumes), *History of the Indies*, De Lome's *Constitution of England*, and a *Poetical Miscellany*. Here was a great variety of reading matter for study or for diversion.

Books were lent in Detroit then as they are now, and were probably as tardily returned. To serve as a reminder in case the memory of the borrower or that of the lender failed, John Askin made a note on the last page of his Journal for 1796–97 of persons to whom he had lent books. Colonel Hamtramck borrowed Sully's *Memoirs;* James May, *The Laws of Upper Canada;* Peter Audrain, *The Court Circuit Companion;* Thomas Smith, *A Law of Congress in December 1795;* and Dr. Harffy, *Major Temple, or the Imposter*.

Probably the stores had few books for sale on their shelves besides the spelling and arithmetic texts for school children. The only other books mentioned in the merchant's journals which have been cited were a large Bible purchased at Askin's by Braddock Chapell, carpenter, and a prayer book charged to Robert Nichol, one of Askin's clerks.

There was no newspaper in Detroit, and there was only one in the whole Territory—*Freeman's Journal*, published in Cincinnati.[5] For lack of a newspaper public notices were posted on the fire-engine house, advertisements were read at the

---

[5] This newspaper was first issued June 18, 1796, replacing the *Centinel of the North-Western Territory*, which had first appeared on November 9, 1793.

church door on Sunday after mass, and a drummer was paid to pass along the streets announcing that a sale was about to commence.

News of the outer world came to Detroit in newspapers sent with consignments of goods, months old perhaps, but news just the same. Vague rumors and exaggerated accounts of events sometimes circulated widely before the facts were known. For example, Prideaux Selby reported to Colonel McKee that "The French King [Louis XVI] was put to death on the 21st Jan'y [1793], in the house of assembly of the national convention, one of the members cut off his head with a pen knife, tis also said the Queen & the Royal family were murdered two days afterwards."

Although there was no newspaper in Detroit, John McCall, a printer, was working there in 1796.[6] James May took orders for him and paid him for his work. Besides the sheriff bonds, writs, and summonses which he printed for the officers of Wayne County, the only other known product of McCall's press is a pamphlet of sixteen pages entitled *An Act Passed at the First*

[6] The press which he used may have belonged at one time to William Macomb. Silas Farmer, *History of Detroit and Michigan* (Detroit, 1884), p. 694, credits the Macombs with having had a press as early as 1785. If they had one, they probably sold it, for there is no press listed in the Macomb Estate Ledger, 1796, Burton Hist. Coll. Perhaps James May owned it in 1796. On July 14, 1800, May charged Sylvester Tiffany, a printer from Niagara, Upper Canada, £5 to ship "1 Small printing press with Types &c." down the lake on May's schooner, the *General Wilkinson*. James May's Day Book, 1798-1804, Burton Hist. Coll. This was probably the press used by McCall.

Douglas C. McMurtrie has expressed the opinion that legal forms were printed in Detroit until 1805, when the press was probably destroyed by fire. *Early Printing in Michigan* (Chicago, 1931), p. 23. It seems more likely, however, that McCall was in Detroit for only a short time in 1796, and that after he left printing was done at Cincinnati on the press of Samuel and Edmund Freeman, publishers of *Freeman's Journal*.

In 1798 General John Wilkins, Jr., paid "E. Freeman," at Detroit, three dollars "for printing 300 bills of exchange for the paymaster gen." *Quarter Master General's Report, 1796-1802* (Washington, 1803), p. 219. "E. Freeman" may have been either Edmund Freeman of Cincinnati, one of the publishers of *Freeman's Journal*, or Ezra Fitz Freeman, lawyer, and probably a relative of the publishers, who was in Detroit in 1798. During the same year, "E. Freeman" and "S. Freeman" were paid at Cincinnati for advertising and for printing. *Ibid.*, pp. 219, 220. Only on the supposition that Edmund Freeman visited Detroit, or that Ezra Fitz Freeman was a printer as well as a lawyer, could one say, on the available evidence, that printing was done in Detroit between 1796 and 1809, the year in which Father Gabriel Richard brought a press to the town.

Session of the Fourth Congress of the United States of America.[7] It was intended "to regulate trade and intercourse with the Indian tribes, and to preserve peace on the frontiers." Very probably it had been printed by order of Winthrop Sargent for the instruction of the inhabitants of the newly established county.[8] Perhaps this was the *Law of Congress in December 1795* which John Askin lent to Thomas Smith,[9] for it is likely that the British subjects were anxious to learn what effect the law would have on their business.

The only secular social organization in Detroit at this time was Zion Lodge, Number 10, Ancient Free and Accepted Masons, which had been established in 1794. Seven members were present at the first meeting, which was held on December 19, at the inn of James Donaldson, under sanction of the Grand Lodge of Lower Canada.[10]

The membership was small, and all the brothers were English-speaking residents of the town: James May, Patrick McNiff, Captain Peter Curry, James Donaldson, Israel Ruland, Samuel Choate, John Wheaton, Captain William Mills, Hugh Heward, Joseph Rowe, Nathan Williams, and George Meldrum. Meetings were held each month at Donaldson's inn. According to the minutes, they were adjourned promptly at ten o'clock.

No Americans attended the meetings during the first two months of occupation. In September, however, three of them were admitted as visitors; and at the St. John's Day banquet on December 27, 1796, Ezra Fitz Freeman was present as a visitor from Harmony Lodge, Number 10, of Cincinnati. During the remainder of the winter neither he nor any other

---

[7] The only extant copy of this pamphlet is in the Burton Historical Collection

[8] On September 30, 1796, Sargent wrote to the Secretary of State from Detroit: "I am ... printing the Law regulating Indian Intercourse &ca which I trust may be attended with Statutory [sic] Effects." C. E. Carter (ed.), *The Territorial Papers of the United States*, II, 580. A footnote identifies the law as the one passed May 19, 1796. This is the act which was printed by McCall.

[9] The law was passed, not in December, 1795, but during the session which began in December, 1795.

[10] C. M. Burton (compiler), Zion Lodge, Detroit, Vol. I, 1794–1802, Burton Hist. Coll. This manuscript is a typed transcript of the minutes of the meetings.

Zion Lodge was the successor of an earlier one which had been founded in 1764 by British army officers in Detroit, but which had been discontinued. C. M. Burton (compiler), Zion Lodge, A. F. & A. M. (Detroit No. 1), 1794–1829. An Account of its Members and Visitors with an Historical Introduction, p. 1, Burton Hist. Coll.

American went to the Lodge; and it was only during the spring and summer of 1797 that names of the newcomers began to appear regularly in the minutes. Although Detroit was now in the United States, Zion remained subject to the authority of the Grand Lodge of Lower Canada.

3

The winter came early in 1796. On December 5 the schooner *Nancy*, sailing for Detroit from Fort Erie, was caught in the ice among the islands near the mouth of the Detroit River. One of the passengers was Eli Curtis, who had missed the ill-fated *Swan*. He and three others attempted to reach the Canadian shore across the ice. The temperature was so low that two of the four froze to death, and a third was saved by Curtis, who reached a house and brought back a sled to carry him to safety. Curtis' hands and one side of his face were frozen. He finally arrived at Detroit on December 28.[11]

As soon as the Indians, the *voyageurs*, the clerks, and other *engagés* had left for the winter hunt, the *habitants* and the merchants who remained settled down to a leisurely way of living. If sufficient wood had been cut during the fall, there was little to do besides keeping the fires burning, feeding the animals, and making occasional trips to the stores.

The long winter evenings provided plenty of time for recreation. Families would gather round the great flaming fireplace or the glowing stove[12] to listen to grandfather's stories of travels in the wilderness and of Indian attacks, or to grandmother's wondrous tales of weird creatures and their mysterious ways. She might tell of *Le Nain Rouge*, the Red Dwarf of Detroit, an ill-tempered demon whose appearance was always a presage of

---

[11] The weather at Detroit was as variable then as now. The year before, on January 30, 1796, Prideaux Selby wrote that there was "no appearance of Winter" until about January 20. *Mich. Pio. and Hist. Soc. Colls.*, XII, 196.

[12] There seem to have been a number of stoves in Detroit at this time. Louvigny Montigny left three there to be sold. Wm. Robertson Papers, May 28, 1796, Burton Hist. Coll. A stove was included in William Macomb's inventory, *ibid.*; Thomas Swaine rented a stove from Robert Gouie, Sibley Papers, December 1, 1796; John Askin sent a round stove to be used in the "Boat Mill," Journal, December 31, 1796; and General Wilkins sent twenty stoves for the garrison, Wilkins Papers, September 31, 1797, *ibid.*

impending disaster. Grand'mère was certain that he had been seen scurrying along the shore on the eve of Captain Dalyell's rout at the Bloody Bridge.[13]

There were also stories of the fearful *Loup Garou*, or werewolf, a man who had taken the form of a wolf and who sometimes made off with a bride-to-be on the eve of her wedding day.

Grandmother might tell also of *Le Lutin*, the goblin who would steal a horse out of the stable at night and ride him until he was so lathered with sweat that he was still trembling with fear and fatigue when his master came to feed him in the morning. The only protection against this ghostly jockey, as everyone knew, was a cross branded on the animal's flank.

Grand'mère knew tales also about *Le feu follet*, the eerie Will-o'-the-Wisp, that caught the attention of the late traveler and led him astray into treacherous marshes; and of *Les Dames Blanches*, white fairies of the wood who compelled the hapless person that chanced upon their revels to dance with them around and around until he collapsed from exhaustion. The children, and the older folks, too, listened intently to the familiar stories and remembered well grandmother's admonition to make the sign of the cross at the first appearance of one of these imps of Satan. The mere sight of that holy gesture would cause the foulest fiend to vanish instantly.

The men spent many evenings at the taverns, where they consumed a prodigious quantity of liquor. John Askwith, for instance, frequented the taverns of James Donaldson and Thomas Smith. During October, 1794, the former charged to Askwith's account from one to four bowls of punch on each of twenty-one days. Sometimes he bought a glass of bitters or a quart of rum in addition to the punch. In November Askwith was at Donaldson's on fourteen different days. In several places there is a charge in his account for "Your Part of Reckoning," indicating that he was one of a convivial party. At various times during these same months Askwith bought "2 Slings" and rum at Smith's.

---

[13] This story and those which follow are from Mrs. M. C. W. Hamlin, *Legends of Le Détroit* (Detroit, 1884). Mrs. Hamlin's historical references are not always exact; but as a descendant of the old Godfroy family, she was intimately acquainted with the legends and the customs of the French.

Isaac Williams, Jr., was another heavy drinker. James May charged him £13 17s. 6d. for nine and a quarter gallons of wine, his "share of Wine drank wile in Town at 2 different Times." So usual was the heavy consumption of alcoholic beverages that one of the local mariners, Captain John Drake, was considered "remarkable for using no kind of drink but water." Jacob Lindley, who made the observation, seemed surprised that, in spite of his peculiar habits, he was "a healthy robust Man."

In the homes of the *habitants*, there were many impromptu dances to the lively tunes of French fiddles; and formal balls or assemblies were held from time to time during the winter season at the Council House. The gentlemen attended with powdered hair, long-tailed coats, knee breeches, white silk stockings, and buckled shoes; the ladies dressed their hair in the latest mode and wore gowns made according to the most recent fashion news from London.[14]

There were also outdoor sports during the winter. The frozen river provided plenty of room for skating; and it was a convenient highway for the *traineaux*, heavy sleds used for hauling firewood, grain, and other supplies. The light *carioles*, too, skimmed over the ice, drawn by sturdy little Canadian horses. There was great rivalry among the owners of fast animals, and races were frequent, especially on the River Rouge below the town.[15] Gabriel Godfroy and some of his friends bet heavily on Jacques Lasselle's horse, which was entered in a race set for Saturday, January 20, 1797.

Christmas was not celebrated in these years by Detroiters. No mention of the day is made in the orderly book of the First Regiment. In fact, a court-martial seems to have been held on December 25; and although it was Sunday, the stores were open in the town.

As long as the French were the most numerous element of the population, New Year's Day, *le jour de l'An*, was the great

[14] Archange Meredith, John Askin's daughter, writing from Woolwich, England, February 3, 1795, made the following request: "Be so good, my dear Mother, as to tell my dear sister Thérèse, that this part of my letter is for her, and how she is to dress in style for the next Detroit ball." Askin Papers, Burton Hist. Coll.

[15] Colonel Arent Schuyler de Peyster, commandant at Detroit during the Revolutionary War, celebrated in verse the "swift carioling" on the River Rouge. Arent Schuyler de Peyster, *Miscellanies by an Officer* (Dumfries, Scotland, 1813), p. 35.

holiday. On New Year's Eve every *habitant* expected a call from *la d'Ignolée*, a group of young men masked and armed with stout staves, who sang a song at each door. After the master of the house invited them to come in, they asked for gifts. The food and clothing which were always ready for them they piled into their cart, and later distributed the accumulation among the poor.

It was on New Year's Eve, too, that the *habitants* expected to see in the sky *le Canot du Nord*, the phantom canoe from the north country which, they firmly believed, appeared at this time bearing the spirits of the young men of the neighborhood who had gone out for the hunt and had failed to return. On this night of rejoicing, however, their ghostly forms reappeared for a fleeting moment to greet the loved ones in the homes they would never enter again.[16]

It was so cold on January 1, 1797, that Colonel Hamtramck canceled an inspection of the troops which he had previously ordered. Nevertheless, in keeping with the spirit of the holiday, he issued a special order: "The Colonel takes this occation to pay to both Officers and Soldiers the Complements of the Season and assures them that their prosperity is one of the first wishes of his heart and he sincerely hopes that providence will take them by the hand and carry them through all the vicisetudes of this life to the Summit of their wishes."

4

During the winter Detroit was practically isolated from the rest of the world. In a letter to François Chabert, Winthrop Sargent complained that almost all communication was cut off by the extreme rigor of the weather. Sargent's reason for writing was to reprimand Chabert, commander of the county militia, for delinquencies in his department. The Secretary was especially critical of the refusal of Captain James May's sergeants to execute his "Warrants of Distress." Sargent admonished the Lieutenant Colonel to see to the disciplining of his men. Apparently the *habitants* were no more eager to serve the United States than they had been to serve King George.

[16] Henry O. Chapoton, "The Legend of Le Canot du Nord," *Burton Hist. Coll. Leaf.*, May, 1939, pp. 5–6.

It was undoubtedly the severity of the winter that delayed the arrival of news of Wayne's death. The Commander in Chief had reached Presqu' Isle on November 18 so ill that he could travel no farther. There he died, December 15, 1796, but not until February 5 did the news reach Detroit. In the orders for February 6 Colonel Hamtramck included a tribute to the memory of "that Gallant Soldier our Commanding General." As a mark of mourning every officer was directed to wear crape on his sleeve and on his sword for a month. The field officers at once held a council of war and decided that Hamtramck should assume command of the army until orders to the contrary were received from a superior authority.

Meanwhile, in spite of the inclement weather, James Henry managed to reach Detroit by way of Greenville on January 6, 1797. He was a son of the late William Henry of Lancaster, Pennsylvania, a gunsmith who had served the Continental army as armorer during the Revolution. James Henry had been employed by James O'Hara, who directed him to make a tour of the western posts and to remain in Detroit to superintend the work of supplying the garrisons with food. Henry's salary was $50 a month and expenses. O'Hara, at Pittsburgh, wrote on January 20: "We are still froze up in this Country a quantity of Whisky and Stores for Detroit lays on french Creek and the Alleghany since June." During the preceding summer O'Hara had complained that low water in the streams had prevented the forwarding of supplies.

Father Levadoux, like the rest, was vexed by the uncertainty of communication. Since the death of Father Dufaux there was no other priest within several hundred miles.[17] He was alone, and he received no word from Bishop Carroll. On December 3, 1796, he wrote that he had already sent three letters but had received no reply. It was not until January that the Bishop's first letter, written October 19, arrived. Finally, in May a letter from Baltimore, dated January 4, was delivered to the Curé—the answer to his second and third letters. There is little wonder that the priest in Detroit was exasperated by the lack of a regular postal service.

Father Levadoux was still, however, an enthusiastic supporter of the Government of the United States. He was happy

[17] Father J. B. Marchand succeeded Father Dufaux in L'Assomption Parish on Christmas Day, 1796.

to learn from the first letter that Bishop Carroll approved of the special service he had held in honor of Washington and Wayne, but he reported to the Bishop that partisans of the British had denounced him to his confreres at Montreal as an enemy to royalty and "a veritable revolutionary." Some of them apparently believed the accusation, for even his good friends did not write to him. Nevertheless, the loyal priest had no intention of deviating from his course. "I am an inhabitant of the United States," he wrote. "I would be ungrateful if I abandoned their interests to sustain those of the crown whose yoke they have thrown off. I try to do my duty honorably and graciously according to my conscience." Father Levadoux reported that the officers at the Fort approved of his policy and were his friends. His parishioners also, he believed, were satisfied with his program.

5

Colonel Hamtramck decided to celebrate the birthday of George Washington with the greatest solemnity in 1797 because this would be the last opportunity while the President was in public life. Besides, it would be the first celebration in Detroit of his anniversary. Consequently, on February 14 he announced that he would review and maneuver the troops on February 22, "if the weather permits." On February 18 the Commandant canceled the review, but ordered the troops to rehearse the evolutions to be performed on the anniversary.

The observance of the occasion throughout the country was especially elaborate in 1797. In New York it included the firing of salutes, parades, a display of flags and streamers by ships in the harbor, and, in the evening, a grand ball followed by supper.

Philadelphia, capital of the United States, had an advantage over other cities: The great man was in her midst. On the aniversary of his birth delegations waited on him at his house, where they presented complimentary addresses which he answered in kind. The Governor and the legislature of Pennsylvania went in a body; and congressmen, officers of the militia, and members of the Society of the Cincinnati called upon the chief executive to congratulate him. There were also parades and maneuvers by the troops, the firing of cannon, and the ringing of bells.

So enthusiastic was the celebration that a motion was carried in Congress to adjourn because of "the noise without, & the indisposition which there seemed to be in members to attend to business (the noise alluded to was the firing of cannon, drums beating and fifes playing, in commemoration of the President's birthday) it was doubtful whether it [the report of a committee which was being considered] would meet with proper attention."[18]

In the evening a ball was held in Rickett's Amphitheatre, "which for Splendour, Taste and Elegance, was, perhaps, never excelled by any similar Entertainment in the United States."

Detroit, of course, could not celebrate on so lavish a scale as the populous and wealthy cities of the eastern seaboard; but, although the same "Splendour" was not attained, and some of the "Elegance" may have been lacking for want of means to provide it, the ceremonies were managed with sincerity and good taste.

At eleven-thirty on the morning of February 22 the entire force of infantry, riflemen, dragoons, and artillery assembled for the maneuvers, which were performed on the Esplanade. Perhaps the militia also participated in the celebration. However that may have been, at twelve o'clock a national salute of fifteen guns was fired from the Fort, the number of guns being intended to represent the states of the Union. Although at the time the nation consisted of sixteen states (Tennessee having been admitted in 1796), apparently Colonel Hamtramck was unaware of the existence of the new member.[19] What other ceremonies there were during the week are not recorded; but there was probably a ball in the Council House on the night of Saturday, February 25.

The final act of celebration took place on Sunday afternoon, February 26, in Ste Anne's Church. An orderly thus quaintly phrased the announcement in the regimental record for February 25:

> The preast of the place having communicated to the Colonel his wish to pay homage in a public maner to the aniversity of the president's Birthday by Singing a

---

[18] *Claypoole's American Daily Advertiser*, Philadelphia, February 24, 1797.
[19] In Philadelphia sixteen guns were fired. *Ibid.*, February 23, 1797.

tedium in church on the 26th Inst. In presence of all the Military Gentlemen The Colonel hopes and wishes every officer to Join the Intended Celebration and Requests all the Gentlemen to meet at his Quarters at 2 Oclock in order to march together to Church where a place will be made ready for the reception of the Officers.

Father Levadoux sang the "Te Deum" in the presence of the officers and his parishioners. The Curé thought it a proper occasion to express his sincere attachment to the United States; and so he read a eulogy of President Washington. It began with a text in Latin from Judges, XIII, 5 which, translated, predicts "he will begin the deliverance of Israel from the Philistines," a prophecy of the mighty deeds to be performed by Samson. The rest of the address was in French. It was a very eloquent and a very florid tribute to the President and the Government of the United States.

Probably not many of the officers besides Colonel Hamtramck and Major Rivardi were able to understand the language of the speech. But all of them surely understood the sincerity of the speaker and the significance of the occasion; for at the close of the service the officers thanked the priest and asked for a copy of the address to be translated and sent to the Secretary of War. Father Levadoux, obviously pleased by their compliments, explained that he could publish nothing without permission of the Bishop; and so he sent the eulogy to Baltimore, where it is still filed away in the archives of the Archdiocese.[20]

The Bishop heartily approved of the "Te Deum" and praised the eulogy in a letter to Father Levadoux, June 6, 1797. He reminded him that, as vicar-general, he had the power to decide for himself whether to publish it or not. Bishop Carroll promised to show the eulogy to the Secretary of War or to President Washington if occasion permitted.

6

Another celebration in Detroit began on the same day that Father Levadoux read his eulogy of President Washington. This was the Mardi Gras carnival which was held on the last three days preceding Lent, or *le carême*, as it was called by the

[20] In February, 1944, the William L. Clements Library published the address in a pamphlet entitled: *Eulogy on George Washington*. It was translated and edited by Professor Edward B. Ham of the University of Michigan.

French. Since it was a period of fasting and penance, the *habitants* used the carnival as the last opportunity to indulge in the amusements they liked so well. Dancing, feasting, and sleighing parties on the river were some of the activities, the officers at the fort and the militia joining with the rest to share the merrymaking.

In many homes on Mardi Gras evening there was sure to be a party happily and noisily engaged in *virant les crêpes*—tossing pancakes baked over the glowing embers of the fireplace in a long-handled frying pan. The trick was to turn the cake by tossing it as high as possible and catching it deftly in the pan. Loud were the cheers when the cook was successful; and laughter greeted the falling of the *crêpe* on the floor, or, perhaps, in someone's lap. The cakes were spread with maple sugar and eaten by the family and the guests. This was the last hilarity permitted before the beginning of Lent on the next day, Ash Wednesday.

During *le carême* Father Levadoux was busy with special services, and he was worried about a problem caused by the arrival of the Americans. The Curé reported to the Bishop that he was constantly embarrassed by the marriage of girls of his parish to officers "who are not of our religion or any other." Most of the officers, he explained, did not even know whether or not they had been baptized. The girls, wrote the priest, were going to a judge to be married without informing him. He asked Bishop Carroll to advise him what to do.

The Bishop answered that marriages before a judge were to be considered valid but sacrilegious. The priest must require public penance and an honorable *amende* before the congregation of all persons who held the sanctity of marriage so slight that they had it celebrated by a heretical minister or by a judge. Nevertheless, when they were not able to reach a priest, the Bishop added, they might be married by a judge.

7

The Court of General Quarter Sessions in 1797 opened its March term on the first Tuesday of the month. Six justices sat for three days, and the Grand Jury again presented its recommendations to the court. It urged that "all nuisances should be speedily removed, particularly the offensive smell arising from the Slaughter Houses, and the quantity of dead Carcasses which are found in every quarter of the town and which must injure the health of the Citizens, as the warm weather is fast approaching."

It also expressed the opinion that the offices of coroner and sheriff could not be held by the same person, and entered a complaint that, although many of the jurors had declared themselves before the court to be British subjects before taking the oath, nevertheless, they "had the mortification to hear reflections thrown against that Government, in the charge from the Bench." This unfriendly attitude of the court, the jury complained, hurt the feelings of the jurors and tended to disturb the harmony existing between the two governments. It was evident that there would be trouble sooner or later because of the large British element in the population of Detroit.

CHAPTER VIII
RUMORS OF WAR

THE long, severe winter of 1796–97 left its mark on the fields around Detroit. In the spring it was discovered that the cold weather had "amasingly injured" the wheat. Some fields had suffered so much that the farmers plowed under the sparse growth to sow the land to corn or other grain. It was estimated that the yield would be less than a third of the previous year's crop, although much more wheat had been sown than ever before.

During the winter, while the ships were frozen in, James Henry had been sending sled loads of flour from Detroit to the dependent posts. Gabriel Godfroy and François Navarre, with their *engagés*, drove heavily laden *traineaux* to Fort Miamis and Fort Defiance to carry provisions to the garrisons. Now with the prospect of a short crop, Henry began to buy all the flour he could find.[1] By April 5 he had procured 400,000 pounds in spite of an attempt by the merchants to corner the supply so that they could raise the price. Although the plan failed because "they could not agree," Henry had found that he could buy more cheaply from the farmers. One of his suppliers was Father Levadoux, who sold him 5,526 pounds of flour for $200. This was the whole or a part of the priest's tithe, the customary one twenty-sixth of their grain which his parishioners had agreed on his arrival to pay him for his support.

---

[1] There were a number of gristmills in the vicinity of Detroit. Most of them were windmills, but Charles Stuart reported in 1757 that two gristmills and two sawmills were run by water power.

A map drawn by Patrick McNiff in 1791 shows six windmills on the Canadian side of the river. On the American side there were a windmill in the Grand Marais, just above the upper end of Belle Isle, and three water mills: one on Bloody Run and two on Trembly's (now Connor's) Creek. One of the last two was probably a sawmill.

In addition, John Askin, in partnership with Meldrum and Park, built a windmill west of Spring Wells in 1792, and Askin and John Hembrow owned a boat mill or floating mill at Grosse Ile in 1796 and 1797.

Because cattle were expensive in Detroit Henry advised O'Hara to send some at once from Kentucky. He remarked that they would be in better condition after the long drive if they came in the spring rather than in the summer, for there would be plenty of grass along the way, and they would thrive among the rushes along the River Raisin until slaughtering time.

Perhaps Henry's supply of salted meat was nearly exhausted. If so, the soldiers certainly would welcome a change. Complaints were frequent about the condition of the salt provisions, and from time to time boards of inquiry were ordered to inspect some that had been issued. Usually, large quantities of it were condemned as unfit to eat, one board reporting that the meat looked more like carrion than like food.

2

During April furs began to come in. Now the merchants would soon know what returns they would receive for the goods sent out the previous fall. The most numerous pelts were raccoon, with deerskins second in number, and muskrat third. Beaver skins, the skins most eagerly sought for during the French régime, were scarce. This year the receipts in general were better than they had been the year before. In the following months the ships of the merchants, his Majesty's vessels, and the sloop *Detroit* would carry from Detroit alone a total of 2,616 packs of furs on the first leg of their course to Montreal and London.[2] On their return trips the same vessels would bring, during the summer and fall, 1,213 barrels of liquor, 2,611 packages of merchandise, and 261 barrels of salt. This was also an increase over the importations of 1796.

In spite of the transfer of sovereignty over the region the British still engrossed the trade. Nevertheless, so far as gathering furs was concerned, it was the influence and the ability of the individual that brought success. The nominal sheriff of Wayne County, George McDougall, who had wintered at Sandusky, reported that he had acquired more than half the

[2] Reports on the Fur Trade, Queenstown, September 24, 1798, *Mich. Pio. and Hist. Soc. Colls.*, XXV, 2c2–203.
In 1796, 1910 packs had been shipped from Detroit.

furs traded there. He attributed his good fortune to the patronage of the "Great Chief Huron," who had adopted him as a son with full ceremonial rites and had conferred upon him the Indian name of Ou-trou-ne-re. The irrepressible McDougall added that all the other traders were jealous of his good fortune.

During the spring returning *voyageurs* and Indians brought in great quantities of maple sugar. The French called it *sucre d'érable* or *sucre du pays*, but the merchants usually wrote it in their books as "Indian sugar." It was packed in bark containers called *mococks*, and the usual retail price was six pence a pound. Sometimes the Indians mixed sand with the sugar to increase the weight. When they were charged with fraud, they coolly shrugged their shoulders and replied that they were simply imitating the traders who watered their rum.

Many of the Indians remained in the neighborhood after their trading was finished. Later in the summer the annuities would be distributed; now they lived on whatever credit they might have with the merchants, or on presents from men to whom they had granted land. Still hoping for official recognition of their claims, the grantees registered them with the recorder, Peter Audrain.

Among the grants was a lease for 990 years from five chiefs of the Chippewa nation to James May, Patrick McNiff, and Jacob Harsen. These men paid 6,000 dollars or "bucks"[3] to the Indians for land on the northwest side of Lake St. Clair. Besides the cash, annual payments were to be made if the title was confirmed by the United States. The lessees, understanding the Indian conception of landownership as the Americans did not, provided in the contract that the chiefs and their tribes might continue to hunt, fish, plant corn, build huts, and make sugar on all parts of the tract which were not improved.

The Indians begged food, when they were hungry, from their American "Father" at Detroit; then many of them would go down the river and cross over to the fort at Amherstburg,

[3] Angus Mackintosh instructed John Conner, his trader at Sandusky, to take "a good fall Buck for 1 dollar." He valued two doeskins or four raccoon skins at one buck. An otter skin was worth five bucks. Mackintosh Letter Book. October 18, 1800, Burton Hist. Coll.

where they appealed to the generosity of their British "Father." Neither government denied their requests, for both were anxious to retain the friendship of the savages.

3

Great Britain was at war with France and Spain. Rumors of impending trouble in the West worried frontier commanders and government officials alike. It was reported in Montreal that Indians in Spanish pay had taken an American fort near the mouth of the Ohio; that the French had got possession of Vincennes and occupied Spanish posts which were to have been transferred to the United States; that the French had won the Creeks over to their interest; that a Frenchman had told the Miami Indians that Quebec and New York were in the hands of the French and had urged them to rise against the British and the Americans; and, finally, that the commandant at Detroit had sent most of his garrison to reinforce other posts.

Matthew Elliot wrote from Malden to Peter Russell, administrator of the civil government of Upper Canada, stating that the French and Spaniards had sent messages to the Indians which implied an intention to invade his province. Elliot had heard of "a great number of [French] troops on the Mississippi moving upward." If war came, he believed that all the Indians except the Wyandots would be loyal to Great Britain. After receiving his letter Russell ordered muskets and cartridges sent to arm the militia about Amherstburg as "the only means within my power at present to obviate the attack with which we are threatened"; and added that "the knowledge of their arrival may possibly encourage the neighboring Indians to continue stedfast in their Attachment."

The Americans were as greatly worried as the British by the possibilities of trouble in the West. Wayne at Detroit had warned Secretary McHenry of the suspicious activities of General Victor Collot, Constantin Volney, and Thomas Power as French and Spanish agents; and he had reported the intimacy of General Wilkinson with Power. Captain Thomas Pasteur had written to Wayne from Vincennes of a report in his vicinity that the French would be in possession of Louisiana in less than two years. According to a current rumor, there were seven thousand troops at New Orleans, and the Spaniards were ready to give up the territory to France. Wayne believed, however, that France and Spain were preparing to unite Canada with Louisiana.[4]

It was rumored that, if such a plan were set in motion, the French would take Mackinac as a base of operations. Certainly the Directory which was ruling France would have no compunction about invading the United States. Ever since the ratification of the Jay Treaty French warships had been seizing American merchantmen in retaliation for our Government's concessions to Great Britain. Confident of their position because of Napoleon's triumphant march through Italy, the Directors treated the new nation with calculated contempt. They ignored Charles Cotesworth Pinckney, Washington's minister to France, and he finally had to leave the country to escape arrest as a foreigner who had no written permission from the government to remain.

The new president, John Adams, called Congress to meet in special session on May 15, 1797, to consider our relations with France. Although he was determined to uphold the honor of his country, he was anxious if possible to maintain peace. In pursuance of this objective he appointed three commissioners to open negotiations with the French. The Senate confirmed the appointments, but Congress took steps to strengthen the nation's military and naval forces.

So far as Spain was concerned, Thomas Pinckney's treaty of 1795 with that nation had removed a threat in the West. There was now no danger of secession. The Kentuckians and Tennesseans were content with the right granted them by the treaty to navigate the Mississippi and to deposit their products at New Orleans. True, the Spaniards were irritatingly slow in delivering Natchez and the other posts to the United States, in accordance with the terms of the treaty; but patience and insistence on our rights would probably solve that problem unless the French and the Spaniards made a united attack.

Officers commanding American frontier posts had orders to stop all foreigners without passports, except British subjects,

[4] Wayne to McHenry, October 28, 1796, Wayne Papers, 47, 43, Hist. Soc. of Pa., Phila.

who had a privileged status under the Jay Treaty. At the suggestion of Secretary McHenry, Robert Liston, the British envoy urged that the same practice be adopted by his government. The recommendation was accepted, and an order was issued by Major David Shank, commander of the troops in Upper Canada.

4

While these dangers were threatening in the West, General James Wilkinson, who had become commander in chief of the American Army after Wayne's death, was making a tour of the frontier posts. Fate had obligingly raised him to the position for which Wayne had thought he was scheming. Now if he wanted to play the traitor, there was no superior officer to check his plans.

Wilkinson had a wide acquaintance in Kentucky, where he had established himself as a merchant in 1783. This venture followed his service in the Revolutionary army, in which he had risen to the rank of brigadier general, but from which he resigned before the end of hostilities. He had married Ann Biddle of Philadelphia and had set up as a gentleman farmer for a short time in Pennsylvania. In Kentucky he built himself a large house at Lexington and entertained lavishly.

Personally attractive, suave, courteous, and generous to friends and followers, Wilkinson soon became a leader in the western country. To enemies or to those who interfered with his plans, however, he was a dangerous foe. He could belabor such marplots with a lash of stinging invective or blacken their reputations by secretly circulated innuendo. Intrigue was a game at which he played with rare talent.

For several years Wilkinson negotiated with the Spanish governor of Louisiana, Esteban Miro, alternately promising to lead Kentucky out of the Union into Spanish control and warning him of attacks which the frontiersmen might make upon the Spanish posts. Because of his apparent attachment to the Government of Spain he received special privileges in trading to New Orleans, and in 1789 Miro advanced him $7,000 for the services he claimed he had performed.

In spite of this foreign connection, which Wilkinson knew

was suspected by his own government as early as 1790, he obtained a commission as lieutenant colonel in the Second United States Infantry Regiment in 1791. In 1792, promoted to brigadier general and ordered to prepare for the arrival of Wayne's punitive expedition against the Indians in the Northwest, he performed the duty so well that he won the praise of the Secretary of War. At this time he was receiving an annual pension of $2,000 from the Spaniards, and other sums from time to time when his importunity made sufficient impression on Carondelet, who had succeeded Miro in December, 1791.

During the summer of 1796 Thomas Power, a Spanish emissary, met Wilkinson at Greenville before Wayne returned from Philadelphia. Together they prepared reports which they hoped would induce the Spanish governor to provide money for plotting in Kentucky. Power later returned from New Orleans to Kentucky with $9,640 hidden in casks of sugar and tobacco. Having been warned of this shipment of money, General Wayne sent an officer who intercepted Power's boat but failed to find the money, of which Wilkinson received a large part for himself. Altogether, he had been paid, since 1790, $26,000 in Spanish gold.

5

General Wilkinson reached Detroit late in June, 1797.[5] His first action was to review the case of Private Henry Sevey, who had been condemned to death by a court-martial in September, 1796 (see p. 60). General Wayne had submitted the proceedings of the court to the President, who had finally approved the verdict. On March 27, 1797, the Secretary of War directed Wilkinson to carry out the sentence. The General ordered Sevey to be shot on July 4.[6]

The Commander in Chief planned to make the birthday of the nation, which he called the "Political Sabbath of the United States," a holiday for the troops. A national salute was to be fired at daybreak, a gill of whisky apiece would be

---

[5] A house was rented from François Baby for General Wilkinson's quarters "from 25th June to 25th September, 1797." *Quarter Master General's Report, 1796–1802*, p. 186.

[6] General Orders, June 29, 1797. General Orders—Gen. James Wilkinson, 1797–1808, War Dept. Archives, Old Records Div., Adjt. Gen's. Office, Washington.

issued to the soldiers, and they would be relieved of all duties except one—attendance at the execution of Private Sevey, which was to be the principal event of the day.

General Wilkinson ordered Major Rivardi to parade the troops in the form of a crescent on the Esplanade facing the glacis. Private Sevey, preceded by his coffin, would be marched to the glacis by a detachment of soldiers commanded by a subaltern. After the preparations were complete, the adjutant would read the sentence of the court, and the firing squad would perform its duty.

In spite of these elaborate arrangements the execution did not take place. On July 4 General Wilkinson countermanded his order of the previous day and pardoned the prisoner with the explanation that he believed mercy would make of him a good soldier. Sevey was simply required to kneel at the flagstaff, grasp it with his right hand, raise his left hand, and renew his oath of allegiance. He then returned to his regiment.

General Wilkinson found a dangerous situation at Detroit. Drunkenness was demoralizing the soldiers, who were buying liquor in the stores and taverns licensed by the county magistrates. The owners, most of whom were British, apparently felt no responsibility to coöperate with the Commandant in maintaining discipline. Besides, British subjects were enticing American soldiers to desert and cross the river, and, finally, many of the leading merchants and other inhabitants, both British and French, were preparing to make a formal declaration of their intention to retain their British allegiance. Because the year of grace during which they must make their decision, according to the Jay Treaty, had almost passed, the leaders of the group were very active in gathering signatures.

The Commander in Chief attacked the first two problems vigorously. He transferred Colonel Hamtramck, with his First Regiment, to Fort Wayne and brought Colonel David Strong, with troops of the Second Regiment, from that post to command at Detroit.[7] He issued an order prohibiting the sale of liquor to soldiers except on written permission of the Commandant, with the purpose, as he phrased it, "To remidy evils replete with consequences so destructive of the National

[7] *Ibid.*, July 9, 1797.

Interests, and so subversive of subordination and discipline...."

In order to keep the soldiers busy and to improve their morale General Wilkinson ordered all the troops to be drilled daily from five to seven o'clock in the morning; from eleven to one in the afternoon; and again from four to six.

On July 12 the Commander in Chief published a proclamation of martial law to apply to everyone within the circuit of the palisades of the town. All such persons were to be considered followers of the army and subject to trial by court-martial for selling liquor to soldiers or for tampering with their allegiance.

The General sent a letter to the justices of the Western District of Upper Canada asking them to coöperate by preventing American deserters from becoming British subjects. He warned that fugitives from the army were numerous on both sides of the river and that "internal commotion" was likely to occur and "involve these Settlements in scenes of Bloodshed & desolation." The justices replied, expressing their sympathy with the General's troubles, but declaring that they had no authority in the matter. They added that they had referred the complaint to Administrator Peter Russell.

On July 15 Wilkinson ordered all deserters from the British army to leave town within twenty-four hours. At the same time he announced that American deserters who desired to return to duty would be pardoned if they appeared within thirty days.

Courts-martial found numerous soldiers guilty of drunkenness and imposed the usual application of lashes. Several civilians also were apprehended and tried for selling liquor contrary to the recent order. At a single session the court found guilty William Mitchell, a sutler; James Fraser, a British merchant of Detroit; and Lydia Connor, "a follower of the Army." They sentenced Mitchell and the Connor woman to be drummed, with the "Rogue's March," through the Citadel before the paraded troops, his left hand tied to her right and a bottle suspended about the neck of each, through the town, through the Fort, then back to Ste Anne Street and out the West Gate, with the order never to return within the line of pickets.

The soldiers witnessed the punishment of Lydia Connor, "a notorious offender," at six o'clock on the evening of July 20; Mitchell, however, escaped the drumming part of his sentence through the intervention of the Commander in Chief. As to James Fraser, who had been in business in Detroit for a number of years, the court decided that his transgression might have been the result of a misunderstanding. Consequently, they sentenced him merely to be reprimanded by the General. Wilkinson reproved him mildly, saying that he was anxious to avoid injustice; but he warned against a repetition and added that, although in the discharge of his duty he desired "to give satisfaction to Citizen and Alien," his first consideration was "the promotion of the national interests, and the approbation of his superiors."

For desertion a military court sentenced Corporal William Kelly of the Second Regiment to be reduced to a private and "to walk the Gauntlet thro' the troops of the Garrison Six times, both ranks striking at the same time." A civilian, Matthew McFall, found guilty of attempting to induce a soldier to desert, was given fifty lashes with wired cats, had the left side of his head and his right eyebrow shaved, was drummed with a noose around his neck through the Citadel and the Fort, then out of town, and ordered never to return.[8] Finally, Wilkinson stationed a sentry at "the tipling house opposite the East angle of the Stockade surrounding the citadel" with orders to stop any soldier who tried to enter.[9] By such stringent measures the General attempted to check drunkenness and desertion.

6

The problem of the British subjects was not so easily solved. They had the right to retain their nationality and to remain in Detroit. If all of them had crossed the river, there would have been little trouble, although the removal would probably have caused a serious economic dislocation. Some did settle in the new town of Sandwich, laid out for them by Administra-

---

[8] *Mich. Pio. and Hist. Soc. Colls.*, XXXIV, 715. McFall, a shoemaker, later returned to Detroit.

[9] The "tipling house" was John Dodemead's tavern.

tor Peter Russell. But, like Askin, many of them would not leave their extensive real-estate holdings about Detroit. Besides, they were well established in business there, and facilities for trade and shipping were excellent. Askin expressed the opinion that the new town was not well situated because a swamp lay between it and the river. The Americans, alarmed at the prospect of a rival trading center so close to their own, promptly dubbed the new town "Smugglingburg."[10]

Under the leadership of John Askin seventeen British merchants who, according to their own estimate, owned about three fourths of the property in Detroit, addressed a courteous but vigorous letter to General Wilkinson protesting against his proclamation of martial law. This action was illegal, they insisted, because it deprived them of rights guaranteed by the Jay Treaty. These men denied that they were hostile to the United States. They recognized the necessity of limiting the sale of liquor to soldiers and promised to obey the order on that subject; but they urged the Commander in Chief to revoke the proclamation of martial law, not only because it was illegal, but also because it had produced a reign of terror among some of the people of Detroit who feared the malice of spies and informers. James Fraser, who had been convicted by court-martial, was one of the signers. Although the merchants complained, in a letter of July 31, that Wilkinson's answer (which has not been found) was not satisfactory, they promised to obey.[11]

Detroiters who elected to become citizens of the United States were irritated by some of their fellow townsmen who "expressed, on every occasion, their contempt for our Government, although our money has enriched them since our taking possession of the Posts."[12] They were annoyed, too, by the fact that the leaders among the British element had urged others to retain their allegiance to the King. John Askin was charged with being the principal in this endeavor. He ad-

[10] Sargent to Pickering, August 14, 1797, C. E. Carter (ed.), *The Territorial Papers of the United States*, II, 624.
[11] Detroit, July 24, 1797. James Wilkinson Papers, Burton Hist. Coll.
[12] Rivardi to Pickering, July 28, 1797, Bernard C. Steiner, *Life and Correspondence of James McHenry* (Cleveland, 1907), p. 265.

mitted having taken a list of signatures to Peter Audrain to be registered; but he denied that he had advised anyone to remain British, although he believed he had a legal right to do so. One hundred men signed declarations of intention.[13] One third of the signers were French. Major Rivardi expressed the opinion that they were little better than the British, and "not in the least to be trusted." Nevertheless, he considered them less dangerous because they were "indolent, cowardly, and (with prudence) little to be dreaded."

The magistrates of Wayne County were alarmed by the situation. On July 12, 1797, they wrote to Winthrop Sargent complaining that the sheriff was able to find scarcely enough citizens to serve on the jury at the recent session of court, and that the militia could not be depended upon if it was called out. They urged the Governor to vest "Sufficient power in the Commander-in-Chief now here, or the commanding-Officer, for the time being to take Such Steps as may check the progress of the present prevailing faction, and prevent a further corruption of the Inhabitants, we by experience finding it out of the power of the civil authority at present to do it."

Undoubtedly there was a great deal of friction between the officials of Wayne County and the merchants who had elected to remain British. The latter element considered the officials disloyal to the King and made light of their authority. John Askin wrote facetiously to Colonel England about some of these officers, and England answered that he doubted if "those new *created Gentlemen* will add much to the Society of Detroit." It is likely that the Colonel had in mind Patrick McNiff especially, who had caused the former commandant sufficient trouble to be remembered.

McNiff's transfer of allegiance had paid him well. In 1796 he had been named surveyor of Wayne County and judge of the Court of Common Pleas. Now General Wilkinson appointed him conductor of military stores and barrack master at $40 a month.

Another resident of Detroit who probably felt the resentment of loyal Britons was Jonathan Schieffelin. During the

---

[13] These declarations were filed with Peter Audrain, who copied them into a record book. Wayne County, Record of Deeds, I, 120–22, Register of Deeds Office, County Building, Detroit.

Revolutionary War he had been a lieutenant in Captain François Chabert's company of volunteers and had participated in raids on American settlements in Kentucky. As recently as June 21, 1797, he had signed a declaration of intention to remain a British subject. Nevertheless, before August 1, 1797, he had accepted from General Wilkinson the positions of Indian agent and interpreter for the United States Government.[14]

George McDougall and François Navarre were probably also in Colonel England's mind when he wrote disparagingly of the new "Gentlemen" of Detroit. They and the other officials who had been British subjects very likely overplayed their parts in attempting to require respect for the authority which they knew was irritating to many people in the town.

The magistrates did not wait for action from Cincinnati to solve their problem. On August 24 they held a special sitting of the Court of General Quarter Sessions before which Askin and William Park were summoned to appear, and Peter Audrain was ordered to bring to court the papers filed in his office respecting British subjects. Unfortunately, no record of the proceedings or of the action taken by the court has been found.

Judge Joseph Gilman, one of the territorial judges, was directed to hold a general court at Detroit in August. Winthrop Sargent, in Cincinnati, feared that he would find "uneasiness in that Quarter." The Secretary even doubted that civil authority would be adequate to govern Wayne County. Judge Gilman, however, did not go to Detroit, nor did any other judge appear during 1797 to hold a session of the general court.

7

Despite the difficulties with British civilians at Detroit General Wilkinson maintained friendly relations with Captain William Mayne, commandant at Fort Malden. The General told him there was no truth in the rumors that the French, Spaniards, and Indians would attack the frontier posts. The only basis for the report, he said, was the collecting of troops

---

[14] *Quarter Master General's Report, 1796–1802*, p. 203.

by the Spanish authorities during the previous autumn to protect their territory from an expected invasion by British and American forces. Wilkinson assured Mayne that secret agents among the Spaniards gave him early and exact information. The Commander in Chief, in order to check disturbing rumors, had a Canadian, François Razice, drummed out of town for giving false information that the French and the Spaniards intended to attack Mackinac and Fort Wayne.

On August 4 General Wilkinson sailed for Mackinac on the sloop *Detroit*, accompanied by Major Caleb Swan. Perhaps he felt that the situation at Detroit was under control, and he must have welcomed the prospect of a voyage away from the summer heat.

Quartermaster General John Wilkins, Jr., had accompanied Wilkinson to Detroit. Matthew Ernest, who had served as an officer during the Revolution, was now assistant quartermaster there, having been sent in May to replace Audrain, whose work had not been satisfactory. Wilkins informed Ernest that his task included the supplying of all the posts dependent on Detroit: Forts Mackinac, Miamis, Defiance, Wayne, Knox, and Lorimers.

Ernest was instructed to strengthen the glacis in front of the Fort, to repair the public buildings, and to enclose the shipyard completely with pickets. Work was begun at once. Since it was impossible to hire skilled men in Detroit, the repairs were made by soldiers, who were paid for their services. In the absence of Captain Moses Porter, who had sailed for Mackinac with his company on July 25, and of Major Rivardi, who was ordered to Fort Niagara to take command there, Lieutenant Tallman of the artillery was in charge of the working parties.

At this time Colonel Strong ordered that no washing be done in the Citadel by "the Soldiery or Women." The women referred to were either wives of private soldiers or unattached women who accompanied the regiments as laundresses. According to army regulations, the number of women with each regiment was proportional to the number of men: an infantry regiment, which contained five hundred and two enlisted men, was entitled to thirty women; a regiment of artillery, consisting of one thousand and two men, might have fifty-nine. Each woman was furnished one ration a day by the commissary.

An order issued by General Wilkinson on July 28 probably caused plenty of grumbling among the merchants. All gunpowder, the order read, must be deposited in the public magazine, the owners to pay fifty cents a keg for storage when it was withdrawn. The storing of the powder was probably meant to protect the town from fire; but the hostile attitude of the British and of some of the French may have had some weight. Furthermore, the Indians were still restless. Major Rivardi reported that "they all expect to see their *Fathers, the French.*"

8

On September 3 General Wilkinson returned to Detroit, where he met his *"reported Spy,"* Thomas Power, who had arrived a fortnight before from New Orleans with dispatches from Baron Carondelet. The Spanish governor entreated Wilkinson to send no more troops down the Mississippi, and to delay the occupation of Natchez and the other posts. Carondelet offered him a grant of land and $4,000 a year if he would aid the Spaniards in detaching Kentucky and Tennessee from the Union.

This was a golden opportunity for General Wilkinson if he wished to betray his country. Always eager for money and land, he might have had both with little immediate danger of discovery. True, the Kentuckians and Tennesseans were not likely to revolt while they could use the Mississippi; but Wilkinson might have aroused some unruly persons to action in that quarter and collected his reward on the strength of promises, as he had done before. The Commander in Chief, however, rejected the offer. He advised Carondelet to carry out the terms of Pinckney's treaty by withdrawing from the forts which the United States was entitled to occupy.

Nevertheless, he promised to protect the territory of Spain from a possible British attack by way of Mackinac. He also suggested that he might be of service to the Spaniards at some future time, hoping to maintain his golden connection with the Dons. Wilkinson ordered his aide, Captain Bartholomew Shaumburgh, to conduct Power to New Madrid, and to prevent him from communicating with anyone along the way. This order may have been meant to impress American officials with Wilkinson's zeal to balk any attempt of the spy to gather information. On the other hand, the General may have feared that Power might divulge compromising secrets.

However that may have been, Wilkinson did not play the traitor; but he had several times come dangerously near to treasonable actions. Apparently his debts, a sordid love of money, and a zest for intrigue had impelled him to set his own interests above those of his country. He cheated the gullible Spaniards of their gold, and he might have involved his country in a war. In spite of his conniving and his pension from the King of Spain, he was clever enough to keep the confidence of the President, John Adams, who informed him that he gave no credence to widespread rumors of his dealings with the Spaniards.[15]

In 1797 the distribution of the annuity to the Wyandots, Chippewa, and Ottawa, according to the terms of the Treaty of Greenville, was made at Detroit from September 6 to 9. On those days selling of liquor to the Indians was prohibited by order of General Wilkinson. Jonathan Schieffelin assisted Colonel Return Jonathan Meigs, clothier general of the United States Army, in distributing the goods.

During the summer orders had reached John Askin, lieutenant colonel of Canadian militia, to prepare his regiment for possible action. From his desk in Detroit he had dispatched messengers across the river to his majors and captains to be on the alert. Finally, on September 8, he ordered Major Parent to assemble his officers and their men in front of the church at Sandwich next Sunday after mass. Lieutenant Colonel Askin promised to be there to select forty-five men who must be ready to march at a moment's notice. Orders from headquarters, he informed the Major, required him to take this action. On September 26 he ordered Captain Daniel Fields at the River Thames to warn twenty-five of his men to be ready for duty.

[15] Adams to Wilkinson, February 4, 1798, E. A. Cruikshank (ed.), *The Correspondence of the Honourable Peter Russell* (Toronto, 1932), II, 75–76.

This military activity of the arch-British subject on American soil was certainly known to the officials in Detroit. Although it was fear of French and Spanish attacks that produced the orders to Askin, and although the United States would certainly have fought beside Britain if an invasion had occurred, still, the presence of a foreigner in their midst issuing orders to his regiment must have aroused further ill feeling on the part of the American element against John Askin. Askin's brother-in-law, Commodore Alexander Grant, was in the same position. Commander of the British navy of the Upper Lakes, he contined to live in his "castle" at Grosse Pointe, whence he directed the movements of His Majesty's ships.

General Wilkinson left Detroit for Fort Wayne on or about September 26. He had expected to return directly to Pittsburgh; but the report of a rebellion at Kaskaskia made him change his plans and set out to establish a garrison in the Illinois town to maintain order. He complained that this expedition "blows up my schemes of happiness for the Winter I fear and may secure me a seat in the regions of unceasing Joy—What sacrifices of Domestic transport do I make to preserve the Public tranquility, and for What Bread barely."[16] Fortunately for the General, the disturbance at Kaskaskia soon subsided; "his seat in the regions of unceasing Joy" remained vacant, and he was able to proceed to Pittsburgh to join his wife, Ann, and satisfy his longing for domestic happiness.

[16] Wilkinson to Wilkins, September 22, 1797, Wayne and Wilkinson Letter Bock, Burton Hist. Coll.

CHAPTER IX
YANKEE ARRIVALS

WHEN the September, 1797, term of court began, Ezra Fitz Freeman was on hand ready to serve his clients. He rented a small house in town, where he lived and had his office. He boarded at James May's. Apparently he had found sufficient legal business to make it worth his while to remain in Detroit. Besides, he would avoid the journey back and forth from Cincinnati for each session of court.[1]

The most interesting case in the Court of Common Pleas was that of John Burrell against Joseph Campau. The schoolmaster drew up an itemized bill showing that Campau owed him £20 4s. 6d. for services, including the teaching of the merchant and his nephew, John Williams. From this debt he deducted £12 3s. 10d., which he owed Campau for goods purchased in his store. The amount due was £8 8d. Campau, apparently, refused to pay. Burrell swore to the accuracy of the bill before Justice James May, who ordered the sheriff to summon Campau to appear in court.

Campau drew up a counterclaim. In it he charged Burrell £6 because "he was incapable of teaching him [Williams] the rules which he asked to be taught." He charged him an additional £3 because, he alleged, the schoolmaster had frequently failed to come to give Campau his lesson in English. Adding the £9 for Burrell's delinquencies to his store account, with an extra charge of 1s. 6d., Campau presented a bill of £21 5s. 4d. The schoolmaster must have been shocked to learn that he would have saved money if he had never taken uncle and nephew as pupils. If Burrell was incompetent, he deserved the shock; however, Campau was noted for his

[1] Ezra Fitz Freeman's brother, Dr. James C. Freeman, who had been arrested in 1794 and sent down the Lakes by Colonel England, was back in Detroit from March to July, 1797. He apparently was practicing medicine.
A Doctor Coventry also was in Detroit in June, 1797.

2

Gradually Americans came to settle in Detroit. Some of them went into business or established new industries, and one of them, James Henry, did both. In October he opened a store in the town with General John Wilkins, Jr., as a silent partner. Henry purchased in Montreal goods worth £2,143 and was well satisfied with his sales. Nevertheless, there were obstacles to overcome. He discovered that "old Abbott made every exertion to undersell" him. Besides, the *General Wilkinson*, which was carrying his merchandise, was driven ashore in a gale. Three of his packages were left on the beach, and he expected that a case of porter would be ruined by freezing.

In the fall of 1797 Henry was preparing to build a tannery at Detroit. Wilkins, who had an interest in this enterprise also, sent James Kennedy from Pittsburgh to work in the factory. He sent also James Williams, of Hagerstown, Maryland, who had been "over the whole of America gaining information on the tanning business," to manage the plant. Wilkins advised his partner to begin on a small scale. Besides operating the store and the tannery, Henry continued to serve as agent for James O'Hara.

At least three more Americans arrived before the end of the year 1797. One of them was Oliver Wiswell.[2] He engaged in business and was soon active in politics as well. Another was Frederick Bates, the fourth son of Thomas Fleming Bates, a Virginia merchant, who had been ruined by the Revolutionary War. Frederick, nevertheless, acquired a good education. Before his twentieth birthday he left Belmont, the family home, to become postmaster at Goochland Court House. In the fall of 1797 he was appointed to the quartermaster's department in the Northwest Territory at a salary of $30 a month. He made his way to Presqu' Isle on horseback, and from there to Detroit by boat. A third newcomer was David

---

[2] He is not the hero of Kenneth Roberts' novel.

parsimony, and it is likely that he exaggerated the teacher's faults. Unfortunately the decree of the court has not been found.

Powers, an attorney from Tioga County, New York, who remained in Detroit for several years practicing law.

The American element was also increased by discharged soldiers who found employment in the town. One of them, Patrick O'Brian, rented of John Askin "a small Brick room," where he worked as a shoemaker.

3

The land jobbers continued to be active in Detroit. Some were agents of eastern men, one of whom was Henry Brockholst Livingston, of the distinguished New York family. Colonel William S. Smith, son-in-law of President John Adams, came to Detroit, apparently acting in Livingston's interest. William Robertson warned John Askin that the speculators from the East had no credit in their own communities. He described Smith as being "remembered now for his extravagance & insolvency!"

When John Adams learned what his son-in-law was doing in Detroit, he wrote him a sharp rebuke. The President was particularly distressed because Smith had intimated that Adams had sent him on an official errand. He warned the Colonel that his actions would injure the reputations of both of them.

In 1797 winter again came early to the region of the Lakes. In November a ship carrying Sergeant Thomas Nowlan and a detachment of men from the First Regiment was caught in the ice near the mouth of the River Raisin. Colonel Strong wrote to François Navarre asking him to carry provisions to them.

The sudden appearance of winter also delayed the construction of a ship which the Government had decided to build at Detroit. Quartermaster General Wilkins expected that the new vessel, a schooner of about seventy tons burden, would save money for his department. She and the sloop *Detroit* should be able to carry most of the military supplies, and thus would avoid the payment of freight charges.

In the fall Wilkins sent the requisite materials to Presqu' Isle, where they remained until spring. The sloop *Russell* of Detroit, apparently caught by the unseasonable ice in Presqu' Isle harbor, advertised in the Pittsburgh *Gazette* that she would sail for Detroit on April 1. Wilkins promised to load the materials for the new ship on the *Russell,* and he urged Matthew Ernest to rush the schooner to completion. The latter, in obedience to his advice, engaged Captain James Guthrie to command the *Detroit* when navigation opened in the spring, so that Captain Peter Curry could give his attention exclusively to work on the schooner. Ernest and Curry established a shipyard on the River Rouge, below Detroit, where men were set at work preparing timbers.[3]

Again the winter almost isolated Detroit from the outer world. During the summer expresses were fairly frequent, Sylvester Ash and Robert McCrea making the journey from time to time between Pittsburgh and Detroit, carrying dispatches. Their pay was $30 a month and a ration and a half a day. The Government provided saddle horses, and sometimes a packhorse was sent along to carry forage and provisions. Enos, an Indian runner, made the trip for $10. The express service was satisfactory for official communications, but Quartermaster General Wilkins complained that "safe conveyances [for money] do not offer more than once in Six months, especially during the Winter Season."

A bonus was paid to speed the riders during difficult weather. In January, 1798, two expresses, Pierson and Schabel, were promised $10 each in addition to their wages if they reached Detroit in twenty days from Pittsburgh. Private persons writing to friends or relatives sent their letters by these expresses or by individuals who could mail them at the first postoffice they reached.

4

The animosity existing in Detroit between the British and the American elements continued to flare up from time to time. During the winter of 1797–98 dissension occurred in the congregation of Ste Anne's because of divided allegiance.

Father Levadoux considered the affair serious enough to warrant reporting it to Bishop Carroll. The trouble began when Philip Belanger, a *marguiller* or trustee of Ste Anne's Church, declared his intention to remain a British subject

---

[3] Woodmere Cemetery today occupies the site of the shipyard.

and one of the American judges urged the priest to replace him with a citizen of the United States. Belanger, hearing of the request, asked Father Levadoux to call a meeting of the *marguillers* so that he might resign. To the great surprise of Belanger, the trustees accepted his resignation instead of rejecting it, as he had expected, thus compromising the priest with the civil authorities. Belanger then withdrew his resignation. The priest informed the court, which immediately decided that no subject of the king of England might hold any position of trust in the county.

When Father Levadoux assembled the *marguillers* and read the decision to them, they decided to obey the ruling of the court. So far as they were concerned, Belanger had legally resigned. Consequently they immediately appointed an American citizen to take his place.

Instead of accepting the action of the trustees, the British supporters of Belanger held a meeting at his house and voted to reinstate him. The court now called a special session before which Belanger and two others were summoned to appear. When they agreed to obey the order of the court, they were dismissed.

The agitation ceased for the moment; but while Father Levadoux was absent at the River Raisin, the leaders of the opposition circulated a petition to the Bishop, urging him to reverse the action of the assembly. As soon as the priest returned to Detroit, he wrote his story of the affair to Bishop Carroll and sent a letter by express to Governor St. Clair. No further action was necessary, however, for the dissension soon subsided, and by spring there was no more trouble. Father Levadoux declared that his parishioners had supported him in his stand.[4]

Numerous desertions from both the British and the American armies worried the commanding officers and aroused the inhabitants on both sides of the river. In the spring of 1798 American deserters in Canada were reported to be committing "every Species of Crime that can blacken a Newgate Kalendar."[5] When the courthouse and jail at Sandwich

---

[4] Levadoux to Carroll, July 29, 1798, Letters to Carroll, 4Y13, Archives of the Archbishopric of Baltimore and Washington.

[5] Peter Russell to the Duke of Portland, March 21, 1798, E. A. Cruikshank (ed.), *The Correspondence of the Honourable Peter Russell*, II, 125.

burned, the civil authorities had no place to confine these desperate characters when they caught them, and so they petitioned Administrator Russell for assistance. He at once had the blockhouse at Chatham removed to Sandwich to be used as a jail.

Captain Hector McLean, who had succeeded Captain William Mayne as commandant at Fort Malden, was angered by the desertion of some native Canadians. Their compatriots on the American side of the river, "Canadians of the worst description," he complained, enticed these men to desert. On application to Colonel Strong at Detroit he was permitted to send a detachment of soldiers over to try to apprehend the deserters "without molesting any of the peaceable Inhabitants of the United States." Two were captured and taken to Fort Malden for trial. This invasion, even though the American commandant had given his consent, probably kept alive resentment against the British. It undoubedly also aggravated the animosity between the civilians and the military.

5

During the spring and early summer of 1798 great quantities of furs were collected in Detroit, whence they were shipped to Montreal. The winter catch was even larger than that of 1796–97.[6] Askin's account book contains numerous entries of pelts received. Quantities of "Bears Oyle" and maple sugar also came from his partner, John Anderson, on the Maumee River. Anderson complained that George McDougall and Ronald McDonnell were carrying on a cutthroat trade at Fort Defiance, each trying to ruin the other by selling to the Indians "For Merley Nothing." Anderson refused to lower his prices, and the Indians threatened to go to Defiance. The trader wrote that he would probably have little business, for he would not trade at a loss.

The market for furs was worse than it had been in 1797. In London deerskins were selling for 20 per cent less, and the price of other pelts was expected to be lower too. There was

---

[6] Report signed by Robert Hamilton, Queenstown, September 24, 1798, *Mich. Pio. and Hist. Soc. Colls.*, XXV, 203.

Hamilton reported that by September 24, 1798, 2,707 packs had been carried over the Niagara Portage, compared with 2,616 packs for the whole year of 1797.

one ray of hope for Askin, however, in this dark prospect. The *Ariadne*, carrying £12,000 worth of furs shipped by Todd and McGill, was captured by the French. Some of Askin's packs were a part of the cargo. When Isaac Todd informed Askin of the incident, he predicted that they would be able to collect more insurance than the furs would have brought.[7] Besides, the other fur ship, the *Euretta*, escaped and reached England safely. Her cargo was likely to bring a higher price because of the loss of the *Ariadne*.

Nevertheless, the outlook for the future was not favorable. It seemed almost certain that the United States would be drawn into war with France. Instead of receiving the three envoys whom President Adams had commissioned to negotiate with the Directory, Talleyrand, the foreign minister, sent them word that only a bribe of $250,000 to him and a loan of $10,000,000 to the government would secure them an audience. They rejected these proposals and sent a report of their experiences to the President.

When Adams, early in March, received news of the treatment of his envoys, he immediately laid the whole affair before Congress. The publication of the story aroused a storm of indignation against France. Congress, during the spring and summer, passed legislation intended to put the nation in a state of defense. The Navy Department was created; new warships were voted; merchant ships were armed; and the President was directed to order our warships to attack French privateers and naval vessels that interfered with our sea-borne trade. An army of ten thousand volunteers was authorized by law, with George Washington as commander in chief; but recruits came in slowly.

The President gave his support to the program for defense, but he labored diligently to prevent war. In order to impress upon his fellow countrymen the dangerous state of national affairs he issued a proclamation naming Wednesday, May 9, "as a day of solemn humiliation, fasting, and prayer." Citizens were urged to refrain from their usual wordly pursuits, and religious congregations were asked to hold services of

---

[7] Although ships and cargoes on the Upper Lakes were not insured, furs and merchandise crossing the ocean were. Askin's furs on the *Ariadne* were valued at £1391 8s. 6d.

thanksgiving to God for His goodness in the past, and to pray for His continued protection against the dangers which were threatening the nation.

In the East the day was observed as the President had requested, and meetings were held at which resolutions were adopted pledging support for his policy. At Detroit Father Levadoux was unable to hold a service on May 9; but on Monday, May 14, he assembled his congregation in Ste Anne's Church and, with the officers of the garrison in attendance, he offered "with all possible zeal" the prayers recommended by the President.

War in Europe, the near approach of the United States to war, and overspeculation precipitated the panic of 1797. People in Detroit felt the pinch of poverty. In the spring of 1798 the expense of supporting the indigent became burdensome. The Grand Jury, in its presentment at the March term of court, urged the justices to instruct the overseers of the poor not to accept as a public charge any adult able to earn a living or children old enough to be put to work.[8] Nevertheless, since the need was great and since there was little hope for improved conditions, the jury advised that, instead of collecting a second tax to provide for the poor, one third of the county revenue be used for that purpose. Although the same presentment emphasized the necessity of building a road around the town so that wagons might pass when the gates were closed, no one, it seems, considered using the unemployed on this public work.

In spite of the gloomy outlook for business James Henry began operating his tannery in the spring of 1798.[9] James

[8] Children were taken as apprentices at an early age. Copies of the indentures of Antoine Fontenoy, eight years old, to Louis Chapoton, and of his sister Mariane, whose age is not given, to Alexis Delisle, in Wayne County, Record of Deeds, I, 192, Register of Deeds Office, County Building, Detroit, are typical.

The masters agreed to instruct the children in the principles of the Roman Catholic religion, and in reading and writing. They promised to provide food, clothing, and lodging.

The children were required to serve their masters faithfully. They were forbidden to gamble at cards or dice, to frequent taverns, or to marry. The boy was bound to serve until he was 21; the girl, until she was 18. At the end of the period of service the masters were to provide them with "the customary suit of clothes from head to foot."

[9] The tannery was at the mouth of May's Creek, near the foot of 11th Street. The spot was called Point Industry.

Williams had arrived during the winter and was in charge of the new establishment. He was an experienced tanner, but Henry was displeased with his "bad habits & wild conduct." James Kennedy and Michael Newman, tanners who had been engaged in Pittsburgh, did not reach Detroit until late in the spring. Although Wilkins still recommended caution, he suggested that the rapidly increasing population south of Lake Erie would provide a market for a large quantity of leather.

Wilkins advised Henry to purchase as much of the stock for their store as possible in the United States. He believed it advisable to give up the Montreal connection if the cost of American goods was about the same. Iron, lead, whisky, and glass, he declared, could be bought in Pittsburgh at reasonable prices.

The store, apparently, was prospering. When Matthew Ernest returned to Detroit in the spring, Wilkins sent George Wallace, Jr., with him to be an assistant to Henry. The new clerk was instructed by his patron to work faithfully, to begin at once to learn French, and to stay away from the billiard table.

Judges Joseph Gilman and Return Jonathan Meigs, Jr., came to Detroit in May, 1798, to hold a session of the Territorial Circuit Court, the first sitting of the Court in Wayne County. The session began on Tuesday, May 29. Quickly discovering that one of the principal problems confronting them was the feud between the civil and the military authorities, the judges tried to adjust existing differences, and to mark out the duty of each group so that future clashes might be avoided.[10]

6

Almost two years had elapsed since Father Levadoux's arrival in Detroit. Although he had immediately asked for an assistant, he was still alone. The priest was anxious to have Father Gabriel Richard for his coworker. Both were refugees from the revolution in France; both belonged to the Order of St. Sulpice; and together they had served the parishes of the

[10] Audrain to François Navarre, May 23, 1798, Navarre Papers, Burton Hist. Coll. Gilman to Sibley, August 23, 1798, Sibley Papers, *ibid.*

Illinois country—Kaskaskia, Cahokia, and Prairie du Rocher—
since 1792. They had become close friends, and Father
Levadoux admired the ability of the younger man. Besides,
he hoped that Father Richard's knowledge of English would
make him especially useful in Detroit.

In June, 1797, Bishop Carroll consented to transfer Richard;
but it was not until the middle of the following May that a
letter arrived informing Father Levadoux that his good friend
was really coming. The Bishop wrote also that Father Jean
Dilhet, who had recently arrived in Baltimore from France, was
on his way to serve the River Raisin settlement. These two
priests would take a great part of the burden from Father
Levadoux's shoulders.

It was about the middle of June, 1798, when Father Richard
reached Detroit.[11] He had left Prairie du Rocher on March
21 and, traveling by way of the Ohio and the Wabash, reached
Vincennes by April 20. He was sad at leaving the congregation which he had been serving. In quaint English he
wrote, "it was little flock but grateful and faithful. I was to
much happy with that people."[12] Forebodings of failure at
Detroit troubled him, and he begged the Bishop to pray
especially for him in his new position.

From Vincennes Father Richard followed the usual route
by the Wabash and the Maumee to Lake Erie, and thence to
Detroit. Father Levadoux was very happy to have his companionship and his help. He was well pleased with the work
of his assistant, but disappointed because of his limited knowledge of English. Father Richard had learned the language
"only passably," he reported.

Tall and spare of frame, Father Richard had the appearance
of an ascetic. He was zealous in his priestly office; but he was
interested also in the physical and mental needs of the people,

[11] Levadoux writing to Carroll, July 29, 1798, reported that Richard had arrived "about six weeks ago," 4Y13, Archives of the Archbishopric of Baltimore and Washington.
Father Richard's notebook contains entries of weather data for Detroit. The first entry is for June 19, 1798. Archives of Notre Dame University.

[12] Richard to Carroll, April 20, 1798, 7B5, Archives of the Archbishopric of Baltimore and Washington. In a postscript to a letter dated March 23, 1797, Richard informed Bishop Carroll that he was beginning "to writt [*sic*] the English tolerably," and asked the Bishop to write to him in English. 7B3, *ibid*.

and his active mind was always busy with ideas for their betterment. Nevertheless, while he was under Father Levadoux's direction, he subordinated himself to his superior.

7

During the summer there arrived in Detroit Solomon Sibley, a New Englander who was destined to become prominent in local politics. A graduate of Rhode Island College, now Brown University, he had gone from his home in Massachusetts to Marietta, on the Ohio River, to practice law. Desiring to establish himself where there were greater opportunities for one of his profession, he wrote to Judge Return Jonathan Meigs, Jr., asking about the situation at Detroit. Meigs informed him that there was "a very considerable Business in the Courts" there. As only one lawyer was residing in the town, the Judge urged Sibley to go to Detroit and open an office.

It was probably during July that Sibley arrived. He was not greatly impressed with the village, which had been built "without taste or elegance"; but he admitted that there was "something in its appearance exceedingly pleasing as you approach it." The attractiveness of the place increased rapidly. About a week later Sibley wrote: "I should feel myself perfectly contented to spend the residue of my days in this Country—But for one thing, we have no ladies here that I care a fig for—have been in company with some of the young French three or four times since my arrival, but take no pleasure in listening to their French nonsense—They speak no English & I speak no french." He expressed the opinion that he would have to return to Massachusetts to find himself a wife. The twenty-nine-year-old lawyer was eager to marry; but he feared that he would be left "in the old Bachellors row."

Sibley took lodging at Major William Winston's tavern and began the practice of law. Almost immediately he received an official appointment. Arthur St. Clair, Jr., attorney general of the Territory, named him his deputy for Wayne County. Warning Sibley that he would "find considerable trouble from the ignorance of the Sheriff," St. Clair advised his deputy to compel him to do his duty. A clash soon occurred when Sheriff Eberts refused to serve writs unless traveling expenses

REV. GABRIEL RICHARD
(Courtesy of Ste Anne's Church, Detroit. Photograph by S. Lucas)

SOLOMON SIBLEY
(Courtesy of Miss Frances W. Sibley, Detroit)

were paid in advance. The deputy attorney general complained to Governor St. Clair and urged that Eberts be removed. The Governor acted, probably before this letter was received, for on August 15 he revoked Eberts' commission and appointed in his stead Lewis Bond, who had served as an officer under Hamtramck.

On the same day St. Clair revoked Patrick McNiff's commission as surveyor. This was the second time that he had been discharged from this office; the United States Government seemed to value his services no more highly than the British had. At the same time the Governor commissioned Matthew Ernest a justice of the peace and a judge of the Court of Common Pleas. He also appointed James Henry to the same offices.

When the Court of Common Pleas sat for the September session, it tried, among other cases, a suit for slander brought by George McDougall against Ronald McDonnell. Apparently their cutthroat competition at Fort Defiance was the cause of the trouble. McDougall declared that McDonnell had used "false, feigned, scandalous, malicious, and opprobious English words" to describe the plaintiff, who had always had a good reputation. The defendant, the complaint continued, had publicly asserted that he was "a Damned Rascal, a Damned liar, a Damned Coward, and a Murderer, and that the said George was everything but a Gentleman." McDougall affirmed that McDonnell, moved by envy of his success, was trying to ruin his reputation and his business. The plaintiff asked for $3,000 damages. The jury seemed not to be greatly swayed by the "opprobious English words" or by the efforts of Ezra Fitz Freeman, McDougall's attorney, for the foreman, George Meldrum, reported a verdict for the plaintiff of $37.

8

The United States shipyard on the River Rouge was a busy place during 1798. Two ships were under construction, and for a time more than one hundred men were employed. In August Meldrum and Park provided "masts, booms, bowsprits, timber, &c." worth $529.50. Under the direction of Captain Curry work on the ships continued during the winter.

The fall of 1798 was marked by an unusual number of shipwrecks. Askin's little fleet was especially unfortunate. First, his schooner *Weazell*, bound for Saginaw Bay with a cargo of trade goods, was cast away on the shore of Lake Huron. Anchors, sails, and rigging were lost, and the cargo was damaged.

In October Askin's sloop *Annette* was wrecked in Lake Erie. Sailing for Detroit from Presqu' Isle under the command of Captain Timothy Grummond, she was carrying stores for the United States quartermaster's department. Overtaken by a storm, the sloop was driven ashore on Long Point and pounded to pieces. The captain, who was drunk at the time, according to the testimony of one of his sailors, sold the cargo to the inhabitants of the neighborhood, pocketed the proceeds, and escaped with Peggy, his wife, to the United States. Only a few pieces of equipment were saved from the wreck. Among the goods sold by Grummond was nearly £100 worth of quartermaster's stores consigned to Matthew Ernest.

As if this were not sufficient loss for one year, the sloop *Saguinah*, which belonged to the firm of Askin, and Meldrum and Park, was so badly damaged that a crew of shipwrights was occupied from December 28 to June 4 in repairing her. In view of all his losses Askin certainly understated his misfortunes when he wrote that "*madame bad luck* took a passage in all my small vessels this fall."

Because no insurance was carried on these or on any other vessels of the Upper Lakes, the financial loss was heavy. Nevertheless, bottoms had to be ready for the opening of shipping in the spring, and so Askin entered into a contract with William Dealy to build him a small ship during the winter.

The vessel was to be of twelve tons burden, twenty-eight feet long at the keel, with a ten-foot beam and a four-and-one-half-foot hold, "deep enough to Stow two Rows of Barrels over each other." The quarter-deck was to be a foot higher than the main deck, and a small cabin with two berths was specified in the contract. The ship was to be built of white oak. Askin agreed to pay £110, New York currency, to Dealy, who would furnish all the materials and deliver the ship at Detroit by May 15, 1799. Dealy immediately went up the Thames River to "the pinery" to begin construction.

Damage to another one of the lake fleet provided some excitement for the people of Detroit. The schooner *Charlotte*, owned by the North West Company, was tied up at the wharf with half her cargo still to be unloaded. Between eleven and twelve o'clock on the night of November 26 sparks from a stove in the cabin ignited the mainsail. Bits of flaming canvas fell into the companionway, setting the stairs, partitions, and bulkheads afire. Soon the flames spread to the barrels of liquor and the packages of drygoods in the hold.

Captain Jesse Burbank, asleep in the cabin, awoke only when the fire broke through into his quarters. Since the flames were between him and the door, a window offered the only means of escape. Burbank scrambled through to the deck, but not before he had been burned on the hands, side, and thigh.

From the deck he hailed the sentinel inside the palisade. The sentinel called the officer of the guard, the drummer beat the alarm, and soldiers and citizens turned out to save the burning vessel.

Colonel Strong soon reached the wharf and organized the soldiers into a bucket brigade. Captain William Mills of the *Nancy*, who was directing the fire fighters, refused to scuttle the ship, as some suggested. Instead, he had a hole chopped in the deck through which water was poured on the fire. Captain James Guthrie of the *Detroit* and Captain James Rough of the *Russell* also lent a hand. The ship was saved, but extensive repairs were required to make her ready for the next season.

9

There was still a possibility that the United States would be drawn into war with France. Alexander Hamilton, second in command to Washington in the new army, was pressing the War Department for action. President Adams, however, still hoped for peace. His patience was rewarded when, in October, he received word that Talleyrand would receive an American minister.

The Indians of the West, who would be a serious threat if war occurred, were still worrying both the British and the American governments. During the summer the braves swarmed into Detroit to collect their annuity. Some of them then crossed the river to Amherstburg, where they complained that the Americans had given them insufficient provisions. Here was an opportunity for the British Indian department to wean the natives from their new allegiance, but Colonel McKee declared that he tried to send them away. The Indians, knowing that they could tip the balance one way or the other in the western country, demanded presents on both sides of the river, and both American and British officials did what they could to appease them.

In the fall of 1798 Colonel Strong sent six chiefs to Philadelphia in charge of Jonathan Schieffelin, Indian agent. They were received by President Adams, to whom they complained about the policy of the Government which forbade them to sell their land to individuals. The President was opposed to changing the law; and so they went away displeased. On the journey the chiefs stopped in New York to visit Alexander Macomb, a former resident of Detroit, who entertained them so royally that they brought back a glowing account of his hospitality.

What the British authorities did to appease the Indians is not known; but they certainly did nothing to arouse their hostility, for General Robert Prescott was expecting trouble. It was rumored that General Victor Collot had promised the natives he would return in 1799, and had urged them to be ready to attack in Upper Canada when the French ascended the St. Lawrence. Prescott had heard that the Indians were preparing to coöperate.

Meanwhile, in Upper Canada Administrator Peter Russell was taking measures for defense against the savages. He issued orders to county lieutenants to have one hundred men of each militia battalion ready for instant service. The Administrator complained to Prescott that the forces of Colonels McKee and Baby of the western District "have been greatly reduced in numbers by the secession of those who have become subjects of the United States."

CHAPTER X
EXPERIMENT IN DEMOCRACY

EVER since the first arrival of Governor Arthur St. Clair at Marietta on July 9, 1788, the Northwest Territory, of which Wayne County was a part, had been under the rule of the Governor and three judges, as provided in the Ordinance of 1787. St. Clair and his colleagues were Federalists. Since most of the settlers who came into the Territory were Republicans, they became dissatisfied with what they considered an arbitrary form of government, and began to demand a voice in making the laws under which they lived.

According to the Ordinance, an assembly should be chosen as soon as there were in the Territory five thousand free males twenty-one years old. In the fall of 1798 Governor St. Clair, heeding the clamor of the people, ordered a census to be taken. A letter to Peter Audrain set the census taking in motion in Wayne County, where the constable of the townships counted the free men twenty-one years of age and over. Peter Audrain sent the returns to Cincinnati on November 1.

Because the census of the other counties indicated that the population of the Territory met the requirements of the Ordinance, without waiting for the figures from Wayne County Governor St. Clair issued a proclamation of election on October 29. Wayne County was allotted one representative. On November 26 Sheriff Lewis Bond posted a notice that the election would be held at the courthouse in Detroit from ten o'clock in the morning until four in the afternoon on Monday, December 17, Tuesday, December 18, and Wednesday, December 19.

This notice must have caused a stir in the community, which was seething with personal animosities. On November 22 Peter Audrain, as prothonotary, notified Patrick McNiff that Judges Louis Beaufait, James May, and Charles François Girardin would not sit with him on the bench at the next term of the Court of Common Pleas. When only McNiff and Nathan Williams appeared on the bench, for lack of a quorum no December session of the court was held.[1]

To have revenge on Judge May, McNiff informed Sibley, the deputy attorney general, that May had attacked Robert Abbott on January 9, 1798, and had knocked him "on the Broad of his Back." McNiff asked that the matter be laid before the Grand Jury. He also charged that the judges of the Court of General Quarter Sessions had concealed an indictment found against Hermann Eberts in the September session. These charges, he probably expected, would make some trouble for the Judge and the ex-Sheriff, two of his bitter enemies. The third, Peter Audrain, he apparently was unable to reach legally; but his son Robert allegedly assaulted Audrain's son James "at the Instigation of said Patrick," and McNiff was tried for breach of the peace in the December term of the Court of General Quarter Sessions.

Judge May, in turn, informed Sibley that McNiff had married Corporal John Deal, of the United States Artillery, and Mary Poulins, on or about August 1, 1798, without previously having published their intention to marry, and without a license. Both McNiff and May were indicted and tried on the charges they had filed against each other, and both were acquitted. The result of the trial of McNiff for breach of the peace is not known.

As a result of McNiff's charge against the judges of Quarter Sessions, the whole bench was presented by the Grand Jury. Judge May, who was presiding as chief justice, became so angry at Sibley, the deputy attorney general, that he "vented his spleen" on him in open court. Sibley, resenting the abusive language, replied to "Sir James" in the same style.

These preliminaries presaged a lively contest at the first election to be held in Detroit under the jurisdiction of the United States.

2

Two and a half years had passed since Captain Porter's detachment of United States troops took possession of Detroit.

[1] Apparently James Henry and Matthew Ernest, who had been appointed to the bench, had not yet been sworn in.

Nevertheless, except for the flag which now flew from the staff in the Fort, where the Union Jack had formerly waved, and the blue coats of the soldiers which had replaced the red, little change was evident. Nothing less than a large number of settlers from the American states would be likely to alter the well-rooted customs of the French and the British residents.

As a matter of fact, few Americans came to Detroit. At the end of 1798 no more than seventeen can be definitely identified.[2] Some of them had government positions or were employed by the army contractor: Solomon Sibley was deputy prosecutor; Lewis Bond was sheriff; Matthew Ernest, Frederick Bates, and Elias Wallen were in the quartermaster department; and James Henry was the agent of James O'Hara, army contractor. Henry was also a merchant and operated a tannery. Michael Newman, James Williams, and James Kennedy were employed in this industry, and George Wallace, Jr., worked in Henry's store. Benjamin Huntington and Oliver Wiswell were merchants. Elijah Brush, David Powers, and Ezra Fitz Freeman were practicing law, as was Solomon Sibley also. Major William Winston and Warham Strong were tavern keepers.[3]

This small group of Americans scarcely felt at home in Detroit. Some of them still looked upon the British residents as "Tories." Even those among them who had become citizens of the United States and accepted office under the Government were not popular. Sibley nicknamed Chief Justice May "Sir James," and May considered Sibley an interloper and a disturber of the office holders. Patrick McNiff also disliked the Americans, whom he dubbed "Yankee foreigners."[4]

Nevertheless, in general relations were friendly. The attendance of "brothers" from the states at meetings of Zion Lodge has already been mentioned, and when the British sub-

[2] There must have been others in the town and in the vicinity. Angus Mackintosh wrote in 1799 of "the number of the lower class of Americans that have come to this Quarter last fall & this spring." Mackintosh to Alexander Macomb, June 25, 1799, Mackintosh's Letter Book, Burton Hist. Coll.

[3] Winston had served in the Revolution and in Wayne's western campaign. He was honorably discharged, November 1, 1796. In the spring of 1798 he opened a tavern in Detroit. Audrain to William Jones, June 12, 1798, Sibley Papers, *ibid.*

Strong was probably a relative of Colonel Strong, the commandant.

[4] On the other hand, it will be remembered that May and McNiff were hostile to each other.

jects across the river celebrated the Queen's birthday on the evening of January 18, 1799, many of the Americans were invited to join in the festivities. All the officers at the Fort, except Colonel Strong and three others, attended. Of the civilians, Matthew Ernest and his wife, Lewis Bond and Mrs. Bond, James Henry, and Major William Winston accepted the invitation. They spent the evening in dining and dancing. Peter Audrain, who remained at home, reported that he could hear "the noise of the Drum."

As for the French the difference in language was a bar to friendly relations with the Americans, at least in the beginning. The complaint of Solomon Sibley, who spoke no French, about his unhappy experience in the company of some young ladies has already been quoted. Different customs also kept them apart. Frederick Bates reported that he could make "but little progress with the french girls," who had a strong dislike for Americans. "They think them a rough, unpolished, brutal set of people," he explained. Nevertheless, Bates was enthusiastic in his praise of the young ladies of Detroit. He was particularly attracted by Commodore Grant's daughters, whom he described as "the finest girls in this country."

Although he was not a Catholic, Bates attended church, apparently for the purpose of seeing these fair *demoiselles*. On Christmas Eve in 1798 he went early to the midnight Mass and seated himself in the Grant pew. When the family arrived, the girls asked him to move. He apologized for his intrusion and sat down in the pew next to theirs. He had scarcely settled himself when they warned him by gestures to move again, as he was in the pew of a lady who was just coming in. This they did three times, having great fun at the expense of the embarrassed young American.

On another occasion Bates and George Wallace took "Miss Navarre's" pew. When she arrived, they seated themselves elsewhere. Before the end of the service the young lady discovered that her dress was stained by the tobacco juice which the intruders had carelessly spat upon the kneeling bench. Miss Navarre told her friends that Bates and Wallace "had more ill-manners & less decency than even the Yankees generally had." Thus a young gentleman from Virginia and his friend from Pittsburgh helped to widen the social breach between the French and the Americans.

In spite of Bates' frequent rebuffs by the French girls, which he frankly reported to his sister Sally, the young Virginian admired these people. He was amazed at the confidence, grace, and politeness of even the ordinary Frenchman, but he did find their ceremonious courtesy somewhat tiresome.[5]

Solomon Sibley, with a New England background, was less tolerant of the strange habits of the French in Detroit. He characterized the people as "exceedingly ignorant and lazy." Provisions were scarce, he decided, not because the soil was barren, but because the farmers were idle. He declared that they threw manure into the river instead of spreading it on their fields.[6] Besides, he suspected their loyalty. He believed that, if French troops should invade the country, the *habitants* and the Indians would unite against the British and the Americans.

Although the establishing of social relations was difficult, life in Detroit for the Americans was not limited to business activities. General John Wilkins, who had spent some time there, probably had good reasons for warning his protégé, George Wallace, Jr., to avoid the billiard table. There was betting also on races and on shooting matches, and in the fall of 1798 a horse was raffled.

Drinking was another social activity. At this pastime the Americans were undoubtedly as proficient as the French and the British. Frederick Bates informed his sister Sally that "The Gentlemen are convivially disposed." He continued frankly: "I do not often get beastly drunk, but I must acknowledge that I am sometimes gentlemanly gay." Then, to allay her probable alarm about his carousings, he added: "I shall not lose sight of those restraints which a young fellow should impose on his conduct."

[5] Bates' opinion of the French girls and his account of his misadventures are contained in a letter to his sister Sally, May 5, 1799, Bates Papers, Missouri Historical Society, St. Louis.

[6] This practice was not peculiar to the Detroit region. Henry Adams, writing of agricultural practices in the country as a whole, declared that: "Except among the best farmers, drainage, manures, and rotation of crops were uncommon." He reported that a New England farmer had even been known to remove his barn when the accumulation of manure became too great. Henry Adams, *History of the United States of America*, I, 18.

The Americans had a shower bath somewhere in town, devised, perhaps, to clear their heads in the morning after a night spent at a tavern. According to Frederick Bates, it consisted of a "Barrel of Water [which] is turned upon you from a height of fifteen feet." The shock, he confessed "leaves you almost insensible." Nevertheless, he enjoyed this Spartan bath. "I seldom neglect to pay my morning devotions in this invigorating temple," Bates declared.

3

In the preëlection campaign during the first half of December, 1798, the three elements—British, French, and American—divided to some extent according to their previous national origins; but the alignments were not exclusive. The former British subjects, by a strict interpretation of the Ordinance of 1787, could not be candidates. This law required that to be eligible a man must have been a citizen of one of the states for three years and must reside in the county; or, he must have been a resident of the county for three years. Since Wayne County had existed for less than two and a half years, only Americans who had come from other parts of the Union would seem to have been qualified to run for office. An additional requirement was that a candidate must own two hundred acres of land in the county.

The qualifications for electors, on the other hand, did not exclude former British subjects. In order to vote, only two years' residence in the county was required for those who had not previously been citizens of a state. Besides, electors must own fifty acres of land in the county. Governor St. Clair, in order not to deprive townsmen of the franchise, interpreted this clause to include those who owned houses and lots in town equal in value to fifty acres of land.

Although it would appear that he could not satisfy the residence requirement, James May was supported as a candidate by Peter Audrain, by most of the judges, and by the English-speaking citizens who had formerly been British subjects.

Most of the French-speaking citizens and all the Americans opposed May. They prevailed upon Solomon Sibley to be their candidate. George McDougall exerted himself among the French in Sibley's interest. A month before the election he reported: "I have already excited much allarm & apprehension in the minds of several of my Countrymen here, should they be so weak as to choose the three-penny judge for their Representative." Other men must have worked to secure votes for the candidates, and, to judge from the animosities that flared up during the December term of the courts, the campaign was probably a lively one.

Although this was to be the first election during the American régime, it was not the first time the people of Detroit had voted. Under British rule they had gone to the polls in 1792 to elect representatives to the Assembly of Upper Canada. One of the candidates was Lieutenant David W. Smith, who was serving at Fort Niagara. He had formerly been stationed at Detroit and was well known in the community. Since he could not appeal to the voters in person, he induced his good friend John Askin to conduct the campaign. Smith's letters to Askin contain some interesting information about his ideas on the subject.

He exhorted Askin not to spare expense for beef and rum— "let them have plenty." The "gentry," he suggested, might be transported to the polls in boats, but "The french people can easily walk." "The more broken heads & bloody noses there is the more election like," Smith wrote. He desired, if he was elected, that a celebration be held on the Common with a bonfire and rum. Askin spent money freely, the bill for campaign expenditures being £233 4s. 5d. Lieutenant Smith was elected, and he reimbursed his able manager promptly.[7]

What means were used to influence voters during the campaign preceding the first American election can only be conjectured. At the polls, as the voting was viva voce, the officials knew for whom each elector voted. Since there was no secret ballot, pressure could be exerted. If Judge May's testimony is credible, on the three days of election—December 17, 18, and 19—liquor was provided freely by Sibley's friends, some of May's supporters were turned away as not qualified, discharged soldiers with clubs threatened those who intended

[7] M. M. Quaife, "Detroit's First Election," *Burton Hist. Coll. Leaf.*, V, No. 2, pp. 30–31.

to vote for the Judge, and many illegal votes for Sibley were accepted.

Although the man who was elected would represent all of Wayne County, Detroit was the only place where votes could be cast. The residents of Mackinac had no voice in the election, and it is unlikely that many citizens came up from the River Raisin settlement to vote.

When the officials had canvassed the returns of the election, they found that Solomon Sibley had defeated James May by fifty-one votes. In the short span of five months the New England lawyer had apparently earned the respect and the confidence of the majority of the voters.

Sibley took the responsibility of his office seriously. On Christmas Day he issued an address to the citizens suggesting that they convene and draw up instructions for him concerning the interests and the welfare of the people of Wayne County. . At the same time he expressed the hope that they would always keep him informed, so that he would be able to perform his duty.

A meeting of the inhabitants was accordingly held. They chose a committee consisting largely of French-speaking people, but including Benjamin Huntington and Ezra Fitz Freeman, Americans from the States, and John Dodemead, coroner, formerly a British subject. These men drew up recommendations for the representative. They instructed him to request the Governor to remove the county treasurer; to present to the Governor the names of the ten men nominated by the committee for judges;[8] to recommend that Audrain be removed as judge of Probate; and to ask for a lot at Detroit on which public buildings might be erected.

Early in January, 1799, Solomon Sibley set out on the three-hundred-mile journey to Cincinnati to attend the first session of the territorial legislature. Shortly afterwards James May, Louis Beaufait, Jr., and Antoine Beaubien took the same route, carrying with them letters of introduction from Peter Audrain to Governor St. Clair, and to William Henry Harrison, secre-

---

[8] Seven of the nominees were French. The others were James Henry, Matthew Ernest, and Jacob Visger. Oliver Wiswell reported that the British element was greatly dissatisfied with these nominations. Wiswell to Sibley, January 23, 1799, Sibley Papers, Burton Hist. Coll.

tary of the territory. Their purpose was to file a protest with the assembly against Sibley's being seated, and to ask for an investigation of the election at Detroit.

4

It was probably after Sibley's departure that Sheriff Lewis Bond received a supplementary writ from Governor St. Clair assigning three representatives to Wayne County instead of one. The census returns, which had reached the capital after the original proclamation had been issued, showed that the county was entitled to two additional representatives. The Sheriff, to whom the writ was addressed, accordingly called another election for January 14 and 15.

"The friends of good order" held a caucus and nominated François Chabert and Jacob Visger. This action, according to Oliver Wiswell, gave universal offense "to the English people." Nevertheless, they apparently named no candidate of their own. Wiswell, although he had agreed to support Chabert and Visger, accepted the suggestion of the French from the River Rouge, who were not satisfied with the nominees, that he be their candidate.[9]

The polls were opened at eleven o'clock on the morning of January 14, in Dodemead's tavern, where the courts regularly sat. Sheriff Lewis Bond was in charge; Justices Matthew Ernest and Patrick McNiff were judges of the election. The first voter, according to Peter Audrain, was Justice Louis Beaufait, who named his son, Louis, Jr., and James May. The judges refused to accept a vote for May because he was contesting the result of the first election. Thirteen others, most of them French, also tried, unsuccessfully, to vote for the Chief Justice. Only twenty-five votes were cast the first day because of torrential rain. The weather was so inclement that no one from the River Raisin settlement appeared at the polls.

On Tuesday citizens from the River Rouge came to vote. Justices Louis Beaufait and Joseph Voyer sat as judges of the election. Although they were supporters of James May, they too refused to receive votes for him. Strangely enough, they declared that Chabert and young Beaufait were ineligible

[9] *Ibid.*, Wiswell explained that there was some doubt about Chabert's eligibility.

because they had lived less than three years in the Territory under American rule, but they accepted votes for Jacob Visger. The latter, it is true, had been born in New York; however, he had come to Detroit and lived as a subject of the British King.

Most of the men from the River Rouge apparently voted for Wiswell and Visger, but some of them named Chabert as their choice. Chabert, however, sometime before the polls closed, announced that he would withdraw because he considered himself ineligible.

The polls would be closed at four o'clock. At about three-thirty, according to Audrain, Justice McNiff came out and advised friends of Wiswell to bring in more votes for him, as the Frenchmen were leading. Audrain declared further that he had proof of an offer by Joseph Cissne and Christian Clemens to pay $100 for ten votes for Wiswell.

When the votes were counted, it was found that Chabert had 68, Visger 63, Wiswell 37, and Beaufait 30. Since Chabert had withdrawn from the contest, the Sheriff issued certificates of election to Jacob Visger and Oliver Wiswell.

Oliver Wiswell decided not to go to Cincinnati. He informed Sibley by letter that he considered the office a burden, and, furthermore, the session would probably be over before he could arrive. Besides, the assembly might seat Chabert, who, persuaded by Audrain and others, resolved to go to the capital and file his claim. After a petition had been circulated among the French in his behalf, he and Visger went to Cincinnati; but they did not arrive "untill the house adjourned."

Shortly after the election Patrick McNiff drew up a set of instructions for the new representatives. He urged them, in conjunction with Sibley, to recommend the following legislation: a more severe militia law to compel men to report for drill; a law to require the building of roads; a law to regulate weights and measures; a law to prohibit British subjects from voting; a law empowering the justices of Quarter Sessions to order galleries removed from the fronts of houses where they partially blocked the narrow streets; and a law to prevent "the Profanation of the Sabath day, by Horse racing, Dancing and a thing too Common on that day—Drunkness."

This was an ambitious program to lay before the first assembly. Some of the instructions were undoubtedly timely and important; but McNiff was certainly optimistic if he expected the customary practices of the French to be suppressed simply by the passing of a law. As a matter of fact, no laws were passed at the first session. The assembly met on February 4, nominated ten persons from whom the President would choose five for the legislative council, and adjourned until September.

James May's charges against Sibley were referred to the Committee on Election. They appointed three commissioners in Detroit to take evidence and to report. Although the commission apparently sat during September, 1799, nothing was done, and Sibley retained his seat.[10]

5

"The Devil to pay, and no pitch hot, since you took your departure from hence,"[11] wrote Colonel Strong to Solomon Sibley. Thus did the Commandant figuratively characterize events that had recently occurred. It was an old story. The feud between the commanding officer and certain of the civilians that had plagued Colonel England, Colonel Hamtramck, and General Wilkinson now involved Colonel Strong. Provoked by the continual drunkenness of his men, he issued a proclamation threatening trial by court-martial of anyone found selling liquor to soldiers. John Dodemead, coroner of Wayne County and keeper of the tavern in which the courts held their sessions, defied the Commandant. A few days after the proclamation three soldiers detailed for the guard appeared on parade too drunk to perform their duty. They admitted that Dodemead had sold them liquor, at the same time declaring "he cared not for the orders of the Colo."

Colonel Strong then posted a sentinel in the street back of Dodemead's tavern. Thereupon Dodemead and others who had previously sold liquor to soldiers contrary to orders, "with the Assistance of that Dam'd P-t-r A-d-n," endeavored to arouse the people against the Commandant. Four of the judges dispatched a letter to the Governor protesting against the proclamation of "martial law" in Detroit. Governor St.

[10] Matthew Ernest, Robert Abbott, and Jacob Visger were the commissioners.
[11] The "Devil" was the longest seam of a ship. It was difficult to "pay"; i.e. to calk.

Clair forwarded their complaint to the Secretary of State, who answered that he supposed the Secretary of War could "correct the error" of the Commandant.

Not satisfied with arousing discord, Dodemead filed suit against Colonel Strong for trespass with force and arms, demanding damages of $5,000. Solomon Sibley engaged Jacob Burnet of Cincinnati to represent the Commandant in the case.

Dodemead and his supporters had yet another scheme. When the Court of Common Pleas convened in March at Dodemead's tavern, the judges laid before Solomon Sibley, deputy attorney general, a series of questions to be answered. The most important of them were whether the presence of a sentinel outside the "Court House" could be interpreted as placing the Court under duress and, consequently, whether a sitting of the Court would be legal. The reply was verbose and indecisive. Sibley pointed out the fact that the sentry was at the back door, and not at the front door, by which one entered the Court. He thought the question of duress would have to be decided by a jury. Nevertheless, as Detroit had always been a garrison town and as courts had held sessions here both under British and under American authority, he could not, without consulting other gentlemen of the law, give an opinion that might throw doubt upon the legality of the proceedings of those courts. The problem was solved, for the moment, by holding the March sessions of both courts in Major Winston's tavern.

The bitterness, however, remained. John Askin wrote in April: "There is a constant war between most of the town citizens or rather magistracy and the military." As a part of this "war," someone attacked Colonel Strong in "an anonymous Pasquinade" which was posted on the door of the engine house. Frederick Bates turned his literary talent to the defense of the Commandant, refuting the calumnies of the anonymous writer in three equally anonymous "pieces" which won the applause of the "few particular friends" to whom he divulged his authorship.

On September 20, 1799, an express rider brought to Colonel Strong, along with other dispatches, a letter from the Secretary of War directed to Judges May, Beaufait, Voyer, and Girardin. There was also a large package for them. They were very happy about the Secretary's gift, and waited expectantly until Sheriff Bond opened it in their presence. When they saw that it was only the *Articles of War*, "The Executive Directory," as Sheriff Bond called these justices, was greatly disappointed. The accompanying letter was a reply to their complaint against Colonel Strong. Secretary McHenry assured them that the Government desired to preserve the rights of the civil authorities, and he promised to report the Colonel's conduct to Major General Alexander Hamilton for investigation. Nevertheless, he informed the judges that a commandant, if it was necessary for the good of the service, must prevent too frequent intercourse of soldiers with civilians. For guidance in their future relations with the Military the Secretary referred them to the Articles. Certainly here was small consolation for the magistrates and their supporters.

Dodemead's writ against Colonel Strong was "quashed for irregularity" in June, and the sentinel remained at his post during the remainder of the year. Then Dodemead "made concessions," the guard was withdrawn on January 1, 1800, and Colonel Strong reported: "All like Kingdom come."

During January, 1799, Colonel Strong had another matter on his mind in addition to the drunkenness of his soldiers and the damage suit filed against him. According to reports, the Indians were meditating hostilities. In order to avoid providing shelter for a war party that might attack the town the Commandant forbade the erection of a stockade around the new Catholic cemetery, which he had permitted to be laid out on the Common just east of the palisade. He directed that it be surrounded by only "a flying fence."

Peter Audrain reported that, when Father Levadoux read the order in church, the people were alarmed.[12] Audrain had heard that a new stockade was to be built to protect the town. He did not deny the necessity for it, but he feared it would cost "a pretty penny."

Not all the alarm, however, was on the American side of the river. On the British side the captains of militia were ordered to send men to help complete the fortifications at Malden. Captain Hector McLean kept his soldiers busy dur-

---

[12] Audrain had reported to the Governor that the Commandant had granted an acre of ground for the new cemetery. The old one, "adjoining their church and within the pickets, is so full that it is a real public nuisance, and has been presented as such by several grand juries." Audrain to St. Clair, November 1, 1798, William H. Smith, (ed.), *The St. Clair Papers*, II, 435.

ing the winter cutting and hauling pickets in accordance with orders from his superiors, so that by March fifty-five hundred were ready to be placed.

Rumors of probable Indian attacks continued to circulate in the neighborhood of the British post, and reports reaching the officials at York caused some apprehension. The British commandant believed, however, that there was no real danger. He accused the Indian Department of trying to frighten the Government into the immediate appointment of a successor to Colonel Alexander McKee, deputy superintendent, who had died on January 13, 1799. Captain McLean wrote that the Americans had the earliest and most accurate intelligence of Indian affairs and that it was always reported to him by Colonel Strong, "between whom and us there is a very good understanding." The American colonel, he added, now treated the idea of an attack "with the utmost redicule."

Nevertheless, recurring rumors of impending raids caused officials to urge Captain McLean to be vigilant. Again he asserted that the danger was manufactured by such men as Prideaux Selby, Indian agent, and Matthew Elliot, who had been removed from his post in the Indian Department for falsifying reports.[13] These two, McLean declared, influenced Captain Thomas McKee, who had succeeded to his father's position.

At Detroit there was still some anxiety during the summer of 1799. Solomon Sibley informed his father that, although the Indians were then at peace, he was "apprehensive it will be otherwise e're long—as they both murmur and threaten." He promised that, if an attack should occur, he would stay clear of the scalping knives of the savages.

If there was really any danger of an Indian attack, it must have been only a local threat. Colonel Strong had probably learned by this time that Talleyrand had agreed to receive American commissioners and that President Adams had given orders for them to proceed to Paris. The prospect was for peace with France. There was little likelihood now of a general Indian outbreak supported by the French and the Spanish governments.

---

[13] Elliot was removed by Peter Russell after charges had been made by Captain McLean. Russell to Elliot, February 6, 1799, *Mich. Pio. and Hist. Soc. Colls.*, XXV, 165.

CHAPTER XI

CONTROVERSY AND COÖPERATION

IN THE spring of 1799 John Askin was pessimistic about business conditions in Detroit. "This place is become very dull," he wrote to his son-in-law, Robert Hamilton, "trade bad and no news." Angus Mackintosh had the same opinion. Returns from the Indian country would "turn out far short of paying for the goods sent out last Fall," he reported. News from Montreal about fur prices was not entirely reassuring. Although deerskins were more valuable than they had been the year before, raccoon pelts were cheaper. Since raccoon skins were very plentiful at Detroit, the lower price was injurious to the community.

John Askin was now sixty, and he was feeling the burden of increasing years. His eyes troubled him so much that for a time he was scarcely able to write, and he had to remain indoors during cold weather. By the end of June, however, he was feeling somewhat better. He had recovered his sight, but he had become hard of hearing. "When I have Stopt Old Age geting in at one door," he wrote, "she gets [in] at an Other."

In spite of illness Askin did not retire from business, but he decided to restrict his fur trading. Experience had taught him that "at this place, he who trades most loses most." In August he began negotiating with John Anderson at Fort Miamis to wind up their partnership. Shortly afterward he had to terminate his long connection with James and Andrew McGill of Montreal since he could not meet the terms of their new contracts, which required payment during the current year for all goods purchased from them. Nevertheless, he hoped to retain the friendship of the partners, and he promised to wind up his affairs with them as soon as he could sell some of his property.

Askin intended to concentrate on supplying the British and the American governments, preferring this sort of business because of the certainty of payment. Besides, they were almost the only customers who paid cash. In order to have sufficient men to prepare the supplies they would require, Askin requested the McGills to send out from Montreal six or eight *engagés* in the spring. If more came than he could use, he would sell their services at a good profit. The Detroit merchant wanted men capable of mowing hay, cutting wood, and doing general work. He also asked for a baker and a blacksmith. In conclusion, he suggested cannily: "Smart young Boys does nearly as Well as men and are much cheaper and easier managed."

During the winter Askin had a gang of *engagés* at the pinery on the St. Clair River cutting timber, and in July he floated it down to Fort Malden in rafts. He offered the United States Government seventy thousand "Excellent Bricks and well burnt" at eight dollars a thousand at the kilns on the River Rouge, or ten dollars delivered on the wharf at Detroit.

The loss of the *Annette* and the *Weazell* in 1798 left only the *Saguinah* of Askin's fleet, and the need for extensive repairs kept her out of service until June 10. The aging merchant viewed the situation philosophically. The vessels, he wrote, were old, freight was decreasing and men's wages rising. "I think I have Suffered very little," he concluded.[1]

In April William Dealy sailed the small sloop of twelve tons burden which he had been building for Askin on the Thames River to a shipyard on the River Rouge below Detroit. Although much remained to be done before she would be ready to carry merchandise for her owner, the builder quit for lack of money. When Askin agreed to pay him a dollar a day and provide the iron necessary to finish the ship, he resumed work; but progress was slow, and it was not until the spring of 1800 that the sloop *Surprise* was ready.

Several other ships, besides Askin's, were being built at the River Rouge. Captain McLean at Amherstburg complained that it was difficult to procure carpenters to work on the *Ottawa* because of the number of vessels being built on the American side, where wages were high. The larger of the two United States Government ships under construction there,

[1] Nevertheless, he did try to apprehend Captain Louis Derineau, whom he held responsible for the loss of the *Weazell*. Askin to Louis Barthe, May 30, 1799, Askin Papers, Burton Hist. Coll.

a brig of about one hundred and fifty tons burden, the *President Adams*, was launched on June 25, 1799.²

Another vessel at the River Rouge was the snow *Caledonia*, which Angus Mackintosh launched on October 18 and towed across the river to his own dock at Sandwich to be completed. On the day of the launching this loyal Briton moved his family from Detroit to their new home in Sandwich.³

Perhaps an altercation with Colonel Hamtramck in August hastened his departure. The Colonel, now commander of the Western Army, was in Detroit during the summer of 1799. One day he sent Lieutenant Lukens to Mackintosh's house to ask him to take the Colonel aboard the *Charlotte* and carry him to Presqu' Isle. Mackintosh refused. The ship, he explained, was laden with North West Company furs, which had to be delivered directly to Fort Erie. The Lieutenant carried the message to Colonel Hamtramck, who sent him back with an order that the *Charlotte* must leave the wharf immediately. Mackintosh promised to move her, but made no haste about it.

In half an hour a sergeant appeared. He informed Mackintosh that, since the ship had not sailed, he was going to cut the hawser. Before the angry merchant could act, the sergeant with four soldiers carrying axes was at the wharf. The sailors on board cast off at once and anchored in the stream. Colonel Hamtramck posted a guard to warn people away, and the next morning, when Mackintosh himself tried to go aboard, he was turned back and had to row out to her from another point. Naturally he was furious, especially since Colonel Strong had given him permission to use the wharf when the Government had no need of it. Perhaps he was still smarting from Hamtramck's cavalier treatment of him when he wrote sometime later, from Sandwich, that since he had his own dock now, he would not use those of the Yankees.

2

Although Detroit had been within the jurisdiction of the United States for three years, trade was still carried on largely

² *Pittsburgh Gazette*, July 20, 1799.
³ Mackintosh to Mrs. William Macomb, October 24, 1799, Letter Book, Burton Hist. Coll.

through Montreal. In the summer of 1799 Joseph Campau sailed for that city to purchase merchandise, leaving his seventeen-year-old nephew, John Williams, in charge of his store. For the past two and a half years the boy had been assisting his uncle, who declared that John knew the business as well as he himself did. He believed also that his nephew was loyal and trustworthy. Nevertheless, during the voyage the thrifty merchant had time to wonder what was happening in the store during his absence. While the ship waited at Fort Erie for a favorable breeze, Campau wrote John a long letter in which expressions of complete confidence in the lad were interspersed with anxious instructions.

He advised Williams to keep a complete assortment of goods in the store to prevent the other merchants of the town from taking advantage of the owner's absence. If John needed more merchandise, he was to obtain it from Robert Innis on credit unless he could buy it cheaper elsewhere. In that case he should pay cash. Campau warned his nephew to give credit only to reliable persons. He admonished the boy to be patient with all customers, but especially with Indians, who might take offense if the clerk was brusque, and leave the store without trading. John Williams dutifully answered this letter, and assured his uncle that the business was being managed carefully.[4]

Even the native Americans bought and sold in Montreal. James Henry, for example, continued his connection with Leith, Jameson & Company. In July, however, the firm complained that his order was small.[5] They asserted that he could not purchase goods more cheaply in the United States unless the Government imposed a duty on goods entering Detroit from Canada. Perhaps Henry was now procuring some of his merchandise from Pittsburgh, as his partner John Wilkins, Jr., had suggested, or from Albany.

Merchants from the latter place were doing business in Detroit. According to John Askin, they could reach the

---

[4] At this time Williams began to pay for his sister Elizabeth's board and schooling with Mme Bellecour, at the rate of £25 a year. Receipt, April 1, 1800, John R. Williams Papers, Mich. Hist. Colls., University of Michigan.

[5] In spite of their complaint, Henry's debt to them in January, 1800, was £3922 1s. 9d. L. J. & Co., to Henry, January 23, 1800, Sibley Papers, Burton Hist. Coll.

town earlier than the agents from Montreal, and spirits from Albany were three or four shillings cheaper. Mackintosh, however, learned by experience that the heavier cost of transportation, interest, and commissions, in addition to "the great leakage" which occurred on the way, made liquor from New York actually more expensive.

During the autumn of 1799 John Wilkins, Jr., wrote to James Henry asking for an accounting of the business of the store and of the tannery, in which he had an interest. Wilkins, believing that he should receive a dividend, demanded an immediate apportionment of the profits. Henry replied that he could not yet make a statement, but that he would do so as soon as possible. He reported progress on the digging of ten vats, which, with those already in use, would hold nine hundred hides. Henry declared that there was little demand for leather unless it was turned into useful articles. Consequently, he had had some of it made into saddles, and he had engaged people in Detroit to make "the common Canadian Shoe Pack."[6]

In September, 1799, Colonel Ebenezer Denny of Pittsburgh, a retired army officer, visited Detroit. His description of the town is not flattering:

> I was much disappointed in the place. It is filthy beyond measure & calculated to accomodate a few Traders. A square of about 300 by 400 yards divided by narrow streets, one only that a cart can turn about in, and the lots no larger than sufficient for a tolerable house to stand on. One or two houses excepted, they resemble the buildings at Vincennes. Pickets round the whole. There is a small regular work back of the town, but it's lost to appearance & covers only the side next itself. It seems to have been designed for a retreat for the commanding officer. They say there is a covered way to it from what's called the citadel. This last place is nothing more than the barracks & small parade within the Town Square, separated from the dwellings by pickets. There is a great quantity of goods taken to Detroit yearly, but no trade there. It is made a place of deposit. Deputy traders, who go out into the Indian country, are fitted off from thence. The plan answered the first intention—the traders jam'ed up together in order to fence in the whole & keep out drunken Indians. The place is crowded at present & not an inch of ground to extend their buildings. I stayed ten days.[7]

---

[6] The shoepack was a moccasin with an upper added to it.

[7] Ebenezer Denny to Josiah Harmar, December 20, 1799, Harmar Papers, Vol. 18, Wm. L. Clements Library, University of Michigan.

Denny had served under General Anthony Wayne in the Revolutionary War, and under both General Josiah Harmar and General Arthur St. Clair during their campaigns in the West. He retired from the army in 1793. His wife was a sister of John Wilkins, Jr.

3

Father Richard was absent from Detroit during the whole summer of 1799. On June 20, at the order of Father Levadoux, he sailed for Mackinac aboard the sloop *Detroit*. Ten days later he arrived at the island, where he found nearly a thousand men: traders, *engagés*, *voyageurs*, and Indians, for it was the time of year when furs were brought in from the more northerly and westerly regions. As Father Richard explained, Mackinac is "the Grand Rendezvous of Several traders of Lac Michigan, Mississippi and Lac Superior &c."

When he left Detroit, the priest had expected to remain at Mackinac only a month, but he found so much work there that he wrote to Father Levadoux asking permission to remain during the winter. Forty children on the island, he reported, needed instruction. Some of them could not even say "Our Father"; others scarcely knew how to make the sign of the Cross. Besides, the church was nearly in ruins and would probably collapse if it were not repaired. He sent his request by an Indian named *Oni-g-wi-gan*, and asked Father Levadoux to return his reply by the same messenger.

Father Levadoux, although he recognized the need for a missionary in the North, could not spare his industrious assistant. Fearing, perhaps, that Father Richard would ask the Bishop to transfer him to Mackinac, Father Levadoux wrote to Bishop Carroll urging the importance of Father Richard's work in Detroit. No one, he insisted, could replace the younger priest, who was indispensable because of the facility with which he spoke both English and French, the confidence which everyone reposed in him, and the close friendship of the two men for each other. On his own authority Father Levadoux directed his assistant to return.

Obedient to the order of his superior, Father Richard embarked on the schooner *Charlotte*, which arrived at Detroit on October 21. After he had resumed his round of parish duties, he requested Bishop Carroll to send him fifty or sixty *Cantiques Français*, which had been printed by John Hayes in 1798 for the use of St. Patrick's Church in Baltimore. He believed they would be useful for his parishioners, who were very fond of singing. The priest approved the practice, but he objected to some of the lyrics which were being sung. These books, he suggested hopefully, "could Stop Some bad Songs they are used to Sing."

Jimmy and Johnny, the sons of William Burnett and his Indian wife Kakima, were still living with James May. They were attending school, apparently throughout the year. During 1798 they had studied under John Burrell; in January, 1799, they were sent to a new master, Peter Joseph Dillon, who had come to Detroit in 1798, helping Hugh Callahan drive a herd of cattle from Hamilton. He was married, and his wife was also a teacher.

As James May paid Dillon only about four pounds each quarter for instructing his two wards, the schoolmaster was anxious to find additional pupils. During the summer of 1799 Dillon drew up a proposal for conducting a school which he sent to John Askin with the suggestion that he circulate it among his friends. The schoolmaster, with a nice sense of propriety, expressed his aversion to advertising himself; but he believed that no one could take offense at this sort of indirect solicitation.

Perhaps it was simply a coincidence that William Robertson, who was visiting Detroit, made an offer to John Askin to rent or sell his "house on the domain" to be used for a school. On the other hand, Dillon may have discussed the matter with him. Although it is true that Robertson was a shrewd business man, and that he was probably anxious to dispose of the house before he left town, his letter seems to reflect a deep interest in education. "The great importance of education & instruction of youth," he wrote, "is so generally acknowledged in all civilized nations that it would be superfluous to write upon such a topic. It is to be lamented that so many obstacles oppose themselves in countries newly settled to the establishment of proper seminaries & the procuring proper teachers."

What came of Robertson's proposal is not known; but it is certain that other people in Detroit were distressed by the lack of schools and the means to provide them. At the December term of the Court of Quarter Sessions the Grand Jury drew up a petition on the subject and addressed it to "the Senate & House of Representatives of the Territory

North West of the River Ohio." The jurors declared that "the Inhabitants of this County are generally in the greatest want of Education, and of Course incapable of giving the necessary support to the operation of the Laws of this Territory ... for the benefit of the Youth, an Acadamy is much wanted in the Town of D'Etroit."

In addition, they urged the importance of "a Prodestant Church for the Use of the People of that persuation whose number is daily increasing." The Roman Catholic Church, the only one in town, they reported, was "old & going into decay." The petitioners humbly prayed that the legislature pass a law authorizing the holding of a lottery or other means to raise money to build an academy and a Protestant Church, and to repair the Catholic Church or to build a new one.

The jurors expressed the hope that the legislators would take into consideration "the Importance of the rising Generation & natural Growth of this place." In conclusion, they declared: "... this also is the request of the Court now Sitting and of all the well wishers for a Good operation of the Laws & the Prosperity of the County of Wayne."

This petition was addressed to Solomon Sibley and Jacob Visger, representatives of Wayne County in the legislature at Cincinnati. Peter Audrain, in an accompanying letter, urged them to press the matter, suggesting that they petition Congress for a part of the Domain on which to place the buildings. The Prothonotary was sure that a beginning could be made as soon as a law was passed, for "a number of benevolent men are disposed to advance Money for the purpose, to be reimbursed out of the profits on the lotery." In spite of these efforts of Detroiters, there is no evidence that any action was taken on the petition.

4

Wayne County received little attention from the territorial government. Although Judge James May informed the Grand Jury at the March session of the Court of Quarter Sessions in 1799 that Governor St. Clair would visit the county during the summer, he did not come. Neither did the territorial Circuit Court sit in the county during that year. According to Jacob Burnet, Judge John Cleves Symmes kept putting off his departure from Cincinnati to Detroit because of reports that the Indians were hostile. Burnet, who had traveled that route a number of times, apparently thought the Judge simply wanted an excuse for escaping the hardships of the long ride. Ezra F. Freeman, the lawyer who had attended the first session of the Wayne County Court in 1796, was irritated because Judge Symmes could not make up his mind to set out. Freeman waited all summer, intending to accompany him to Detroit, but finally gave up hope when he had made no move in that direction by the end of September.

Jacob Burnet had little respect for Judge Symmes, who had recently confirmed a judgment entered against one of the lawyer's clients by the Wayne County Court of Common Pleas. When Burnet protested, the Judge explained his decision by saying that "it would discourage the Court of Wayne County if so many of their Judgments were reversed." In Burnet's opinion this was "a reason which ought to damn him to all eternity as a Judge."[8]

The Wayne County Court of Common Pleas, during the June term, 1799, heard a great many suits. Most of them were begun for the purpose of compelling individuals to pay their debts. The reason for the recourse to law was probably the scarcity of cash in Detroit. Even an honest debtor could hardly find money to satisfy a creditor. John Askin, James May, and Solomon Sibley declared that there were neither sufficient coins nor bills in town with which to meet their obligations.

The small number of cases tried by the Court of General Quarter Sessions suggests that the community was law-abiding. Judge May, however, reported that he had had two men arrested for making counterfeit silver dollars. In view of the scarcity of cash these people probably anticipated an excellent market for their product.

The only other evidence of criminal activities is the sworn return of Constable Louis Guignier *dit* Bourguignon. "... there is in my Street," he wrote, "a Woman ... who is not of good fame." The constable related how he was called out of bed on a Sunday night to arrest a man who was causing

[8] Jared Brooks received the same answer from Judge Symmes in a similar case. Brooks to Sibley, October 28, 1799, Sibley Papers, Burton Hist. Coll.

a disturbance at her house. Besides, the woman had a little girl who used "very improper language to everyone passing her door, especially to Women and Girls." Guignier could think of only one other practice "contrary to the orders of the honorable Court"—the selling of liquor without a license by a newly arrived merchant. "I myself have bought of him," the constable added candidly. If these were the only crimes committed in the town during the summer of 1799, Detroit was indeed a model village.

In the fall, however, a crime was allegedly committed that must have given the townspeople something to talk about. Peter Chartrand, a baker, charged that George Saunders, variously described as "painter & limner" and as a "Play Actor," came to his house on November 1, 1799, and carried away "with force and arms... Rebecca... the wife of him the said Peter, whereby the said Peter hath lost the Comfort and affection of his said wife, the said Rebecca...."[9] Chartrand demanded $1,500 damages. On December 12 Saunders was arrested, was released on a bond of $60, and ordered to appear at the March term of court in 1800.

In September Solomon Sibley set out for Cincinnati to attend the first legislative session of the territorial assembly. Neither Jacob Visger, whose election had been conceded, nor François Chabert, whose eligibility had been questioned, nor Oliver Wiswell, who had been certified as a representative, but who felt that the office would be a burden, accompanied Sibley.

When Sibley arrived, the Assembly was already in session. Jacob Visger finally reached Cincinnati on October 8, but François Chabert, whom Sibley was expecting, remained in Detroit. Consequently Wayne County had only two representatives.

Representative Sibley was not unmindful of the problems of his county. When a tavern bill was being considered, he introduced an amendment intended to prevent drunkenness

[9] Complaint filed by David Powers for Peter Chartrand. N. W. Terr. Records, Wayne County, Court of Common Pleas, March term, 1800, Legal Research Building, University of Michigan.
If this case ever came to trial, the records are missing. Entries in John Askin's Journal show that Saunders was in Detroit as late as July 14, 1800.

among soldiers, but it was defeated. He also drew up a memorial "for the perusal of Capt. Wm. H. Harrison, Esq., Delegate to Congress—when at leisure."[10] In it Sibley called attention to the needs of his constituents which he hoped Harrison would lay before Congress: Commissioners should be sent to Detroit to begin the work of clearing land titles; building lots ought to be laid out on the Common east and west of the town to permit expansion, and a two-acre lot on the Common should be reserved for an academy, a courthouse, and a jail to be built with the proceeds from the sale of the other lots; mail service ought to be extended to Detroit; and land which the Government had acquired from the Indians should be opened to settlers.

Solomon Sibley's correspondence indicates that his friends and his constituents asked him to look after many matters for them. He was probably pretty busy in Cincinnati, but he found time for recreation. During October, November, and December he entertained the "Dancing Club," of which he was a member, and he attended dances given by other members. Friends in Cincinnati, too, George and Jacob Burnet, Arthur St. Clair, Jr., and Captain Samuel C. Vance, invited him to their homes.

Although Sibley was now thirty years old, he was still "in the old Bachellor's row." He must have talked a great deal about his desire to find a wife, for some of his friends teased him about his failure. Dr. William Brown, another Massachusetts man who had recently moved to Detroit, closed a letter with a wish for his "Success in getting a wife notwithstanding your Sad Disappointment."[11] A few months later Ben Huntington thought that Sibley was at last engaged. He had heard that "the fine Girl from Chilacotha has persuaded you to relinquish Detroit as a place of residence." This rumor proved to be false; for Sibley returned to Detroit in the spring of 1800, still a bachelor.

[10] Harrison, who was secretary of the Territory, was chosen Delegate by the element hostile to Governor St. Clair. He defeated Arthur St. Clair, Jr., by only one vote. Sibley to J. Schieffelin, October 9, 1799, Sibley Papers, Burton Hist. Coll.

[11] Brown to Sibley, November 24, 1799, *ibid.* There is nothing in the letter to explain the meaning of the "Sad Disappointment."

J. Schieffelin to Sibley, December 30, 1798; and Sibley to Schieffelin, March 20, 1799, contain references to Sibley's difficulties in finding a wife. *Ibid.*

Most of the letters to Sibley at Cincinnati were filled with stories of dissension, both social and official. Of the first variety there was the ball in November arranged by the "Gentlemen of Detroit," Americans and British subjects alike. They invited the "Military Gentlemen" to attend, but the latter unanimously refused. Furthermore, they persuaded some of the ladies to reject invitations; and it was rumored that they even tried to bribe the musicians to withhold their services. Nevertheless, the ball was held. "An agreeable Company tho not numerous" enjoyed the dancing, an excellent supper, and good wine. The "Gentlemen of the Garrison" then planned a ball of their own, which moved the civilians to contemptuous mirth.[12]

The official troubles centered in the courts. The enmity of Judges McNiff and May toward each other almost cancelled the December sitting of the Court of Common Pleas. The former declared he would not sit in March and asserted that neither would Judges Charles F. Girardin and Louis Beaufait. In that case there would be no session, as three judges must be on the bench to hear cases.

Others, too, were hostile to Judge May and to his confidant, Peter Audrain, who was charged by his enemies with being "the chief Director of all the Factions, Mischiefs, & dissensions which have arisen in Detroit," and so was nicknamed "Monsieur Talleyrand." A number of Frenchmen signed a remonstrance against the acts of these two "tyrants" which François Navarre intended to carry to Cincinnati. Because an attack of rheumatism kept him at home, he sent the paper to Sibley.

Another petition, "from a majority of the respectable people from this County," asking the Governor to remove Judge May was also received by Sibley. The immediate cause of this request was the discharging of the three county commissioners, Joseph Visger, Antoine Dequindre, and Jacques Campau, ostensibly because they did not present the public accounts at the December term of the Court of Quarter Sessions, as required by law. Elijah Brush, who was acting as prosecutor in the absence of Sibley, protested that Visger, who was in Cincinnati, had offered the financial report at the September

---

[12] Colonel Strong's sentry was still posted at the door of Dodemead's Tavern.

term. Since Judge May had refused to accept it then, his action now looked like a trick to snare the commissioners. In Sibley's opinion they were removed because they took his advice and refused to pay the judges, the sheriff, and the prothonotary six or seven hundred dollars in a lump sum for their services. "They love me as the d—— loves truth," Sibley wrote, referring to the judges. Although Judge François Navarre protested vigorously, Judge May induced Judge Joseph Cissne to support him in discharging the commissioners. Robert Abbott, Charles F. Girardin, and Ben Huntington were appointed to replace them, but, according to Elijah Brush, only Abbott took the oath of office.

All these dissensions were purely local in their origin. The causes were a lack of experience in self-government; misunderstandings among the French, the British, and the American elements of the population; the usual incompatability of the civilian and the military points of view; and, most of all, personal jealousies.

The partisanship which embittered the political life of the eastern states was absent from this frontier settlement. So far as one can learn from the extant correspondence of the residents, the passage of the Alien and Sedition Acts and the publication of the Virginia and the Kentucky Resolutions of 1798–99 caused not a ripple of excitement in Detroit. The reasons are clear: the people had no voice in national affairs, and all the officials were Federalists. They were loyal supporters of President Adams and of Governor St. Clair, from whom they had received their commissions. Anyone who had formerly been a Republican found it expedient to change his allegiance. Frederick Bates, friend of Jefferson and a Republican while he lived in Virginia, informed his brother Richard that he could give him plenty of arguments in support of Federalism. At Detroit, he asserted, "nothing democratic will go down with us. A young fellow in this Country whose principles are democratic could scarcely find employment as a Shoe black."[13] French, British, and Americans, all were

[13] F. Bates to R. Bates, December 24, 1799, Bates Papers, Missouri Hist. Soc. St. Louis. Richard answered: "I cannot think your politics are radically changed, but only dissembled for your own convenience while among those miscreants of Detroit, those instruments of popular degradation, those maggots of political corruption . . .."

conservative. As James Henry phrased it, "We Jog on in the old way here."

There were some indications, however, that this condition would not long continue. In the East the Republicans were fast gathering strength; in the Northwest Territory the Republican element elected William Henry Harrison territorial delegate to Congress; and in Wayne County Americans were arriving who held no offices, and who were hungry for land. They were likely to have more democratic ideas than the conservatives who were already firmly established.

Early in the year 1800 a ceremony was held in which all Americans could unite. There was no reason why the French should stand aloof, and even some of the British participated. The event was the procession and solemn rites "representing the funeral" of George Washington, who died on December 14, 1799. The services were held in Detroit on February 12, 1800.

The funeral cortege, "which exceeded any thing of the Kind ever seen at this Place," was led by the officers and soldiers from the Fort. Then came a casket followed by the members of Zion Lodge and other Masons. The officers of the militia and about one hundred citizens of the town brought up the rear. The procession passed along the streets in great solemnity to the Esplanade, where three volleys were fired over the bier. All day long cannon were fired at intervals, paying the last honors to the memory of a great man. One observer remarked: ". . . his loss is generally lamented in this Country, even by Alliens."[14]

---

[14] Lewis Bond to Sibley, February 14, 1800, Sibley Papers, Burton Hist. Coll. At the order of Colonel Strong, Matthew Ernest spent $52.29 for crape, ribbon, and other materials to be used for "representing the funeral" of the late George Washingtion, Feb. 8, 1800. George Washington Papers, *ibid*.

CHAPTER XII
THE FIRST REGIMENT RETURNS

TOWARD the end of February, 1800, John Askin received news from his friend Alexander Henry in Montreal that the prices of furs had fallen because, according to rumor, fur buyers in Hamburg, London, and New York were bankrupt. The price of muskrat pelts, it is true, was good—twenty-four shillings apiece—but only because Henry and John Jacob Astor were competing with each other to purchase them. The Montreal merchant urged Askin to trade his raccoon skins to the Yankees for rum instead of sending them down the Lakes.

In March the merchants of Detroit learned that the United States Government had appointed Matthew Ernest inspector of revenue for the port. He made no attempt to enforce the tariff law, however, until he had received instructions from Washington. Then he sent out a circular requesting each merchant to pay the prescribed duties on all "spirits, wines & teas" in their possession which had been imported since March 2, 1799.

This burden on the trade from Montreal, which the British merchants had long been expecting, undoubtedly affected business in Detroit. Goods that were produced abroad, especially manufactures which could not be replaced by American products, would be more expensive to the consumer. Products which could be procured within the United States would probably now find their way to Detroit. James Henry decided at once that he would order no more goods from Montreal. Because of the duties, he wrote, "the course of trade must be changed."

Although John Askin seldom found satisfaction in reviewing the business situation in Detroit, his account of conditions in the spring of 1800 was even more pessimistic than usual. "The appearances," he declared, "are really bad & I fear will prove so with many Others as well as Myself... this Country is Over-done & he who has sold least in My oppinion has done best. I'm hardly Out of any Article & of some I have a considerable Quantity but no Cash to be got, & to sell for Wheat, corn &ca & give great credits I will not, those who have done so cannot now get a purchase for their Grain.... Among other Evils here are 17 large Merchant vessels to transport the loadings of 3 or 4 at Most. Ruin, Detroit is not far from you."

John Askin's ill success in business could not be attributed to inexperience or to lack of industry. He had been engaged in the Indian trade since 1761, and the great volume of his correspondence, which has been preserved, gives ample evidence of his meticulous attention to the details of his manifold enterprises. So closely did he apply himself to business that he seldom left Detroit. When, during the fall of 1799, he traveled to York to make personal application for recognition of his land claim in Canada, he declared it was "the only Voyage" he had made "for Nineteen Years past."

John Askin undoubtedly lived well, as was the custom of Detroit merchants. Besides, he had numerous children for whose education he spent considerable sums. Still, it is likely that his financial troubles, aside from the hazards of the fur trade, were chiefly the result of his kindly nature. His letters show not only that he was scrupulously honest himself, but also that he trusted other men, at least until they had proved themselves unworthy of his confidence. Generous alike to friends and acquaintances, he was too indulgent to excel in competition with sharp traders.

2

On April 11, 1800, an express arrived at the Fort with orders for Colonel Strong to transfer the Second Regiment to Pittsburgh. The officers were not pleased with the order. After having lived in Detroit for nearly three years, they had become comfortably settled. Now they had to sell their cows and their furniture in preparation for leaving. Besides, they were in debt to the merchants, and, unless the paymaster arrived before their departure, they were likely to be sued.

The order which removed Colonel Strong from Detroit directed Major Thomas Hunt to take command of the Fort with three companies of the First Regiment and half a company of artillery, the smallest American garrison that had been stationed at the post.

After Major Hunt arrived with his troops, Colonel Strong, on May 18, sailed down the river on the brig *President Adams*. Captain Peter Curry was in command of this new ship, which was making her maiden voyage. Rated at one hundred and fifty tons burden, she was much larger than the sloop *Detroit*, the only other United States vessel on the Upper Lakes.[1] The *Adams* carried eighteen guns.

3

In the spring of 1800 John Williams left Detroit for Pittsburgh. Dissatisfied with his position in Uncle Joseph Campau's store, he had quarreled with him. Although the merchant offered to take him as a partner, John's pride would not permit him to accept. Instead, he applied to Colonel Strong for appointment as a cadet in the Second Regiment. The Colonel promised him a commission, and John sailed away for Presqu' Isle.

While he was waiting at Fort Erie for a ship, he wrote two letters to his uncle. In the first he described his pleasant voyage with a number of lively companions; but in the second the eighteen-year-old boy expressed his regret at having rejected his uncle's offer. Although John had considered the army a good school in which a young man could learn about life, he had already discovered unpleasant aspects of a military career. He confessed that business now seemed to be the best occupation for him, and he begged his uncle to make no arrangements that would exclude him from a partnership. John explained that he would go on to Pittsburgh, see Colonel

---

[1] John Askin estimated the cost of the *Adams* at from £8,000 to £10,000. Askin to Todd and McGill, May 2, 1803, Askin Papers, Burton Hist. Coll.

The Government built a smaller ship, the schooner *Senator Tracy*, at the River Rouge yard at about the same time. Probably this was the schooner of about seventy tons burden that General Wilkins had ordered built in the fall of 1797. The *Tracy* was launched during the summer of 1800. *Quarter Master General's Report, 1796–1802*, p. 147.

According to Peter Audrain, the *Detroit* was "rotten and unfit for service without considerable repairs." Audrain to Hamtramck, April 17, 1800, Hamtramck Papers, Burton Hist. Coll. The *Detroit* sank during the summer of 1800, and J. Young was paid "for hire of a boat" to raise it. *Quarter Master General's Report, 1796–1802*, p. 163.

Strong, and, on some pretext or other, have himself discharged. He promised to return to Detroit after a brief visit to his relatives in Albany.

Williams' plans, however, went awry. When he reached Pittsburgh, Colonel Strong had gone to Cincinnati. The Second Regiment was camped near Fort Pitt, and the boy was given a friendly reception by Lieutenant John Whipple of the regiment, Captain Moses Porter of the Artillery, and Colonel Hamtramck, all of whom had known him at Detroit. The Colonel invited the boy to dinner. The attention he received from the officers seems to have banished John's distaste for army life. Now he wrote that there were a number of vacancies and he expected his appointment soon.

But Colonel Strong did not return, the commission was not forthcoming, and John became terribly homesick. During July he wrote again and again, condemning himself for ever having left Detroit, "the only place where I can be happy." He complained that he had received no letters and confessed that, although his family had always reproached him for being ungrateful and cold, he was really very sensitive. To him Detroit was a paradise compared to Pittsburgh, and he disliked the people in the Pennsylvania town. The women, especially, he found quite ugly, and he begged for news of his "Chère Catiche." Williams declared that he was waiting only for word that his uncle still wanted him as a partner.

John at length decided that his uncle and all his other relatives had forgotten him. There seemed to be no other course but to become a soldier. Now, however, he learned that Colonel Strong had no authority to give him a commission. And so he wrote to General Wilkinson explaining the situation and asking how he could become an officer. When Williams received no reply, he again wrote to his uncle begging him to forgive his conduct in Detroit, which, he insisted, was simply that of a foolish young fellow.

4

The judicial machinery of Wayne County seems to have broken down completely in the spring of 1800. If Patrick McNiff, Charles F. Girardin, and Louis Beaufait refused to sit at the March term, as McNiff had assured Sibley they would, there was no March session of the Court of Common Pleas; and for lack of a quorum the Court of General Quarter Sessions adjourned from day to day until March 22. Then Judges James May, Joseph Voyer, and Joseph Cissne appeared on the bench; but the night before, Peter Audrain, clerk of the court, had received an order from Governor St. Clair suspending May and Cissne for dismissing the county commissioners. The clerk informed the judges and posted the order on the enginehouse wall. The session of the Court was over before it had begun. There was nothing for the judges to do but to await a hearing before Judge John Cleves Symmes, Jacob Burnet, and Arthur St. Clair, Jr., whom the Governor had appointed as a commission to inquire into the charges. Audrain also was to be investigated, for Judge Symmes was instructed to question him about the alleged falsification of a record transmitted to the General Court of the territory.

As if this were not enough judicial delinquency, the territorial Circuit Court, which had failed to sit in Detroit during 1799, was apparently going to ignore Wayne County again. On June 5 the Grand Jury addressed a complaint on the subject to the Governor. Two weeks later Solomon Sibley informed St. Clair that Judge Symmes had not arrived. He urged the necessity of a session of the Court to satisfy the people, who felt that the Government was neglecting them.[2]

If Sibley was distressed about Judge Symmes' failure to hold court in Detroit, he could at least appreciate the Judge's reluctance to make the journey; for Sibley had reached home only about two weeks before he wrote to the Governor, after a very unpleasant trip from Cincinnati. Being in a hurry, the lawyer took Zane's Trace up the Mad River, which was said to be "much the nighest." After leaving the Trace, Sibley lost the trail and wandered for five days in "the wilderness." Then he came out on Blanchard Creek, which he followed for two days without being able to cross. Luckily he happened upon a village of friendly Indians, who guided him to the rapids of the Maumee. "My anxiety of mind," he reported, "united to the fatigue of Body has reduced me in point of flesh—but am

[2] Sibley wrote also that he had read in the papers that the Northwest Territory had been divided, but that he had not learned in which part Detroit was placed. Indiana Territory was established on July 4, 1800, Detroit remaining in the Northwest Territory.

tolerably hearty." The journey by the usual route from Cincinnati would not be so difficult; nevertheless, the prospect could hardly have been inviting to the fifty-eight-year-old Judge.

As a matter of fact, he was on his way to Detroit when Sibley wrote to the Governor. With him came Arthur St. Clair, Jr., attorney general of the Territory, and Jacob Burnet. They brought with them a commission appointing Elias Wallen sheriff, instead of Lewis Bond, who had resigned. No record has been discovered of the session of the Circuit Court, or of the findings of the Commissioners who had been authorized to investigate Judges May and Cissne and Prothonotary Audrain.[3]

5

Peter Joseph Dillon was teaching in Detroit in the spring of 1800, perhaps in the house which William Robertson had offered for that purpose. Wherever it was, the schoolmaster was apparently satisfied with the facilities, for he protested to George Meldrum against moving to "the house where Mr. Cook keeps store." Dillon objected that there was neither enough room nor enough light there for the pupils. He expressed his willingness to move to any building "within the stockade" where the conditions were suitable for a school.

On May 18 Dillon entered into a contract with George Meldrum, John Askin, and Matthew Ernest to serve as a schoolmaster for their children, and others who might apply, not to exceed twenty-two, for the ensuing year.[4] His salary

[3] Jacob Burnet, in his *Notes on the Early Settlement of the North-Western Territory* (New York, 1847), pp. 285–286, wrote an account of the celebration at Sandwich of the King's birthday on "June 4, 1800," in which American judges, lawyers, officers, and citizens of Detroit participated. He named Colonel Strong as commandant of the Fort. According to this writer, Captain Curry of the *Adams* carried the judges and visiting lawyers to Fort Malden and then to Maumee Bay.

There are several discrepancies in this account, which was written long after the event. The Judge and the lawyers did not arrive until the last week in June, 1800, and Colonel Strong had been replaced by Major Thomas Hunt in May.

Burnet may have attended such a celebration in 1798. Judges Gilman and Meigs opened court in Detroit on May 23 of that year. However, if that was the correct date, they could not have sailed on the *Adams*. She left Detroit on her first voyage on May 18, 1800.

[4] John Askin apparently removed his children from Matthew Donovan's school in the fall of 1799. On November 15, 1799, Donovan wrote to Askin expressing his

was five hundred dollars, of which fifty dollars would be paid at once, and four dollars each week thereafter. Whatever fees the teacher collected from the parents, other than his sponsors, would be applied toward paying the weekly stipend. The remainder of the five hundred dollars was to be used to pay off a debt which Dillon owed Askin and Ernest. His patrons further agreed to provide "a commodious school house and fire wood as the season requires it."

The schoolmaster promised to teach "the science of reading, writing and speaking the English language, Grammatically; ...Arithmetic, Geography & Trigonometry." He offered instruction also "in any other Branch of Literature that may be thought most useful." Dillon agreed to accept no pupils who were not approved by his three patrons and to dismiss none without their consent.

William Burnett's sons, Jimmy and Johnny, had a vacation during July and August, 1800. Their Indian mother, Kakima, came to Detroit to visit them. Perhaps she brought her other children: Abraham, Isaac, Jacob, Nancy, and Rebecca. Kakima probably felt uncomfortable within the stockade of the town; at any rate she took her children to live with the Indians.[5] It is likely that they stayed with the Potawatomi, who had a village at Spring Wells, two or three miles below Detroit, for Kakima's father, Aniquiba, was an influential Potawatomi chief. Unfortunately, there is no further information about the family's visit; but there can be little doubt that Jimmy and Johnny enjoyed their vacation.

If Father Richard could have found time for it, he might have attended school to practice English. There were so few English Catholics in Detroit, he informed Bishop Carroll, that he feared he would forget the language. Only five or six came to confession. He estimated that there were perhaps a dozen "of our profession, but most of them are certain perpetual

---

surprise that the merchant was arranging to establish a school in opposition to his. Donovan admitted that his "Conduct of the 29th of October was irregular," but excused himself for having drunk too much on that day by explaining that the weather was inclement and that he had no firewood. He promised never to taste liquor again so long as he taught school in Detroit, and begged Askin not to condemn him for his single lapse from sobriety. Askin Papers, Burton Hist. Coll.

[5] Entry against Burnett in James May's Day Book, August 27, 1800: "To Boarding your woman & her children with Indians from 5th July to this day ... & pasturage for Horses ... £23 4s." *Ibid.*

travellers from Ireland, some of whom only recollect of hearing their father or mother to be Romans and Know nothing of Catholic Doctrine nor care much of being instructed in it. They are of different trades viz. taylors, tavern Keepers, Soldiers, &c. You Know very well How much it is easy to make Such people good Christians!" The assistant pastor promised to invite them to come to him for lessons in the teachings of the Church.

Father Richard was distressed by the condition of the Indians who visited Detroit. They were always drunk, he declared, and it was the traders who were to blame. When he reminded them of the law that forbade traders to carry liquor to the Indian villages, they assured him that it was entirely legal to sell the savages all they wanted at Detroit. The priest observed sadly: "No man unacquainted with the trade of our back ward Countryes is able to foretell the cunning means inspired by the exhaustless wish of getting fur."

6

John Williams, who was in Pittsburgh, had to wait until October 26 for a letter from his Uncle Joseph. In it Campau expressed surprise that John had not received a letter he had written in July. He was glad to know that his nephew now realized how foolish he had been to leave Detroit, and he urged him to return. The boy answered at once, writing that he was glad his uncle still wanted him for a partner, and that as soon as the troops moved down the river, he would accompany them to Cincinnati, and then set out for Detroit on horseback.

A few days later another letter from Joseph Campau arrived, and one from John's mother. The uncle had written on July 22, and had sent both letters to Albany, expecting the boy to be there. Campau wrote that he was leaving on a business trip to Montreal. When he returned, he expected to find his nephew at Detroit, and they would then organize the partnership they had talked about. John answered this letter the day after he received it. He reported that James Henry was just leaving for Detroit and that he would accompany him if he had money enough to buy a horse. At any rate, he expected to be at home soon because the troops were leaving in three or four days on their way to Natchez. He still planned to go with them to Cincinnati, and from there to Detroit.

During the next few days something happened to change Williams' plans. He entered the employ of James O'Hara, the contractor who furnished supplies to the army, and left Pittsburgh with the Second Regiment on November 8.

Joseph Campau wrote two more letters urging John to return. In the second he complained that he had received no word from his nephew since his letter of July 24. Campau wondered whether none of the four letters he had written in October had reached John. His uncle had now lost patience. Because he was ill, he needed help in the store. If the boy did not arrive at Detroit before the end of December, Campau declared, he would have to engage someone else.

7

Early in September, 1800, a bilingual petition to Congress was circulated in Detroit and the vicinity. Fifty-one men signed the English version, and one hundred, including Fathers Levadoux and Richard, signed the French. The signers requested that the Government recognize their land titles, including grants from Indians, and that Indian claims in Wayne County be extinguished so that settlers would come in. They declared that the British Government encouraged people to cross into Canada, where grants of land were available. According to the petitioners, "few accepted the offers, preferring rather to embrace the opportunity of gaining rights of Citizenship, under a free Government."

The citizens of Wayne County asked also for one or more townships near Detroit to endow an academy or a college, and an additional township "for the support of the Gospel and for erecting necessary buildings for the celebration of divine service."[6]

In asking for assistance to provide churches, the people

[6] C. E. Carter (ed.), *The Territorial Papers of the United States*, III, 104.
Another request in the petition was for public mail service. In answer either to this or to a separate appeal the Postmaster General replied: "The route proposed from Pittsburgh to Detroit does not appear at this time eligible. The distance is very considerable, the inhabitants at Detroit not very numerous, the route is thro' a Wilderness and only marked by Indian foot paths and without accommodation for a post rider." *Ibid.*, p. 122.

probably intended that one of them should be for some form of Protestant worship, as the Grand Jury had specified in their presentment of the previous year. There was no Protestant minister in the town, but at the time the petition was signed a young man who was later to serve as a preacher was on his way to Detroit. He was David Bacon, a Connecticut schoolmaster. Having been inspired by reading the *Life of David Brainerd* to become a missionary to the Indians, he attracted the attention of the Missionary Society of Connecticut. Under its auspices he was sent to visit the tribes south and west of Lake Erie to discover the possibility of doing missionary work among them. Setting out from Hartford on August 8, he traveled overland to Buffalo Creek, New York, where he took passage on a ship and arrived at Detroit on September 11.

Bacon was hospitably received by the Commandant, Major Thomas Hunt, who took him into his home as a guest. The young man sought advice on his mission from Jonathan Schieffelin, Indian agent, John Askin, and Ben Huntington, "formerly from Norwich." They advised him that the shores of the St. Clair River or Mackinac Island would be more favorable fields for his project than the region to which he had been directed.

At this time Senator Uriah Tracy of Connecticut was in Detroit ready to sail for Mackinac. He had been sent by President Adams to gather information about the copper deposits on the south shore of Lake Superior, and to learn on what terms the Indian title to the land there could be extinguished. When Senator Tracy invited Bacon to accompany him on his voyage, the young man accepted, and John Askin gave him a letter of introduction to the Ottawa of L'Arbre Croche, on Lake Michigan.

"Friends & Brothers," Askin wrote, "The Bearer hereof Mr. Baken is one of the *Great Spirits* representatives on Earth. He asked me where shall I go to render Service to Indians and point out to them & Their Children the Means of happiness here & hereafter. I Answered to my Friends the Ottawas at Arbre a Croche & the Mission where I once lived—they are the Nation best disposed to hear what the *great Spirit* has to say to them & who knows how to behave to his representative. He now goes to see you. *Brothers* Treat him well & dont make me a liar. He will shew you and your Children how to be happy here & hereafter. Adieu Friends & Brothers."

Senator Tracy and David Bacon set sail from Detroit on September 13. At Harsen's Island, in the St. Clair River, Bacon found Bernhardus Harsen, who had been recommended to him as a capable interpreter. Harsen urged upon the young man the advantages of the St. Clair region for his projected work. He assured Bacon that Nanga, chief of the local Chippewa, who was hunting at the time, wanted missionaries for his people.

So effective was Harsen's appeal that Senator Tracy sailed for the North without his companion, who remained to study the Chippewa language with the interpreter. Early in October the Senator stopped for Bacon, and they returned to Detroit. At Mackinac Tracy had broached the subject of a mission at L'Arbre Croche, and the chiefs had been pleased with the idea.

On October 7 Senator Tracy addressed an Indian council at Detroit.[7] He introduced David Bacon to the chiefs and stressed the importance of missionaries and teachers for their instruction. There Bacon met Nanga, who seconded Harsen's invitation to establish a mission on the Island.

Bacon was pleased with the prospect for future missions. Since he had been sent simply to investigate and report, he would probably have left for home if "a number of sober, likely young Indians" had not told him that they wanted an education. Happy at this opportunity to serve the savages, he promised to remain and teach them during the winter; but the Indians soon departed for their hunting grounds, and the teacher was left without pupils. This experience with the

---

[7] Senator Tracy was not favorably impressed by the defenses of Detroit. Writing to Secretary of War James McHenry on November 28, 1800, he explained: "D'Etroit is in a condition not by any means pleasant. The Fort is a kind of shadow of the town, & if assailed, not only the assailants but defenders must batter the Town to pieces, of course. The whole town is picketed in, which is not only expensive, in the first instance, but extends the guards beyond all hearing, & so very thickly placed are the Houses that a single fire must reduce the Town & citadel as it is called beyond all human means of extinguishment; they having no engine, nor any particular means of carrying water." This letter is in the William L. Clements Library, University of Michigan.

In spite of Tracy's statement to the contrary, there was a fire engine in Detroit.

fickle red men seems not to have dampened his ardor. Nevertheless, since there was nothing for him to do in Detroit, he set out for Hartford, promising to return in the spring.

8

The Grand Jury of Wayne County in September, 1800, indicted two women: Sarah Harvey, "wife of John Harvey, Baker,"[8] for selling beer and cider at retail without a license; and Margaret White, spinster, for keeping in Detroit "a common, ill-governed, and disorderly house, and in her said house for lucre and gain certain persons, as well men as women . . . remain drinking, tipling, whoring, and misbehaving themselves . . . ." Mrs. Harvey pleaded guilty and was fined twelve dollars. Miss White was found guilty, but a record of her sentence has not been discovered.

On the night of October 9 an incident occurred which provided a more serious matter for the Grand Jury to consider. Sergeant Cole of the Fort Malden garrison, with several soldiers, broke into a house below the town and attacked the occupant, François Poquette. On the pretext that he was a deserter they attempted to carry him away. Poquette resisted so vigorously that he wounded the Sergeant in the head and face. The soldiers then attacked him with their bayonets and dragged him naked into a canoe, in which they transported him across the river. Dr. William McDowell Scott of Detroit was called to attend both Sergeant Cole and Poquette.[9] The latter was so severely injured that the Doctor counseled the soldiers not to move their prisoner. The Sergeant, however, declared that he had orders to deliver him to Malden dead or

---

[8] John Harvey owned the bakery. Peter Chartrand was his baker.
This woman, who was living with John Harvey, was not legally his wife. His wife, whom he had deserted in England, was still alive. M. M. Quaife, "John Harvey," *Burton Hist. Coll. Leaf.*, IV, No. 1.

[9] Dr. Scott began to practice medicine in Detroit during the summer of 1800. He had come to the United States from Ireland in 1795.

Dr. Scott held various county and town offices. His Ledger, 1803-1812, now in the Burton Historical Collection, contains entries of charges for performing marriage ceremonies as justice of the peace, and for executing court orders as marshal, along with his professional accounts. The Doctor usually charged four shillings for a visit to a patient. The bill for "drawing a tooth" was also four shillngs. On one occasion, however, he charged a patient eight shillings for "Visit and attempt to draw a tooth" (p. 66).

alive. Poquette, accordingly, was carried to the British fort, where he died early the next morning.

A week after the abduction a special session of court was held by four of the judges. Testimony was taken about the affair, and witnesses were put under bond to appear before the Grand Jury, which indicted Sergeant Cole for murder. Governor St. Clair reported the matter to the Secretary of State. According to Jay's Treaty, the American authorities had the right to demand the delivery of the Sergeant; but the Governor took no action because "the measure is delicate, and a refusal on their part might involve very serious consequences." Instead, he asked the Secretary for instructions. "The above affair," he added, "has caused great uneasiness amongst the inhabitants."

Captain Hector McLean, commandant at Fort Malden, was worried by the action taken on the American side of the river. Besides, his enemies in Canada, Prideaux Selby, of the Indian Department, and Matthew Elliot, whom he had had dismissed from that service, unsuccessfully sought a grand jury investigation on the British side. The Captain sent a report to the Commander in Chief, and then wrote a personal letter to Major James Green, asking his support in this "disagreeable circumstance." McLean denied that the Sergeant was ordered to take the man, declaring that he had simply given him and the soldiers a pass. The American military authorities, he added, made no complaint, as they had, at times, seized some of their deserters on British soil.

9

On October 14, 15, and 16 an election was held for representatives to the territorial legislature. The candidates were James May, Jacob Visger, George McDougall, Jonathan Schieffelin, François Chabert, Ben Huntington, and Joseph Cissne. During the campaigning McDougall and Schieffelin appealed especially to the French element. The former promised that he would call a special session of court which would order the sheriff to accept their produce in payment of taxes. The *halitants* were pleased with this offer, for they had little money and were accustomed to a barter economy. Besides, it was said that McDougall had assured the French people at Grosse Pointe that, if he were elected, he would secure their lands to them in spite of the efforts of William Robertson and his unprincipled lawyers to turn them out.

Jonathan Schieffelin also sought the French vote. According to Elijah Brush, his favorite theme was "Keep out the *Sacre* Americans," who, Schieffelin declared, were the sworn enemies of the French. Brush asserted that both Schieffelin and McDougall had "poisoned the minds of the people in this County . . . in their electioneering meetings against the Government and laws of the Territory." McDougall, he maintained, was the greater offender, having aroused the people so that they were "ripe for an insurrection, and like the National Convention of Old France for taking off the head of every American and others who did not fall in with their measures."

The election was held in the Council House. On the first day an altercation occurred near the polling place between McDougall and Ben Huntington, one of the county commissioners. Stories of the affair differ, but, apparently, the quarrel was about the collection of taxes in produce. McDougall loudly insisted that the *habitants* had no cash and that the Court would order the sheriff to take grain or flour. Huntington damned the Court and maintained that the commissioners would refuse to accept anything but money. McDougall warned him that, if the sheriff tried to seize cattle or other property to sell for taxes, he would head a party to oppose him.[10] The dispute was continued with an exchange of blows, but not much blood was shed.[11]

George McDougall, Jonathan Schieffelin, and François Chabert were elected. Immediately Ben Huntington notified Schieffelin that he would contest his election because he was an alien, having filed notice in 1797 of his intention to remain a

[10] A little later Solomon Sibley wrote: "Nothing frightens the Canadians like taxes. They would prefer to be treated like dogs, and kennelled under the whip of a tyrant, than contribute to the support of a free government." Sibley to Jacob Burnet, August 2, 1802. Burnet, *op. cit.*, p. 495. Sibley made no allowance for the poverty of the French at Detroit.

[11] Joseph Campau to John Williams, October 24, 1800, Campau Family Papers, Burton Hist. Coll.

Campau was supporting McDougall, Schieffelin, and Chabert. His letter indicates that he still identified himself with the French element; but he had already taken a step toward closer relations with the newcomers when, on August 4, 1800, he joined Zion Lodge—the first Frenchman in Detroit to enter the Order. On October 6, 1800, he had become a Master Mason.

British subject. Being an alien, he was incapable of owning land, and thus was unable to qualify as a freeholder.[12] Joseph Cissne, at about the same time, informed McDougall that he would contest his election on the grounds that he did not own two hundred acres of land, and that he was of "a pernicious disposition, disquiet mind and conversation," and by his seditious utterances and "unlawful contrivances" tended to arouse hatred and contempt for the Government.

The coroner, John Dodemead, designated Judges James May and Jacob Visger to preside at hearings of the charges against the representatives-elect. Schieffelin's case was heard on October 23, from ten in the morning until five in the afternoon. According to Audrain, the proceedings were "rather noisy."

The charges against McDougall were presented at a session that began at seven in the evening of the same day and continued until two in the morning. The newly elected representative declared that Cissne was simply the tool of Elijah Brush and Oliver Wiswell, who were his enemies. They vigorously denied the charge. The commissioners resumed the hearing at about eleven o'clock on the morning of October 24. Because of "the conduct of Mr. McDougall and his friends," the judges adjourned the session at one in the afternoon "without closing the business."[13]

Before these hearings began Solomon Sibley had left Detroit for Chillicothe to attend the second session of the first legislature of the Territory. Jacob Visger set out to join him on October 25. Sibley wrote from the capital that great opposition was rising against "our present & worthy Governor" and that "Party has run high this session." On December 1 the House Committee on elections reported favorably on seating Schieffelin and McDougall. It is likely that Sibley used his influence in favor of these men, both of whom were his friends.

[12] Huntington to Schieffelin, October 18, 1800, A. D. Fraser Papers, Burton Hist. Coll.

To judge from Huntington's letter, Schieffelin asserted that since his declaration was made more than a year after June 1, 1796, the date set by the two governments for the evacuation, it was not valid. Huntington maintained that since it was made within a year of the actual evacuation on July 11, 1796, he was still a British subject.

[13] Although McDougall apparently was somewhat erratic and blusterous, he seemed to be sincere in his attempt to aid the French people. The fact that he retained the friendship of so steady a character as Solomon Sibley would indicate that he was not so obnoxious as his enemies pretended.

CHAPTER XIII

AN INCORPORATED TOWN

THE usual round of winter social activities helped the inhabitants pass the time pleasantly while there was little communication with the rest of the country. Two assemblies were held in January, 1801—on the sixth and on the twentieth. Corned beef, ham, bread, and apples were served for supper, with coffee, tea, and spirits to wash them down. Three fiddlers provided music for the dancers.

These assemblies were held in the officers' mess house within the stockade, and the participants were officers from the Fort and American citizens from the town and its environs. Peter Audrain reported that the people were still divided socially. Another assembly met at the Grand Marais, on the Côte du Nord-Est; still another at the River Rouge; and a fourth at Sandwich. British subjects very likely crossed the river to attend the last.

The young men took their ladies driving in *carioles* on the frozen river and matched their swift little Canadian ponies in breakneck races on the ice. Dinners, visits, and the New Year's celebration provided a variety of diversion for the inhabitants. Besides, Zion Lodge held monthly meetings, and the taverns were always open for less formal stag parties. Dodemead's offered the special attraction of a billiard table.

For some of the inhabitants of Detroit and the vicinity winter was an unhappy season. There were poor people, especially the aged, who had no means of support except private charity. When that failed, the county officials paid for their keep out of the public funds. No definite scale of payment was established. Instead, when a home had to be found for a pauper, two justices of the peace ordered the inspectors of the poor to post a notice in three public places announcing the date of an auction. On the appointed day bids for the care of the indigent were received, and he was awarded to the householder who would provide a home for him at the lowest cost.

In the spring the merchants resumed their trading, but business was dull. Solomon Sibley was so discouraged by conditions in Detroit that he thought of leaving. In March he wrote to Arthur St. Clair, Jr.: "If Business does not materially increase here before fall I shall close & take up my bed and walk." He asked St. Clair to inform him "what prospects offer &c."

One industry, at least, began to expand at this time. A number of traders on both sides of the river ordered stills from James Henry, who had them made in Pittsburgh by John Hamsher. Here was one result of the American occupation. Angus Mackintosh explained that "whisky which comes in from Fort Pitt via Presque Isle...is become the Choice Liquor of most of the Indians in the environs of this Place." The merchants believed that within the course of a year very little West India rum would be used in the fur trade.

Thus did commerce, at least in ardent spirits, follow the flag. American whisky replaced British rum, as the latter had superseded French brandy. Mackintosh, in spite of his loyalty to Britain, approved of the change. He predicted that the distilleries would consume the surplus of local grain, and that money would be kept at home. As a proof of his faith in the future of the industry he ordered two stills from Henry and asked him to engage a distiller at Pittsburgh.

One of the most annoying circumstances at Detroit—the lack of a regular postal service—was now about to be remedied. During the short session in 1801 Congress provided that mail should be delivered by way of Cincinnati. This was a roundabout route, but it was better than none. Perhaps hereafter Detroiters would not be so long ignorant of what was passing in other parts of the country. For example, Solomon Sibley read in a newspaper an account of his appointment to the Legislative Council of the Territory before his commission arrived. It reached him finally on March 25, 1801, with a letter from Governor St. Clair dated at Cincinnati, February 23. On March 14 the people in Detroit were still wondering who had been elected president.[1]

[1] Jefferson was elected by the House of Representatives, February 17, 1801.

In 1801 there seems to have been no sitting of the circuit court in Detroit. Judge John Cleves Symmes directed Sheriff Wallen, if no judge appeared by the third Tuesday of May, to adjourn court "in a public manner at the Council house in Detroit" from day to day for a month, unless a judge arrived sooner, "to prevent a lapse of the term." The few documents which are extant contain no evidence that any judge put in his appearance.

2

In May, 1801, Jean Baptiste Roucour died. He had been ill and unable to perform his duties at Ste Anne's Church for some months. The *marguillers* had voted in November, 1800, to give him £2 a month out of the funds of the church; Father Levadoux added £1; and the *habitants* were instructed to provide firewood for him until the first of the year.

After the death of the old *chantre* the *marguillers* decided to give him a funeral service and burial gratis in acknowledgment of the zeal with which he had served the church for many years. At the same time they instructed Father Richard to perform the functions of *chantre* and *sacristain* in place of the late M. Roucour.

On May 9 David Bacon returned to Detroit, bringing with him his wife Alice, whom he had married on December 24, 1800, while he was in Connecticut, and her fifteen-year-old brother, Beaumont Parks. During the winter Mr. Bacon had been ordained as an evangelist to the Indians. He hoped that his young brother-in-law would learn the Chippewa language so that he could become a teacher.

Since the Missionary Society of Connecticut expected its evangelist to be partially self-supporting while he was preparing to go among the Indians, Mr. Bacon, during his first visit, had arranged with John Askin and others to open a school on his return. They put a carpenter to work for ten days making benches and desks, and otherwise furnishing a proper place for study, at a total cost of £9 16s. Mr. Bacon had a writing desk and a bench made for himself, and John Askin purchased a bell for £5 14s. 8d.

Classes began on June 1. A month later Mrs. Bacon, who was only eighteen years old, opened a school for girls. Among the pupils of these schools were John, Isaac, and Rebecca Burnett; Alexander, Charles, James, and Eleanor Askin; John Richardson, Askin's grandson; and Alexander Grant, son of the Commodore. James Henry paid tuition for "one scholar" from June 1, 1801, to March 22, 1802.[2] These children were taught reading, writing, arithmetic, English grammar, and geography. The girls, in addition, had lessons in sewing.

The Reverend Mr. Bacon began to preach on Sunday, May 17, 1801, in the courthouse. The congregation was larger than he had expected, and his hearers seemed to be greatly interested in his sermon. He preached regularly every Sunday, always in the morning, for he soon discovered that the people were "in the habit of visiting and riding out for pleasure in the latter part of the day." Although he preached the word of God "without reserve," the attendance increased.

Bacon believed that the people enjoyed his sermons. "Four or five of my hearers," he wrote, "are men of liberal education, but I have not heard that they have made any unfavorable remarks. Indeed, I am treated with much more respect by all classes of people than I had any right to expect." In addition to preaching and teaching, Bacon was also studying the Chippewa language. In June he reported: 'We are making pretty good progress."

During the latter part of June and the first of July Ste Anne's Church was thronged with the faithful of Detroit and the vicinity. Monseigneur Pierre Denaut, bishop of Quebec, had come at the request of Bishop John Carroll of Baltimore to perform the sacrament of confirmation. Since no bishop had visited Detroit for a number of years, many persons had never been confirmed. Consequently, on June 25, 26, and 28 and July 2 Bishop Denaut performed the rite for almost five hundred persons. Some were children in their teens, but the majority were older people. Jacques St. Aubin, ninety years of age, was the oldest.

3

During the summer of 1801 the ships on the Upper Lakes were busily employed. The United States brig *President Adams* was sailing under the command of John Williams,[3] and

[2] Bill and receipt, May 22, 1802, Sibley Papers, Burton Hist. Coll. The identity of this "scholar" is not known. Henry had no children at the time.

[3] This was not Joseph Campau's nephew.

the new United States packet *Senator Tracy* went into service at this time, with John Connelly as captain.

Ships of the Royal Navy were also plying the Upper Lakes. In May Commodore Grant sailed for York aboard His Majesty's snow *Ottawa* to attend a session of the Legislative Council of Upper Canada. To his brother-in-law, John Askin, he delegated two delicate duties. One of them was to try to comfort Mrs. Grant in her grief over the death of their daughter Thérèse, who had been with her husband, Dr. Thomas Wright, surgeon of the Royal American Regiment, in Jamaica. He had died there, and the young widow with her four children set out for Detroit. In New York she and three of the children died of yellow fever. The surviving daughter, Thérèse, was taken care of by the Macombs until she could be sent to her grandparents at Grosse Pointe. The Commodore suggested that Askin invite Mrs. Grant to stay for a time with Mrs. Askin, her sister.

The other task was to write a letter to Dr. William McCoskry, surgeon of the Second United States Infantry, in answer to his written request for the hand of Isabella Grant in marriage. The Doctor had been in Detroit in 1793 with the Quakers who came to assist in making peace between the Indians and the Americans, and again while Colonel Strong was in command at the Fort. It was probably during this latter period of service that he met Miss Grant. His letter to the Commodore was written in a camp on the Ohio River below Fort Massac. John Askin, in collaboration with Mrs. Grant, wrote briefly that the parents would place no obstacle in the suitor's way and that, as their daughter seemed to be favorably disposed toward him, he was welcome to visit her at any time.

In Detroit Solomon Sibley also was a lover separated from his loved one. During the summer of 1801 his thoughts must have wandered often to Marietta, on the Ohio River, the home of Sarah Whipple Sproat. Sibley, who was now thirty-two years old, had determined at last to leave "the old Bachellors row." But Sarah was far away from Detroit, and the cautious lawyer was somewhat timid in his matrimonial approach. Consequently he put the negotiations into the hands of two trusty proxies in Marietta.

Paul Fearing, who was one of them, and apparently as coy

as his principal, asked Colonel Ebenezer Sproat, "how should you like a Councillor &c for a S-n in L-w?" The Colonel, guessing after a slight hesitation that Sibley was meant, answered: "I esteem him highly both for his honesty & for his politicks, but as it respects the matters to which you refer, I have nothing to say, that being the sole province of the Parties." Fearing then inquired whether Sibley's visit as a suitor would be acceptable. He was able to report only that the Colonel "seamed to acquisce." Fearing added that there was a rival for Miss Sproat's affections. Although the local swain's chance of success was slight, Fearing urged Sibley to visit Marietta as soon as possible.

The other agent, Zenas Kimberly, approached the young lady herself. His suit was successful. Exultingly he wrote: "The Bird is yours." Kimberly explained that he must use cryptic language for fear the letter might fall into someone else's hands. He assured the absent lover that the whole affair had been managed with prudence and candor. His only fear was that Sibley might repudiate him.

Sibley promised to visit Marietta, but business prevented his leaving Detroit. Then he fell victim to "the prevailing fever of the Country." He informed Kimberly, however, that he would see Miss Sproat after the territorial legislature adjourned, and would spend most of the winter in Marietta. To set his agent's mind at rest Sibley assured him that he would "religiously adhere to any st'pulation or engagements you have or may enter into in my behalf, so far as consistant with the character of a Gentleman." He asked Kimberly to explain the reasons for his absence so that his "character would remain equally fair and untarnished in the good opinion of Miss S. and her relations as ever."

The laggard lover in Detroit expressed the hope that three or four months' delay would make no difference to the lady. He warned Kimberly "to act with caution and such secrecy as a transaction of this nature requires," and requested him to write as soon as he learned the effect of Sibley's absence.

4

On August 16, 1801, an assembly of the members of Ste Anne's decided to build a new church. They named a standing committee on construction consisting of Louis Tremblé, Charles Moran, Joseph Coté, Simon Drouillard, Jacques Pelletier, and Gabriel Godfroy. These men were instructed to draw up a plan in consultation with builders and to present it to the assembly. A week later "les habitants assemblés" agreed to accept the plan which the committee presented. The building was to be one hundred and six feet long and forty-two feet wide. Although they had intended to build the church of stone, they had to give up that idea, as the only quarry belonged to the Abbotts, who declared that the entire output was contracted for.

The committee was directed to estimate the cost of building and to assign a quota of the expense to each member. The subscription was opened on September 21. Father Richard obtained most of the pledges and signed them as a witness.[4] Colonel Hamtramck, whose signature was at the top of the list, promised to contribute £20. Fathers Levadoux and Richard pledged one fifth of the tithe for the year, estimated at £40. Most of the obligations were expressed in terms of produce or services. For instance, J. F. Lasselle promised £30 in merchandise or grain; Prisque Coté, thirty days of labor, valued at £12; François Chabert, £16 in grain; Louis Chauvin, six days' sawing, worth £1 16s.; Joseph Campau, £18 in merchandise; Jean Yax, the labor of his mulatto slave; Simon Yax, a boatload of stone and six days' labor, valued at £4 8s.; John Shaw, two thousand bricks delivered at Detroit, £6; and Isidore Pelletier, twelve days' work as a mason, worth £7 4s. Nearly everyone, it seems, was willing to assist in the work.

While the Reverend Mr. Bacon continued to preach every Sunday, gradually his congregation dwindled. The first coolness apparently developed after he had refused a number of requests to baptize children of parents who were not church members. Besides, it is likely that after the novelty of attending church wore off, the easygoing people of Detroit tired of Mr. Bacon's Puritan theology. He noticed that some of the principal men of the town no longer attended the services. Nevertheless, they still were courteous to him, and he con-

[4] Souscription pour La Construction d'une Nouvelle Eglise en pierre, Detroit Chancery Archives, I, 3.
This list covers seven large sheets of paper, which are bound together with ribbon.

cluded that "they disliked the message rather than the messenger."[5]

The missionary had other discouragements as well. His wife was ill for a time, and he was making little progress in learning Chippewa. The best way to master the language, he decided, would be to live among the Indians; and so he wrote to the Missionary Society asking for permission to go to L'Arbre Croche.

5

During the latter part of the summer James May was worried by lack of news from the schooner *Harlequin*, under the command of his brother Joseph. Finally, in September, when the sloop *Good Intent* arrived from Presqu' Isle without having heard of her, May gave her up, certain now that Captain Joseph May and the two sailors were drowned. James May was greatly distressed by the disaster which killed his brother and his Negro slave, who was one of the sailors. This man's wife, who also belonged to May, became too ill to work through worrying over the fate of her husband. She was anxious to have with her her son George, who belonged to John Askin. In order to satisfy the mother May offered to buy George from Askin, who refused to sell. But he sent the boy to May's house, where he remained until the middle of October.[6]

On November 20 John Askin received word that part of the rigging and the foremast of the ill-fated schooner had been cast ashore on the Canadian side, and that an Indian had come upon the vessel, which he sold at Buffalo for five dollars. It was reported at the same time that Joseph May's body had been found and buried.

In the fall of 1801 William Burnett seems to have decided that his son John had had sufficient schooling, for on September 30 James May put him to work in his store. Although he was

[5] Bacon reported to his brother that the Reverend Joseph Badger, a missionary to New Connecticut, and the Reverend Thomas E. Hughes, who had studied at Princeton, visited Detroit late in September, 1801. Both preached, but neither of them was well received by the people.

[6] May sold this woman or another one to John Anderson on October 28, 1801, for 200 good raccoon skins valued at £22 6s. 8d. He was to receive 50 more skins if her work was satisfactory. May's Day Book, Burton Hist. Coll.

only "on trial," John apparently kept the position, and in 1804 his father sent May an indenture binding John to work for three years.

In the fall of 1801 the name of Charles Curry begins to appear frequently in the business records of Detroit as a dealer in furs and general merchandise. Curry purchased his stock of goods from Robison & Martin of Albany, and he sold furs valued at £181 12*s.* 6*d.* to John Jacob Astor in New York. Curry complained that the furs were poor. Money, he reported, was scarce, as usual, but the expected arrival of the army paymaster would remedy the condition, at least temporarily. The seasonal attack of fever again was taking its annual toll. As Curry expressed it, "there is a grate many died with the Favour in this place within four weeks."

During October and November the traders, loaded with merchandise, set out for their wintering places. Nicholas Campau's stock for his Sandusky post included flints, fire steels, knives, awls, combs, fishlines and hooks, blankets, "Ostridge" feathers, "Juice Harps," lookingglasses, beads, wampum, crosses, earrings, armbands, powder, balls, and nearly two hundred gallons of whisky. Altogether the goods were valued at £815 3*s.* 11½*d.*

6

Solomon Sibley left Detroit for Chillicothe, capital of the Northwest Territory, in November, 1801, in order to attend the first session of the second General Assembly. This time he would sit in the Legislative Council. Representatives Jonathan Schieffelin, François Chabert, and George McDougall accompanied him. Sibley reported that he and his companions had a disagreeable journey, having spent eleven days on the road.

They found a spirit of dissension among the legislators. The Republican element had increased, and there was strong opposition to the Federalist governor, St. Clair. Sibley, a Federalist also, was distressed to find himself "in the midst of violent Jeffersonism." The people of Chillicothe were hostile to the Governor because they believed he was responsible for bills which provided for the removal of the capital to Cincinnati and for a division of the Territory that would indefinitely postpone statehood. So bitter did this hostility become that a mob attacked the house where the Governor was lodging. Some of the men more daring than the rest forced their way inside. There Jonathan Schieffelin "met them in the passage with a brace of loaded pistols, and drove them back into the street."[7]

During this session of the legislature Solomon Sibley introduced a bill for the incorporation of Detroit.[8] Approved on January 18, 1802, it defined the boundaries of the corporation as the dividing line between John Askin's and Antoine Beaubien's farms on the east, the line between the Macomb farm and the Pierre Chêne farm on the west, the river on the south, and a line two miles distant from the river on the north.

The Act provided for a five-man board of trustees to govern the town. These men, one of whom was to be chairman and another treasurer, had legislative, executive, and judicial authority within the limits of the corporation. Other officers were to be a secretary, an assessor, a collector, and a town marshal, all of whom, together with the trustees, would be elected annually at a town meeting held on the first Monday in May. Freeholders, renters paying $40 a year, "and Such other persons residing within said town, who Shall be admitted to the freedom of Said Corporation by a Majority of the Electors at their annual Meetings," were made eligible to vote for town officers.

All ordinances passed during the preceding year were to be laid before the voters at their annual meeting. If a majority of those present disapproved of any of them, they would thenceforth be null and void. The voters were also to determine in town meeting the amount of money to be spent for public purposes during the ensuing year.[9]

---

[7] Jacob Burnet, *Notes on the Early Settlement of the North-Western Territory*, p. 333. Burnet was a member of the legislative council.

In his account of the riot Governor St. Clair does not mention Schieffelin. He takes the credit himself for dispersing the mob. William H. Smith (ed.), *The St. Clair Papers*, II, 556.

[8] *Corporation of the Town of Detroit, Act of Incorporation and Journal of the Board of Trustees, 1802–1805* (Detroit, 1922), p. 7. A manuscript copy, in Audrain's hand, is in the Burton Hist. Coll.

The people of Detroit had petitioned the Territorial Supreme Court in 1798 or 1799 for a charter, but without effect. *Mich. Pio. and Hist. Soc. Colls.*, VIII, 507–508.

[9] The Board of Trustees was empowered to license and regulate taverns or ale houses, but the fees to be paid for the licenses were to be established by the Court of Quarter Sessions of the county, and the money was to be paid to the county treasurer. The first tavern license issued by the Board was granted to Mrs. Ann Coates, a widow, the only woman who kept a tavern in Detroit at the time.

The Act provided that the charter should be in effect from and after February 1, 1802. It also contained the names of the officers who would serve until the first election. Members of the Board were: John Askin, Sr., John Dodemead, James Henry, Charles François Girardin, and Joseph Campau. Peter Audrain was named secretary; Robert Abbott, assessor; Jacob Clemens, collector; and Elias Wallen, marshal.

Solomon Sibley must have been largely responsible for naming these officials. Why he chose John Askin is puzzling, unless it was to compliment the old merchant; for Askin was still a British subject, intending to move across the river as soon as possible. Whatever the reason for the appointment, it pleased Askin, who wrote to a son-in-law: "The legislature honored me so far as to make me the first of five trustees who they named & to whom they gave great authority."

The Board met for the first time on Tuesday, February 9. The members took the oath of office, elected James Henry chairman, John Dodemead treasurer, and Louis Pelletier messenger. The Trustees ordered a town meeting to convene at eleven o'clock on the morning of February 15. Determined that everyone should be apprised of the session, they directed that a notice, in English and in French, be posted on the engine house, and they instructed the messenger to read the notice to every "house Keeper" within the corporation. When the inhabitants met in the courthouse, Peter Audrain read to them the act of incorporation in English and in French.

The first legislation enacted by the Board was an ordinance "for the better Securing of the Said town against injuries of fire." It consisted of seventeen articles almost identical with those adopted by property owners in November, 1798 (p. 85). The second ordinance required bakers to sell their three-pound loaf of bread for six pence, New York currency, and to stamp their initials on each loaf. On March 20 the Trustees ordered that a market be held every Tuesday and Friday on the river bank, just outside the pickets, "where the old Bake house stands," and prohibited the selling of meat and garden produce at any other place.[10]

[10] A photostat in the Burton Historical Collection of a map of "Fort Du Detroit In 1775" shows the "King's Bake House" on a small point of land between the merchants' wharf and the public wharf. This was apparently the site of the first market in Detroit.

CHAPTER XIV
JOHN WILLIAMS FIGHTS A DUEL

THE winter of 1801-02 was remarkable for its mildness. There was still no frost in the ground on New Year's Day, and as late as February 4 there had been "not one day's Carrioling" [sleighing]. An important social affair of the season was the wedding of Elijah Brush and Adelaide Askin. The ceremony was performed by Father Levadoux on the evening of February 17, in the presence of a large number of relatives and friends. This marriage of a New England lawyer to the daughter of a British father and a French mother was a presage of the eventual fusion of the diverse elements in Detroit.

John Askin was pleased with his new son-in-law. To his old friend Alexander Henry he wrote: "he promises fair, has a good character and is reckoned a good lawyer which is not a bad profession in this quarter."

The bridegroom immediately dispatched to Robison & Martin at Albany an order for household equipment. Among other articles he ordered "one set of fashionable guilt chinea complete with coffee cups &ca; one barrel of loaf Sugar and Coffee; one fourth chest of best hyson tea; a half barrel of best French brandy; one dozen handsome knives and forks; a half dozen small breakfast knives and forks; two large dining table cloths; and six small breakfast cloths."

Solomon Sibley, Brush's colleague at the bar, was still a bachelor. He spent some time in Marietta, as he had promised, after the adjournment of the legislature; but on his return to Detroit he informed a correspondent who had "boiled" him about a wife that he was "still free of an incumbrance of that agreeable nature." It is likely, however, that Sibley had visited his intended bride and, perhaps with some trepidation, had confirmed the proposals of his agents.

Frederick Bates also remained a bachelor, but he enjoyed the company of the young ladies of Detroit and praised their virtues in verses teeming with characters of Greek and Roman mythology. One of the poems, entitled "To Isabelle," begins:

> Miss Bella's fairer than the Cyprian Queen;
> Wittier than Sappho, pride of Mytilene;
> Graceful as Dian, taller than the Nymphs;
> Beauteous as Helen or the mountain Sylphs;
> Purer than lilies, sweeter than beds of flowers;
> Bright as Aurora, mild as gentle showers.

The poet filled several pages with lines in the same style and diction before he concluded this tribute, dedicated, perhaps, to one of Commodore Grant's daughters, for whom he had earlier expressed his admiration.

Another of Bates' poems is "An Heroicomical Excursion," in which he tells the story of a trip to Malden—across the river by boat and then from Sandwich by phaeton. Here again are the classical allusions, and there is a conscious hyperbole for which the reader has been prepared by the title.

> At your commands, the low'ring clouds are fled
> To distant wilds, by blust'ring Eurus led:
> Serenely mild the arching Heavens expand,
> And lazy billows slowly lash the strand.
>   The Boat prepared, our tourists take their seats
> Nor ask a convoy of their country's fleets;
> The lonely Bark a watry waste explores,
> And dauntless seeks the neighbouring British shores.
> No Calinurus now, the voyage requires;
> For Neptune seconds all the Fairs' desires.
>   Blow gentle gales, & waft them o'er the Strait
> And come my Muse, the incidents relate;
> With smooth progression now the Vessel glides;
> Attendant Dolphins hov'ring near her sides
> To rescue beauty from the whelming wave
> (In case of wreck) and loveliness to save.
> Needless precaution! all the stars have given
> Protecting passports, sealed by saints in Heaven.
> Go foolish Dolphins, meaner mortals guard;
> Nor hope those smiles which might a God reward.
>
> See Springfield's landscape lessens to the sight,
> And all its pleasing views no more delight.
> Canadian shores supply the absent scene
> And Sandwich shows what our Detroit *has* been.
> Avast my Muse! suppress the rising sigh,
> The Phaeton waits! Times precious moments fly.
> The car ascended, swift it rolls away,
> Resplendent as the orb of closing day.

FREDERICK BATES
(Courtesy of the Missouri Historical Society, St. Louis)

Governor William Hull, by Gilbert Stuart
(Courtesy of the Burton Historical Collection)

So soon arrived—See Malden's turrets rise;
Hear her artillery shake the vaulted skies
And Erie's waves extend their blue domain
Beyond our vision like the imperial main.

The poet continues with an account of the visit at Malden and of the return to Matthew Ernest's home below Detroit, whence they had set sail. Surely this lively young fellow, who could transform the familiar countryside into a vale of Arcady, must have been a welcome guest at every social function.

John Williams returned to Detroit during the winter of 1802. From the spring of 1801 until some time in the fall of that year he had been at Wilkinsonville, a camp on the Ohio River below Fort Massac, as contractor's agent with the United States troops. He must have been happy indeed to be back again among his friends and relatives in the town which he had praised so feelingly while he was absent. His uncle, Joseph Campau, forgot the disappointment he had suffered when John had failed to return at his demand, and received the prodigal at once into the store, for he had a great affection for his nephew.

Other people liked John too. John Askin described him as "a very fine young man with an excellent Character," and soon after his return to Detroit he was appointed lieutenant in the militia and elected township clerk.

Ben Huntington, who had lived in Detroit since 1798, removed to New York in 1802. In May he informed Solomon Sibley that he had gone into business with a friend and had made a good beginning. Huntington reported that he had seen Jonathan Schieffelin, who passed him on the street without speaking. He probably still bore a grudge against Huntington because of the bitter election contest in Detroit in the fall of 1800.

A Wayne County tax roll that has been preserved provides much interesting information about conditions in Detroit and the vicinity in 1802.[1] Detroit Township, which included the town and a considerable area to the west, contained only one

---

[1] Duplicate of the County Tax in Wayne County, Territory of the United States, Northwest of the River Ohio ... for the year 1802, Gabriel Godfroy Papers, Burton Hist. Coll.
The "Duplicate" is in English. There is also the original roll for Hamtramck Township only, in French, in the Hamtramck Papers, *ibid.*

hundred and four houses. Most of them were valued at amounts ranging from $250 to $800. Richard Donovan's and John Dodemead's, however, were assessed at $1,200, and James May's at $1,000.[2] Many residents of the town had at least one horse and one or two cows.

Only seven slaves were listed in the returns for Detroit Township. John Dodemead owned two. Matthew Ernest, James May, Gabriel Godfroy, François Lafontaine, and Jacques Pelletier each had one.

Five physicians were practicing in Detroit at this time: Dr. William Brown, Dr. William McDowell Scott, Dr. Joseph Wilkinson, Jr., Dr. Hermann Eberts, and Dr. William McCoskry, who had resigned from the army in February, 1802.[3] The first two had each one horse. Doctors Scott and Eberts each kept a cow.

Hamtramck Township, which included the Côte du Nord-Est and Grosse Pointe, contained one hundred and sixteen houses. Most of the taxpayers were farmers. Their farms, in general, varied in width from one to six arpents; but a few were nine or twelve. The depth was usually forty arpents.

The cultivated area was generally small—from ten to twelve square arpents—though some farmers planted thirty or forty square arpents, and Commodore Alexander Grant had one hundred in cultivation.

The Commodore's property at Grosse Pointe was assessed at $1,500. Besides his house, he owned three slaves, six horses, and thirty-five cattle. Only Elijah Brush, who was assessed for the property belonging to John Askin, paid more taxes than Alexander Grant. Louis Tremblé's holdings also were assessed at $1,500. In addition to his farm and his house, he owned one slave, eighteen cows, two oxen, and two horses. He also operated a water mill, a sawmill, and a horse-power mill. Maurice Moran had a water mill and a horse-power mill; Louis Beaufait, Jr., a windmill; and Henry Berthelet, a water mill. Other large taxpayers in Hamtramck Township were

[2] A year later Charles Jouett, Indian agent at Detroit, reported that a majority of the private houses were greatly in need of repairs. The palisade and the public buildings, he declared, were "in a state of decay." *American State Papers, Indian Affairs*, I, 759.

[3] Dr. David Davis was surgeon at the Fort.

Antoine Beaubien and George Meldrum. The latter owned four slaves.

Farm implements were still primitive, but by this time some progress had been made. John Askin bought "a Machine for cleaning wheat, a Fanning Mill," such as the farmers around Queenston were using; and he ordered one of "Tulls two wheeled drill Plows" to be sent from England.

2

In March, 1802, the feud among the judges in Detroit flared up again. Solomon Sibley, prosecutor of Wayne County, informed Governor St. Clair that the justices of the Court of Common Pleas would never sit again with Patrick McNiff because of his "odious character." The justices of the Court of Quarter Sessions, he added, were sending to the Governor a report of the proceedings against McNiff in their recent session. Sibley suggested that St. Clair remove him from the bench.[4]

Homicide was a crime almost unknown in Detroit. Consequently there must have been a great stir among the inhabitants when Kish-ku-kon, a Chippewa, was brought to town charged with killing Antoine Lauzon, a trader for Angus Mackintosh at Saginaw. On May 9, 1802, at a hearing before James Henry, Louis Beaufait charged Kish-ku-kon with murder. The Indian confessed that he had stabbed Lauzon in the back and admitted that he knew the trader had died as a result of the wound. The prisoner gave no reason for his act, but Angus Mackintosh said he had heard that the Indian killed his trader for refusing him liquor.

Kish-ku-kon was locked up in the county jail to await trial. The next day Sheriff Elias Wallen, apparently fearful lest the Indian escape, addressed a requisition to Colonel François Chabert, commandant of the militia. Urging that the jail was "intirely insufficient" for safekeeping the prisoners, he asked for a detail of militia as a guard until the prison should be rebuilt.[5]

---

[4] McNiff died in May, 1803.

In spite of the quarrels among the judges the Court of Common Pleas was apparently efficient. John Askin praised this court as being far superior to the similar one on the Canadian side of the river. Askin to Robert Hamilton, April 8, 1802, Askin Papers, Burton Hist. Coll.

[5] Kish-ku-kon (the name is variously spelled) apparently justified the sheriff's fear by escaping from prison, for he was indicted again for the same crime, and a war-

Peter Chartrand, John Harvey's baker, who had sued the artist-actor George Saunders for stealing his wife, now had cause for another suit. On July 4 William Smith, a hatter, assaulted Chartrand in the street and gave him a severe beating. The baker filed suit in the Court of Common Pleas for $500 damages. When the case was heard in the December term, the jury awarded Chartrand only $35.

The Trustees of the town met weekly to pass ordinances and to levy fines on offenders. On April 8 they adopted a comprehensive measure designed to remedy sundry unsatisfactory conditions in the village:

> Whereas the Streets of that part of the town of Detroit within the Stockade are So narrow that foot passengers have difficulty at times to Keep clear of horsemen & carriages unless they go Slow &c. Sec. 1st. It is therefore ordained by the board of Trustees that if any person or persons Shall ride, or drive a horse or carriage quick, or Shall let or drive his horse or horses loose to water, within the limits before recited from and after the publication of this ordinance, Shall, for every Such offense, forfeit & pay the Sum of two dollars, or any lesser Sum at the discretion of the board of Trustees to be recovered on the oath of a creditable Witness.

Other sections of this ordinance ordered inhabitants to remove from streets, lanes, or alleys adjoining their property any "incumbrance" that might impede a free passage; required proprietors of houses to maintain in good condition their log sidewalks since "the middle of the Streets of the Town of Detroit, within the Pickets are almost impassable, in bad weather for persons on foot"; prohibited the piling of lumber, firewood, and stones along the bank of the river in such a way as to prevent carts from reaching the waterside; and ordered inspectors to make another survey of houses to discover whether

---

rant for his arrest was issued on September 19, 1805. Marshal William McD. Scott arrested him on July 31, 1806. While on the way to Detroit Kish-ku-kon, also known as "the Chippeway Rogue," was rescued by his father, his son, and other Indians. Another warrant was issued on September 24, 1807. William W. Blume (ed.), *Transactions of the Supreme Court of the Territory of Michigan, 1805–1814* (Ann Arbor, 1935), II, 17–19.

On December 28, 1807, Governor Hull wrote to Secretary of War Henry Dearborn asking him to obtain from the President a pardon for Kish-ku-kon on the grounds that he and his father, Little Cedar, were influential chiefs who were friendly to the United States. *Mich. Pio. and Hist. Soc. Colls.*, XL, 240.

In 1826 Kish-ku-kon and his son Big Beaver killed another Indian. Both were jailed in Detroit. While awaiting trial, Kish-ku-kon obtained poison from a member of his tribe and died on May 17. His son escaped on October 6, 1826. Silas Farmer, *History of Detroit*, p. 181.

the law requiring certain fire-fighting equipment was being obeyed.

A number of persons had already been called before the Board and fined for neglecting to protect their property from fire. It is notable that among the number were John Askin, James Henry, Robert Abbott, John Dodemead, and Joseph Campau, all officers of the corporation. Justice was apparently administered impartially in Detroit.

At the first annual town meeting held at the courthouse on the morning of May 3, 1802, the voters returned all the incumbents except Jacob Clemens, collector, and John Askin, trustee, in whose stead they chose respectively William Smith and George Meldrum. Askin was ineligible to hold office, for he had moved across the river, where he had built a house which he called Strabane, named after his birthplace in Ireland. The new house was "opposite the lower End of Hogg Island" (Belle Isle), on a tract of land which his friend Isaac Todd of Montreal had given him the previous year. Elijah Brush and his wife moved into the old Askin homestead on the edge of town.

When John Askin left, Detroit lost a grand old man. The bitterness against him over the question of citizenship had long vanished. Before he crossed the river Askin wrote that "in justice to the Gentlemen on this side I must say I have received nothing but politeness and civility from them above these two years past." Detroiters generally must have been sorry to see him go.

At the town meeting "the Freedom of the Corporation was unanimously voted to Solomon Sibley Esquire, Counsellor at law, and one of the members of the Councill of the territorial legislature, for the Services he rendered the Said Corporation in the framing of, and attending the passing of the bill intitled an act to incorporate the town of Detroit and for other eminent Services to the County of Wayne at large . . . ." The Trustees were directed to give Sibley a copy of the resolution bearing the seal of the corporation.

Matthew Ernest, collector of customs, was unable to convince the British merchants in Detroit and the vicinity that they must pay duties on merchandise imported at Detroit to be sold in the interior of the country. Citing Article 3 of the Jay Treaty, which permitted goods to be carried over portages without being subject to duties, they claimed the right to bring in free the consignments destined to the Mississippi country by way of the Maumee and the Wabash.

In order to obtain a definite ruling on this matter Ernest appealed to Albert Gallatin, Secretary of the Treasury, who replied that goods landed in the United States in course of transportation should be permitted to pass if they were merely on the way to a foreign destination. This situation, he explained, did not exist at Detroit, since the merchandise would be distributed to points within the country. For this reason the merchants could not claim protection under the treaty, and their goods were dutiable.

3

The open winter of 1801–02 was unfavorable for hunting. Charles Curry, complaining that it was the worst in twenty years, reported that "Muskrats is scarcer this year than ever They have been before," and that he had to pay 2*s*. 6*d*. for them. Raccoons could be bought for 3*s*. 3*d*., minks for 4*s*., and otters for 32*s*. In spite of his pessimistic report, Curry shipped to Albany 220 pounds of beaver, 1,425 raccoon skins, 375 mink, 18 bear, 117 otter, 10 fox, 12 fisher, and 16 deerskins.

At some time during 1802 an Indian store, or "factory," was established at Detroit by the United States Government. It was managed by Charles Jouett, Indian agent, who arrived at Detroit in that year. He was a Virginia lawyer and a friend of President Jefferson. This store, like the other five which were in operation at the time, was intended to provide the Indians with necessary goods at fair prices in exchange for their furs. No liquor was sold in the "factory."

The local merchants were hostile to these establishments, for they disliked the competition. Nevertheless, the Indians carried few furs to the Government factories, since they were usually in debt to the merchants, who took their pelts in payment; consequently they had little or nothing left to sell elsewhere. Besides, since they preferred to trade where they could get liquor, they patronized the private traders.

Because of the mild weather, navigation opened earlier than

usual. It was reported that the *Caledonia* would sail for the Sault on April 20. The United States packet *Senator Tracy* with Captain John Connelly in command, was now carrying troops and military supplies. One sailor, and ten soldiers detailed for this duty, made up her crew.

During the summer of 1802 Lieutenant Henry B. Brevoort took command of the brig *Adams*. He was an officer in the regular army who had been master of the galley *Adams* on the Ohio and Mississippi rivers in 1800 and 1801.

Peace with Napoleon caused a rise in the price of furs, and Alexander Henry in Montreal predicted that business in general would improve. Although the Treaty of Amiens between Great Britain and Napoleon was not concluded until March 27, 1802, John Askin had heard rumors of peace during the preceding December. The news had cheered him and others in Detroit who expected that trade would increase as a result. Although cash was scarce in the town, as usual, the expected payment of $44,000 to the troops in June would provide a temporary supply of currency.

Hoping, perhaps, to profit by the brighter prospect for business, Frederick Bates decided in June, 1802, to open a store. He ordered a stock of goods from Lewis Farquharson and Company at Schenectady, to whom he was recommended by Matthew Ernest, assistant quartermaster general, in whose office Bates worked.[6]

In the summer of 1802 Joseph Campau and John Williams finally established the partnership which the merchant had proposed two years earlier. John was glad to take advantage of the offer and to settle down in Detroit. The agreement provided that Campau would furnish the capital to purchase merchandise, and that he would draw 6 per cent interest on his investment. Profits and losses were to be divided equally. For the sake of his health or to care for his other interests the uncle reserved the right to absent himself from the business "when he shall think it proper," but his nephew might devote only five days a year to his own affairs. The agreement, signed on July 20, was to run for three years.

[6] Ernest to Lewis Farquharson & Co., June 20, 1802. Bates Papers, Missouri Hist. Soc., St. Louis.
Ernest wrote: "Mr. Bates is just commencing business . . . ."

Williams must have set out immediately with a quantity of furs to sell in Montreal, where he would purchase a stock of goods; for the next day he was at Malden, bound for Lower Canada. On August 2 he transshipped his seventy-four packs of furs at Queenston and continued his voyage. In Montreal the young merchant sold his furs to good advantage, or at least so he thought, and began to purchase goods to carry back to Detroit. Before Williams left Detroit Campau had instructed his nephew to buy him a rug and some picture frames. Williams bought the rug and fourteen "fine" frames. He informed his uncle that in them he would find portraits of the King and the Queen of England, Napoleon Bonaparte, and General Washington—a prudent selection for cosmopolitan Detroit.

4

The Reverend David Bacon continued to preach and to teach in Detroit during the winter and spring of 1802. On February 19 Mrs. Bacon gave birth to a son, whom they named Leonard.[7] Soon afterwards orders from the Missionary Society arrived directing Bacon to go to L'Arbe Croche to preach to the Ottawa there. The Evangelist decided that he would first visit the Indians at the mouth of the Maumee River; and so he set out early in May with a skilled boatman and his brother-in-law, Beaumont Parks. After a sojourn of nearly two weeks the missionary failed to arouse the interest of the savages, who told him politely but firmly that the white man's way was not for them. Defeated, but not discouraged, Bacon returned to Detroit on May 18. Two weeks later he and his family boarded a ship for Mackinac, whence he would go to establish a mission at L'Arbre Croche.

Father Michel Levadoux left Detroit during May, 1802.[8] The worthy priest who had labored loyally to make Americans of

[7] Leonard Bacon became an "influential professor at Yale University and one of the foremost religious and social leaders of his generation in America." M. M. Quaife, "David Bacon," *Burton Hist. Coll. Leaf.*, IX, 39.

[8] A letter from Charles Curry to Robison & Martin, Detroit, May 17, 1802, bears this note on the cover: "pr. The Revd Mons Lavadoux." Sibley Papers, Burton Hist. Coll.

The last entry signed by Father Levadoux in the Registre de Ste Anne is the record of a wedding on May 17. There is nothing in the Registre or in the Livre des Assemblées to indicate exactly when he left Detroit.

his parishioners was obeying the call of Father Francis Nagot, director of St. Mary's Seminary at Baltimore, to go there as his assistant. Father Gabriel Richard now became the pastor of Ste Anne's. Since he could no longer serve as *chantre*, the *marguillers* agreed to pay Etienne Dubois 450 *livres* a year to fill that office. Besides singing the liturgy, he would be required to instruct the children in the ceremonies of the church, to catechize them on Sundays and saints' days in the absence of the pastor, and to assist with the lectures during Lent.

Save for the new steeple, which was not built until October, the repairing and enlarging of Ste Anne's were completed during the summer of 1802. According to Father Richard, the church was almost entirely new, except the roof, and the seating capacity was increased by the addition of thirty pews.[9] Although the congregation was $500 in debt and although Father Richard expected the "ornamental work" to cost as much more, he estimated that the rents of the new pews would bring in $400 a year; and, besides, there was still $500 to be collected on the pledges.

The priest reported that he had had some difficulties in connection with the building. Several people complained that he meddled too much with the work; others, that he did not do enough. His only answer was: "I have tryed to do for the best." He requested Bishop Carroll to "Pray God for the union between all members of my Congregation and for the conversion of the Sinners who are in a to great number."

5

John Wilkins, Jr., in Pittsburgh, was angry with his partner, James Henry. In September, 1802, he wrote demanding that Henry immediately refund the money which Wilkins had invested in the store and in the tannery, and send him a complete statement of the condition of both enterprises.

Wilkins complained that, although he had asked for reports at various times previously, he had never had one. As a matter of fact, Henry had prepared in June, 1802, a statement of the capital invested in the tannery. It showed nearly seven

---

[9] Apparently the congregation had decided not to build on the Common, for the old church was simply repaired and enlarged. Richard to Carroll, October 20, 1802, Letters to Carroll 7C2, Archives of the Archbishopric of Baltimore and Washington.

hundred hides in stock and more than five hundred in the twenty-one vats. Besides, one hundred and fifty-two skins were in other processes, and Henry had shipped some leather and some deerskins as an "Adventure to Pitt."[10]

This adventure was not a happy one. Because of low water, which permitted only canoes to descend the Allegheny River, most of the shipment remained on the portage. The shoemakers in Pittsburgh were pleased with the quality of the leather which they received, but the uncertainty of the supply discouraged them from contracting for more.

Transportation on the Lakes also was sometimes uncertain. John Wilkins gave a letter written on September 7 to George Wallace, Jr., to deliver to James Henry at Detroit. Wallace reached Presqu' Isle, where he waited for a ship. When none had arrived by September 25, he wrote to Henry, his former employer, that he would have to return to Pittsburgh. He said he was sorry that he would be unable to visit Detroit, "the only place in this world that I have any estimation for." Wallace asked to be remembered particularly to Marie Catherine Audrain, and he instructed Henry to tell Miss Navarre that "I have not forgotten her—nor perhaps never will."

If John Wilkins had waited a little longer, he might have sent his letter by the United States mail; for Frederick Bates was appointed postmaster at Detroit on September 7, 1802, and an office was opened in October.[11] The route as established by Congress was by way of Pittsburgh and Cincinnati, and there were two deliveries a month.

6

Meanwhile John Williams had purchased in Montreal a great variety of goods for the firm of Campau and Williams and set out for Detroit.[12] John McGregor and Jacques

---

[10] At this time the firm of Tuttle and Russell purchased some of Henry's saddle, bridle, and harness leather. Henry's Tannery Ledger, p. 23, Burton Hist. Coll. The partners in this Detroit company were Christopher Tuttle and William Russell.

[11] C. E. Carter, *Territorial Papers of the United States*, VII, 63.

Gideon Granger to Frederick Bates, July 1, 1803, acknowledges the receipt of Bates' postal accounts for the quarter ending December 31, 1802. Bates Papers, Missouri Hist. Soc., St. Louis.

[12] Statement, Joseph Provan to Campau & Williams, September 6, 1802, Campau Family Papers, Burton Hist. Coll. The goods cost £2143 8s. 1½d.

Lasselle, who had also been in Montreal on business, traveled with him. On October 1, at Fort Erie, Williams and Lasselle were on board the schooner *Thames* watching merchandise being loaded into the hold. For want of other diversion the two young fellows began a friendly test of strength by lifting boxes of shot. As both were able to lift them, and as there was nothing heavier with which to try their strength, Lasselle boasted that he could lift more than any other man. Williams asserted that his uncle Toussaint Campau was stronger than Lasselle. To settle the argument they bet two beaver hats on the outcome of the test, which was to be made after they reached Detroit. They then went ashore for dinner at John Crow's tavern.

Williams, Lasselle, John McGregor, François Bizaillon, J. B. Piquette, and a Mr. Carroll sat down together. After dinner the first three remained at table drinking brandy and four or five bottles of port wine. At about dusk word came that the *Thames* was preparing to cast off. Williams bought another pint of brandy, which they drank at once. Flushed with liquor, and apparently forgetful of the schooner, Williams and Lasselle began to argue about the athletic prowess of Lasselle's brother François, who had beaten Williams in a race in Montreal. Williams demanded another test at Detroit, since, he said, he had been ill with ague at Montreal and, besides, Lasselle had started first. At any rate, if Lasselle should beat him again, Williams was certain that his uncle Toussaint Campau could run faster than Lasselle.

Next Lasselle boasted of his brother's skill in shooting. Williams asserted that he had become an expert marksman while with the army on the Ohio. Lasselle then bet $50 that Williams could not put six shots out of twelve into the crown of his hat at twelve yards. This bet was to be settled at Detroit.

The two young fellows now began to extol the fighting ability of their relatives. Lasselle maintained that his father and his brother could whip anyone. Williams declared that the Campaus were better men. Then Lasselle began to praise the Navarres. He wanted to bet that in a fight Touton Navarre could whip any of Williams' uncles. Williams insisted that his Uncle Toussaint could lick any Navarre; but he refused to bet out of respect for his uncles, who, he maintained, never fought unless they were provoked. By this time the two were very angry.

John Crow now brought in some bread and cheese for supper. When Williams began to help himself to the food, Lasselle, in a rage, seized him by the coat and tried to throw him to the floor. Williams shook him off, and Lasselle became furious. He smashed the tumblers on the table and knocked over the candles. He stamped and swore and shouted that not a man in the whole Campau family dared face him. Frightened by his drunken violence, everyone fled the room except Williams. He, feeling himself to have been "grossly insulted, abused & challenged (together with my family), my temper being extremely heated," after a moment's hesitation, ran to the *Thames*, where he got his two loaded pistols and returned to the tavern.

Williams laid both weapons on the table. Lasselle snatched one and cocked it. Williams took the other. Both raised their pistols. Williams saw fire flash in the pan of his opponent's weapon. He fired. Lasselle staggered toward Williams, coughing blood, and collapsed in a heap on the floor.

Lasselle was put to bed in the tavern under the care of Dr. Cyrenius Chapin. Williams was arrested and locked up in the jail in Niagara. Feeling in the community ran high against Williams, apparently because he was an American. In prison he heard that Lasselle was expected to die and that "the whole parish is in combination to have me hanged if they possibly can."[13] Robert Nichol, of Queenston, who had formerly been John Askin's clerk, visited Williams as soon as he heard of the affair and did what he could to make him comfortable.

Dr. Chapin continued to attend Lasselle, and Dr. James Muirhead also was called. By November 11 the patient had recovered sufficiently to be removed to Detroit, Dr. Chapin accompanying him on the voyage and remaining with him until November 30. After Dr. Chapin left, Dr. William Brown took care of Lasselle.

Meanwhile Williams, languishing in prison, wrote to his Uncle Joseph assuring him that, if the witnesses of the duel

---

[13] Williams to Joseph Campau, October 27, 1802, John R. Williams Papers, *ibid*. Robert Nichol to John Askin, October 15, 1802, Askin Papers, *ibid*., mentions the prejudice against Williams.

told the truth, he would be acquitted. As he expected to be in jail all winter, he asked for a prayer book and a hymnal. He promised to take to heart the advice contained in a letter from his uncle, and assured him that "since that unlucky day" he would never again "make use of liquor, but rather ... live a reformed life." He requested his Uncle Joseph to take care of his sisters, as "you always have done," and asked that his Uncle Denis come to visit him, adding that "although a criminal and a prisoner, I hope to have the pleasure of seeing all my relatives."

7

Joseph Campau was greatly distressed by the plight of his favorite nephew. He was worried not only because of his imprisonment, but also by this blow to their partership, for he was too ill to bear the burden of business alone. During the past four years he had consulted all the doctors in town. Although they had dosed him with all sorts of medicines, he felt no better; and so, in desperation, he appealed to Father Richard for spiritual aid. The priest drove a hard bargain. He made Campau promise to have two high masses said for the benefit of his health and to go to confession regularly until March 15, 1803. Besides, he had to agree to give up charging compound interest on debts and to stop selling liquor to the Indians. Father Richard gave him a year's grace in keeping this pledge on Campau's plea that he had $6,000 worth of goods in the hands of the savages. Finally, the priest required the ailing merchant to promise to withdraw his certificate of membership from Zion Lodge and to attend no more meetings.[14]

Campau promised. Within a month, perhaps as a result of his renewed interest in religion, he was chosen a *marguiller* of Ste Anne's Church. Nevertheless he did not withdraw from Zion Lodge. As a matter of fact, he was reëlected treasurer by the brethren on December 6, 1802, and he continued to attend the meetings.[15]

In the fall of 1802 Solomon Sibley journeyed to Marietta,

[14] Prayer for health, Nov. 25, 1802, Campau Family Papers, *ibid.*
[15] C. M. Burton (compiler), Zion Lodge, Detroit, 1794–1829, *ibid.*
Although he had been absent at times because of illness, he began to attend pretty regularly after January 1, 1803.

where he and Miss Sarah Sproat were married on October 31. At last he was out of "the old Bachellors row," but he soon returned to Detroit without his bride, explaining that she would remain with her parents during the winter. Sibley intended to visit her in the spring. In fact, he was thinking of moving to Marietta.

Another Detroiter was less fortunate in his love affair. Although Dr. William McCoskry's suit for the hand of Isabella Grant was successful, and although the couple planned to be married in the fall of 1802, the wedding never occurred. Instead, Isabella married Captain William Gilkinson of Sandwich, master of the schooner *Thames*, in February, 1803.

CHAPTER XV

IN INDIANA TERRITORY

IN 1803 Detroit was included in Indiana Territory. The enabling act of April 30, 1802, which permitted the people of Ohio to draw up a constitution and apply for admission to the Union, provided that "from and after the formation of the said state" the eastern portion of what is now Michigan should be a part of Indiana Territory.[1] The people of Wayne County were not consulted about the transfer. Federalists charged the Republicans in Congress with separating Wayne County from the new state so that the Federalist majority in the county would be excluded from the Ohio constitutional convention.

Solomon Sibley blamed "the interested ambition of a half-a-dozen aspiring individuals" for the haste with which the change was made. He named "Sir Thomas" Worthington and Judges Symmes and Meigs as the leaders in the movement. According to Sibley, the leading men in Detroit believed that the act of April 30, 1802, was "unconstitutional" because it was contrary to the fifth article of compact in the Ordinance of 1787.

In accordance with the enabling act, Governor William Henry Harrison, on January 14, 1803, established Wayne County, Indiana, by proclamation. Although this county was smaller than the original one proclaimed by Winthrop Sargent, it embraced the whole Lower Peninsula, a large part of the upper one, and small portions of Illinois and Wisconsin.

The transfer left local government unchanged, all civil and militia officers retaining their positions. The people of Detroit, however, were greatly dissatisfied with the new connection. While they had been within the Northwest Territory, they had been three hundred miles from Cincinnati, the capital. The governor had never visited Detroit to view conditions at first hand, and the circuit court had held only two sessions

[1] The western part of Michigan had been included in Indiana Territory by an act of Congress, May 7, 1800.

during six years. With the new capital, Vincennes, twice as far away as the former one, the people of Detroit might expect to receive even less attention than before. Besides, Wayne County would now have no representatives in a legislature. Since Indiana Territory was in the first stage of government, Detroit was under the rule of a distant governor and judges.

As a result of their discontent, the leaders circulated a memorial to Congress, in English and in French, praying that Wayne County be erected into a separate territory. The petition cited the disadvantages already mentioned and suggested that more settlers would enter the region and that commerce would increase if conditions were made more favorable. Three hundred and eleven men signed the petition.[2]

2

Colonel John Francis Hamtramck was now in command of the Department of the Lakes. To him at his headquarters in Detroit early in 1803 came orders from Secretary of War Henry Dearborn to build a fort at the mouth of the Chicago River. The Colonel made the necessary arrangements and named Captain John Whistler to head the expedition. Because of his connection with the building of Fort Dearborn, "the real beginning of civilized Chicago," Dr. Milo M. Quaife has suggested that Hamtramck may be called the founder of that metropolis.

The Colonel, however, was not permitted to have any further hand in the work, for he died on April 11, 1803. Major Zebulon Pike, senior officer at the Fort, assumed command and ordered the officers to wear mourning bands of crape on their sleeves.

A high requiem Mass was said in Ste Anne's on April 13, Father J. B. Marchand of Sandwich assisting Father Richard in the service. The officers attended in a body, and Father Richard pronounced a eulogy over the remains of the patriot who had served his adopted country loyally for many years. Colonel Hamtramck was buried with full military honors in Ste

---

[2] A manuscript copy of another petition, undated and without signatures, but certainly drawn up in 1803, is in the A. D. Fraser Papers, Burton Hist. Coll. It is printed in *Mich. Pio. and Hist. Soc. Colls.*, VIII, 511–513. This petition asked that Detroit, as the most important town for trade and defense, be made the residence of the governor and the seat of the courts, or that Wayne County be made a separate territory.

Tomb of John Francis Hamtramck in Mt. Elliott Cemetery, Detroit
(Photograph by Frederick E. Moncrieff)

"A View of Detroit and the Straits, Taken from the Huron Church June 22nd 1804," by Edward Walsh
(Courtesy of the Clements Library)

Anne's cemetery. To cover his tomb the officers of his regiment provided a marble slab upon which they had carved an epitaph which reviewed his military career and praised him as "a valuable officer & a good citizen."[3] In spite of his peppery temper and stern military bearing, the late Colonel had many friends in the town. Joseph Campau reported that everybody mourned his passing.

Colonel Hamtramck left a wife and four children: two daughters, Julienne and Henriette by his first marriage, and John Francis and Alexis H. by his second.[4] An inventory of his personal property contains some significant items. He had a collection of more than sixty books, including *Laws of the United States*, *The Life of Frederick II of Prussia*, *Military Tactics*, Thompson's *Seasons*, Montesquieu's *Spirit of Laws*, *The Art of Surveying*, Cicero's works, *The American Revolution*, a French Bible, and Mirabeau's works.

Among his other possessions were a pair of silver-mounted spectacles, a silver-mounted sword, a gold-headed cane, window curtains "with springs," and a "Bathing Tub." He also had a "large Bay Horse," two cows, twenty-one sheep, and ten lambs.

When the news of Colonel Hamtramck's death reached Washington, Secretary of War Dearborn ordered Colonel Henry Burbeck to Detroit to take command of the Department of the Lakes. The expedition under the command of Captain John Whistler, which Colonel Hamtramck had organized, left Detroit in July for the mouth of the Chicago River to build and garrison Fort Dearborn. The Captain and his family, together with stores and artillery, were carried around the Lakes aboard the schooner *Tracy*. The soldiers marched overland along the Indian trail, led by Lieutenant James S. Swearingen.

The garrison at Detroit now consisted of one company of artillery and three companies of infantry, a total of 199 officers and men. This was probably the smallest force stationed at the post since the arrival of Hamtramck in 1796.

Civilians and soldiers alike viewed with alarm the reduction of the local garrison, a result of President Jefferson's policy of economy. Civilians quarreled incessantly with the military authorities, but they were largely dependent for a medium of

[3] Colonel Hamtramck's tomb is now in Mt. Elliott Cemetery, Detroit.
[4] In 1797 Colonel Hamtramck had married Miss Rebecca Mackenzie.

exchange upon the hard cash with which the Government paid the troops and purchased supplies. More than a year earlier Frederick Bates had reported the "consternation which seized the Gentlemen of the army on the arrival (yesterday) of the President's Speech" (Jefferson's first message to Congress). Bates, who was still a clerk in the quartermaster's department, feared that the "contemplated reforms will send many of us to the grubbing Hoe and the broad Axe."

In spite of this dire possibility Bates favored Jefferson's recommendations because he felt that they were intended to increase democracy. Since the triumph of the Republican Party in the election of 1800 Bates had abandoned his arguments in favor of Federalism. Now he announced: "I have been singing 20 Peans to the Genius of Democracy."

Solomon Sibley, on the other hand, was still a staunch Federalist. He had denounced in scathing language the repeal of the Judiciary Act. To his friend, Representative Seth Hastings of Massachusetts, he wrote: "If Congress proceed to prostrate the barriers of our Constitution, as they have begun, the consequences are evident & I fear no less than a Civil War. I am surprised at those Jacobin or anti Constitutional principles finding so many disiples in New England." Sibley had expected that "the general information united to a cool investigating spirit would have protected that part of America at least from the wild and fashionable frenzy of modern republican philosophy." He predicted gloomily: "If New England does not stand firm, our boasted Constitution is forever lost."

Now he informed Samuel Vance that "Mister Thomas Jefferson reduces our garrison daily and if the report of Louisiana being ceded is true, a further reduction will undoubtedly be the case. Should the troops be entirely removed and our prayer for a new Territory rejected, this country will be completely damned."

Sibley's fear that the garrison would be withdrawn had some basis in fact. Secretary Dearborn, in April, had directed Colonel Hamtramck to recommend a suitable site in the neighborhood for a fort, because he was contemplating the removal of the post from the vicinity of the town. The Secretary suggested that "the Island claimed by Mr. McComb or others" might be a satisfactory place.[5] If he was referring to Grosse Ile, he might have been interested to know that the French had thought of building a fort there instead of at Detroit, but had abandoned the idea "for fear that the timber would some day give out."[6] Charles Jouett, Indian agent at Detroit, in his report to Dearborn in 1803, recommended Hog Island (Belle Isle) as "highly eligible for a garrison, as the elevation of its western end has a complete command of the river." Nevertheless, Fort Lernoult was not removed.

During the winter Secretary Dearborn ordered the brig *Adams* sold. When she was offered at auction in the spring of 1803, the highest bid was $2,300. Since she had cost between eight and ten thousand pounds, according to John Askin, the Government bid her in and maintained her in service. At this time the *Adams* and the *Tracy* composed the United States Navy of the Upper Lakes. The British naval force also consisted of only two ships—the snow *Camden* and the schooner *Maria* under Commodore Grant.

3

Governor William Henry Harrison did not neglect the new county which he had proclaimed. In May he came to Detroit bringing Judge John Griffin with him.[7] Perhaps a session of the circuit court was held at that time. The Governor was probably invited to numerous social gatherings, for no people enjoyed entertaining more than did Detroiters. Whatever

---

[5] The late William Macomb and his heirs claimed ownership of a number of islands including Grosse Ile and Isle aux Cochons, now Belle Isle.

[6] Memoir by Captain Jacques Charles Sabrevois, 1718. *Coll. of the State Hist. Soc. of Wis.*, XVI, 366.
De Sabrevois was commandant at Detroit from 1715 to 1717.

[7] Historians have doubted that Governor Harrison visited Detroit. For example, Beverly W. Bond, Jr., in *The Civilization of the Old Northwest* (New York: 1934), p. 208, wrote: "... the territorial officers at Vincennes do not appear to have attempted the long and dangerous journey to Detroit." The following documents show that he spent some time there.
On May 10, 1803, Harrison signed "at Detroit" an authorization for Audrain to administer oaths of office. Peter Audrain Papers, Burton Hist. Coll.
On May 14 the Governor purchased from James May 11 pounds of "Tamarands," 1 pound of orange peel, 1 pound of lemon peel, 2 bottles of sweet oil, 1 bottle of capers, 1 bottle of anchovies, and three quarters of a bushel of peas. Judge Griffin bought 4 pounds of hair powder. May's Day Book, May 14, 1803, *ibid*.

else they may have done, it is certain that they gave a ball in his honor.

Although the circulating of petitions for separation from Indiana was probably in full swing at the time Governor Harrison reached Detroit, there is no record of his attitude toward the project. Logically, he should not have opposed it, for he had been one of the leaders in the movement to separate Indiana from the Northwest Territory. Whether he approved or not, he was probably urbane and gracious. Harrison was not the unbending autocrat that Governor St. Clair had been. Understanding the spirit of the western people, he was ready to obey their will.

Whatever was Governor Harrison's attitude, his visit did not diminish the desire of the people for separation and their efforts to accomplish it. Solomon Sibley was so sure a new territory would be established that he decided to take his wife to Detroit and remain there. Having developed a feeling of attachment to the town and a deep interest in its future, he requested Senator Worthington to recommend him for secretary of the territory.

In September Sibley sent two petitions requesting the erection of a separate territory to the Senator, who had promised to sponsor them in Congress. The lawyer declared that "there is not a man of sense in the County who does not fervently pray for success to the measure." He was happy to learn some time later that the petitions were "well received" in Washington; but he wondered why Senator Worthington failed to mention the secretaryship, especially since the Court, the Grand Jury, and friends at Detroit had recommended him.

Frederick Bates also wanted to be secretary of the hoped-for territory. His brother Tarleton in Pittsburgh promised to do what he could to aid him, but he was not optimistic about Frederick's chance of success. Frederick, however, probably expected that his earlier Republicanism and his recent return to the fold would be of some assistance to him, especially since Sibley was a staunch Federalist.

The second town meeting for electing officers was held on Monday, May 2, 1803, in the courthouse, on St. Joseph Street between St. Honoré and St. Antoine. The voters chose a whole new board of trustees: Robert Abbott, Charles Curry, James May, Dr. William McDowell Scott, and Elijah Brush. A motion to give Jonathan Schieffelin, "one of the representatives in the late Legislature of the northwest Territory," the freedom of the corporation was carried "by a large Majority of the Electors present." In spite of the fact that they reëlected none of the Trustees, the voters unanimously approved all the transactions and ordinances of the Board during the previous year.

The Trustees in their capacity of municipal magistrates sentenced men of both low and high degree for galloping or cantering their horses in the streets of the town. François Delisle, an apprentice, and a "Negro-man" of Jean Michel Yax were each fined one dollar for this breach of the peace on June 20, 1803. A month later, among others James Henry and Dr. William Brown were fined for the same offense.

Many inhabitants of the town continued to be called before the Trustees to answer complaints about defective chimneys and unsatisfactory fire equipment. On July 20, 1803, Frederick Bates, Robert Abbott, James Abbott, George Meldrum, and Robert Munro were among those fined sums ranging from fifty cents to three dollars. Open drains and "necessary houses" were other subjects of complaint. The Board ordered these "nuisances" abated as soon as possible.

Reflecting the increasing American influence, especially among the governing class, the Board passed an ordinance intended to reduce "drunkness, idleness, and profanity on the Sabbath day." It forbade tavern keepers to permit anyone except strangers and travelers to meet together in companies in their taverns on the Sabbath day or on either of the evenings preceding or following, for drinking and tippling. This ordinance also required taverns to close at ten o'clock at night, and forbade publicans to permit "minors, apprentices, servants, or Negroes to Set drinking in their houses," or to furnish liquor to them without special permission of their parents or masters. The penalty for disobedience was a fine of ten dollars (half of which would be paid to the informer), and possible loss of the tavern license. For a breach of this law Martin Myers, convicted of selling liquor on Sunday, was fined but permitted to retain his license.

4

Charles Curry returned to Detroit in December, 1802, after a business trip to Albany. He reached Amherstburg on the sixth, but was unable to proceed farther because there was ice in the river. Consequently he made the rest of the journey by land, leaving his merchandise until there should be enough snow for *traineaux* to bring it to his store.

Curry sent Robison and Martin at Albany a considerable amount of business from Detroit. In January, 1803, Robert and James Abbott ordered some goods. In February Curry recommended Thomas McCrae, Jr., and Frederick Bates to his friends. He explained that "they find that the dutie coms Verry hard on them, and they must get their goods from Albany." Orders to Albany increased in number and in size. Although James Henry bought a consignment worth £818 12s. 4½d., he was still buying in Montreal. In January, 1803, he owed Forsyth, Richardson, and Company £1590 4d., and the late firm of Leith, Jameson, and Company £1130, 12s. 8d. Henry's credit was good, for in spite of these large debts the former company placed an order in London for additional merchandise which he requested.

The Montreal merchants credited Henry's account with £13 7s. 4d. for a bale of sole leather which he had sent them to sell. After Henry had been disappointed in his shipments of leather to Pittsburgh because the uncertainties of transportation made regular deliveries impossible, he had decided to send all his leather to Montreal, which he believed was a better market. Although the distance was double that to Pittsburgh, he found that transportation was regular, the cost was no greater, and the selling price was higher. A few months later Henry learned that there were uncertainties also in his new course of trade. Out of a shipment of eight bales of sole leather five sides were stolen on the way, and Forsyth, Richardson, and Company were unable to sell the consignment for some time. Though he now purchased dry goods from Montreal and Albany, Henry continued to order stills and whisky from Pittsburgh.

Except that whisky was replacing rum in the Indian trade and also, perhaps, among the white people in Detroit, tastes seem to have changed little during the American régime. In January, 1803, however, Charles Curry reported that "pigtail" tobacco was preferred. He explained that it sold for sixpence a yard and there were eleven yards to a pound. During the British régime "carrot" tobacco, so called from its shape, had been the common variety. The preference which Curry mentioned could not have been unanimous, however, for Bates ordered plug as well as pigtail tobacco.

Merchants left a great deal to the judgment of the wholesaler when they ordered merchandise. Among other articles, Frederick Bates asked Robison and Martin to send him simply three dozen men's shoes, "best kind," and two dozen ladies' slippers, "fashionable." Charles Curry, after ordering large quantities of raisins, figs, prunes, and almonds, wrote that "the Remainder Mr. Wm. Robison Will recalect as he nows what I want as well as I dow."

Robison and Martin seem to have enjoyed the confidence of many of the people of Detroit. Elijah Brush ordered all sorts of goods from the firm. Although there were several silversmiths in Detroit, he sent to them at Albany for a dozen dessert spoons and a dozen teaspoons engraved with his initials. He explained his boycott of the local artisans thus: "if you give a Silver Smith in this Country Silver to work you'll never get either work or Silver. I know this by Experience."

Apparently this New England lawyer was making money. During the summer a *calèche* which he had ordered from Robison and Martin was delivered to him.[8] He probably called it a shay.

Merchants' accounts contain records of few goods for children except clothing and arithmetic and spelling books. Toys, it seems, were not part of their stock. One may be sure, however, that the girls had dolls of some sort, and that the boys had wooden swords and guns, and probably wooden whistles and other playthings which could be made at home. The first consignment of toys shipped into the region of Detroit seems to have arrived in 1803. Although it was directed to Moses David at Sandwich, perhaps a part of it was intended for the Detroit

[8] The *calèche* or *calash* was a light two-wheeled vehicle with a folding top. Only the wealthier people of Detroit owned them. The farmers used their heavier two-wheeled carts for hauling produce to market and for carrying their families to church.

trade. We may be certain that, if children of Detroit saw these toys in the hands of their friends and relatives on the other side of the river, there would soon be a demand which Detroit merchants would hasten to supply.

The invoice listed the following items: two and three-quarters gross of common assorted wood toys—carts, trunks, tables, knockers, chaises, cradles, coaches, cupboards, and horses; six dozen whistles, six dozen pails, three dozen wax figures in boxes, six dozen glass pictures, twelve dozen "Skreekers," nine dozen "Bellows Birds," eight dozen large trumpets, eight dozen churns, six dozen "Bullett Birds," three dozen "Bulls & Butchers," a half dozen "Aaron Bells," one dozen swords, one dozen wooden guns, three dozen whips, ten dozen lead watches, ten thousand marbles, and two thousand "Allies." This was an assortment that surely would have delighted any youngster. If some of these toys were not sold to merchants in Detroit, it is practically certain that Detroit fathers in Sandwich on business brought back some of them to boys and girls at home.

In the fall of 1803 Solomon Sibley was very pessimistic about the prospect for business in Detroit, blaming the union with Indiana for the unfavorable condition. "The disagreeable situation which the late law of Congress, authorizing the eastern district [Ohio] to enter into a state Gov't has thrown this part of the Country into," he wrote to his friend Seth Hastings, "is easier felt than described. Business of every description is fast declining and must eventually dwindle to a mere nothing unless Congress speedily interpose in our behalf." He explained the difficulty of carrying appeals to the court at Vincennes and urged the Congressman to use his influence to make Michigan a separate territory. Sibley suggested that Hastings might advocate economy as an argument since that had been used recently "as a Vehicle for carrying all measures."

Sibley expressed the opinion that territorial courts at Detroit would aid in suppressing smuggling, which he knew was pretty common. As a matter of fact, he had prosecuted two such cases recently in the Court of Common Pleas. One was against Jacques and François Lasselle, who were charged by the collector, Matthew Ernest, with bringing in, without paying duties, a consignment of merchandise worth £87 8s. from Sandwich. The jury in the September term of court found the merchants guilty and decided that the goods were forfeit to the United States. The other case was against John Gentle, who was alleged to have smuggled ten kegs of brown sugar from Sandwich.

John Askin, on the other hand, was optimistic about the future of Detroit. Having heard that commissioners would soon arrive to take testimony on land claims on the American side of the river, he warned Alexander Henry not to "throw away" his lands there. Askin believed that the value would soon "rise much."

5

The social life of Detroit in the early part of 1803 was marked by the wedding rites of Charles Jouett and Elizabeth Dodemead. The groom was the United States Indian agent; the bride was one of the daughters of John Dodemead, tavern keeper, coroner of Wayne County, and a trustee of the town.

Zion Lodge was the only social organization in Detroit. Although nearly seven years had passed since the British had relinquished sovereignty, it was still under the jurisdiction of the Grand Lodge of Lower Canada. Since most of the members were Americans, they decided, on May 2, 1803, to apply for an American charter. Jonathan Schieffelin, whose brother Jacob was a merchant in New York, was instructed to write to the Grand Lodge of New York requesting a warrant for Zion Lodge.[9] Joseph Campau was present at this meeting. In fact, he attended pretty regularly during 1803, going also to confession on April 5, and again on May 11. Thus he kept part of his promise to Father Richard.

In May, 1803, Solomon Sibley left for Marietta to bring his wife to Detroit. They traveled up the Ohio to Pittsburgh, and from there up the Allegheny River and French Creek to Le Boeuf, the head of navigation. The journey from Le Boeuf to Presqu' Isle, where they could embark for Detroit, was overland. Besides three large trunks, they brought Mrs. Sibley's piano. As Dr. William Harffy's harpsichord had been carried to the Canadian side, this was probably the only instrument of the kind in Detroit.

[9] A charter from the Grand Lodge of New York was not received until July 6, 1807, when the chapter became Zion Lodge Number 1.

The Sibleys found the trip quite fatiguing because of the hot weather and the low water in the Allegheny. After a short time in Detroit Mrs. Sibley was reported to be "pleased with the Country & its inhabitants, so far as acquainted."

In the spring of 1803 Peter Chartrand was in trouble again. Charles Curry and David Van Derhyden had him imprisoned for debt. When he petitioned the Court of Quarter Sessions for release under the poor debtors' law, the judges, after he had taken the pauper's oath, liberated him in September.

John Reed, a runaway slave belonging to a Colonel Grant of Kentucky, appeared in Detroit during the summer. After having read an advertisement promising a reward to anyone who should catch him, James May had him put in jail. Daniel Ransom provided bond for the Negro's release and had Solomon Sibley write to Colonel Grant offering to buy the man. Sibley explained that he could not be held in Detroit as a slave, but that Ransom could probably persuade him to indent himself for a term of years. The lawyer suggested that Grant would probably be willing to pay the reward, plus about fifty dollars, for goods which Reed had stolen from a merchant, and still sell the Negro cheap rather than run the risk of taking him home through the Indian country.

Father Gabriel Richard had been serving in Ste Anne's parish for five years, first as assistant to Father Levadoux and, since his departure, as pastor. To Bishop Carroll he wrote, "My flock becomes every day dearer to me." Nevertheless there were some difficulties to overcome, and some friction existed in the congregation.

The priest had alienated a number of his parishioners by attempting to suppress the practice of taking the offering by a *queteuse*. The custom, according to Father Richard, was for several families in the congregation to agree in advance to take turns in providing the *pains benits*, the holy bread for communion. On the appointed Sunday a daughter of the family presented the *pains benits* to the priest, who gave her an image of the Virgin, called La Paix, to kiss. She then collected the offering. At Christmas in 1802 Father Richard had refused to permit a girl to do this because of "her indecent dress." Although he thought that all except her relatives would approve of his decision, only one of the *marguillers* was willing to take the offering.

Father Richard tried to abolish the practice because he believed that the custom of the *queteuse* "gives to young Girles an opportunity of displaying an uncommon Luxury, which may be offensive to many people, particularly to the Protestants who are not used to have such customs in their Churches." His parishioners, however, were stubborn. On Sunday, September 11, 1803, because Father Richard refused to permit the collection by a *queteuse*, Pierre Chêne, whose daughter was to serve that day, carried his *pains benits* out of the church thirty minutes before the service began.

Finally the priest compromised. He permitted the collection by either a girl or a *marguiller*, but he urged them to accept the latter, explaining that in other parts of the United States trustees took the offering. Because they were loath to change he asked Bishop Carroll to write a pastoral letter to his congregation stating that men only should perform that duty. He also requested the Bishop to "exhort them to a more exact docility to their pastor." Father Richard informed the Bishop that Father Jean Dilhet had changed the custom at the River Raisin, where now only *marguillers* or their wives took the offering.

6

In spite of the efforts of John Williams' attorney, W. D. Powell, Jr., the young Detroiter remained in prison at Niagara. In April, 1803, Joseph Campau wrote again offering to post a bond to guarantee his nephew's appearance in court whenever it was required. Campau reported that Jacques Lasselle was able to walk, to eat heartily, and to drink. He had admitted to the merchant that he was responsible for the quarrel; nevertheless, he was going to sue John for $3,000 damages. Campau believed that under the circumstances his nephew was the one who should sue. He expressed his sympathy for Williams in his confinement and sent $200 by Captain Connelly for John's use.

According to Thomas Clark of Queenston, the magistrates would never free Williams unless he had affidavits from officials on the British side of the river to prove that Lasselle had recovered. He urged Campau to consult with John Askin, whose "strong desire to serve Mr. Williams may be very serviceable." Furthermore, Clark offered to be a surety for Williams' appearance in court, and he expressed the opinion that Thomas Dickson would no longer refuse to be a surety if Campau would make himself responsible for whatever bond the magistrates might set.

Meanwhile Williams was very uncomfortable in his cell. It became very hot in June, and as the door was opened only when his meals were brought, the air was stifling. Hoping to obtain relief, he wrote a letter to the magistrates of the Court of Quarter Sessions requesting that they devise "some plan, the most acceptable in your judgment, in order to admit Circulation of air in the room I now have the misfortune of being Confined."

Following the advice of Mr. Clark, Joseph Campau wrote to him and to Thomas Dickson asking them to do their best to procure Williams' release on bond, promising to be responsible for his nephew's appearance whenever the court should require it. Their efforts were successful, and John was released in September.

John Williams had been in Detroit only a short while when he was served with a warrant in Lasselle's damage suit against him, and the case was called for the December term of the Court of Common Pleas. Solomon Sibley presented Jacques Lasselle's complaint. He asked for $3,000 because of Lasselle's suffering and heavy medical expenses, and because he was still unable to attend to his business as a result of the wound. Elijah Brush answered by declaring that Williams had fired only in self-defense. The case was finally heard in the June term, 1804, and the jury gave a verdict for the defendant, John Williams.

CHAPTER XVI

END OF THE CUYAHOGA DREAM

TRUE to his promise to Solomon Sibley, Senator Thomas Worthington presented the memorials of the people of Wayne County to the Senate. Moreover, as chairman of the committee appointed to consider the erection of a new territory, he brought in a favorable report, which was adopted by the Senate, and his committee drew up a bill which was passed on December 6, 1803. In the House this bill was defeated by one vote, in spite of the efforts of Representative J. B. C. Lucas of Pennsylvania, chairman of the committee which reported it.

The aspirants for office in the hoped-for territory, however, were not discouraged. Solomon Sibley, Frederick Bates, James Henry, and Peter Audrain were actively seeking the position of secretary. Sibley had the support of the magistrates of Wayne County. He had asked Senator Worthington also to recommend him, but the Senator, a staunch Republican, ignored the request.

Tarleton Bates labored assiduously to muster support for his brother Frederick. He informed Frederick that Representative Lucas of Pennsylvania would speak for him, as would Senator Abraham Baldwin of Georgia, Representatives Oliver Phelps of New York, John Smilie of Pennsylvania, and others. From Detroit Samuel Tupper, contractor's agent, wrote directly to President Jefferson, recommending Bates as a young man highly regarded for his integrity and his ability. Tupper also reported that Bates' "attachment to republican measures is unquestionable."

What assistance the other two applicants expected is not known. Perhaps Audrain believed that, since he was already clerk of every governmental agency in the county and the town, he had a prior claim to the secretaryship of the territory.

On March 26, 1804, Congress provided for the opening of a

new postal route to Detroit by way of Warren and Cleveland, Ohio, the same act discontinuing the old route from Cincinnati.[1] The delivery of mail from Cincinnati had been very irregular. William Ruffin apologized to Postmaster Bates for the poor service and expressed the hope that it would be remedied by the change, which was to take effect on October 1.

John Rice Jones, attorney general of Indiana Territory, expected to be in Detroit during the summer of 1804 for a session of the territorial circuit court. He informed Solomon Sibley that Judge Henry Vanderburgh would go to the seat of Wayne County if there were any criminals in jail who should be tried. Sibley's reply is not among his papers. Whether there were criminals in prison or not, the court did not sit during the summer.

2

The Trustees of Detroit were occupied with the numerous details of providing for the health and safety of the inhabitants. At nearly every session they fined a number of citizens reported by the inspectors to be delinquent in their fire-fighting equipment. The heaviest assessment was for one's chimney "Ketching fire"—usually three dollars. These fines were the principal source of income, which, during the fiscal year 1803–04, was $137.25. The expenses of government were correspondingly low. Aside from fees paid to the various officers, the only expenditure was $15 for repairing the fire engine, and the treasurer on May 5, 1804, reported a surplus of $35.56.

In April a part of the eastern stockade and the Pontiac Gate were removed by order of Colonel Hunt. During the previous October the Board had protested against an order from the Colonel, who was then at Mackinac, to remove the lower section of this line of the palisade and to reset it so that it would fence in part of the Common and extend to the storehouse in the old shipyard. The Trustees had then asserted that such action would be contrary to the charter of the corporation, which vested in them the control of the Common, and also a violation

[1] The route from Cincinnati to Detroit had cost the Government $1,200 from July 1, 1802, to July 1, 1803, and it had produced a revenue of only $150.12. C. E. Carter, (ed.), *Territorial Papers of the United States*, VII, 156.

of an ordinance passed on April 20, 1802, prohibiting the inclosure of any part of this area.

Because the protest had been of no avail, a town meeting was convened on April 28 to determine whether or not the pickets and the gate should be replaced. Twenty-five freeholders or their proxies attended and voted thirteen to twelve against replacing them. This was a shrewd decision, for an affirmative vote would probably have resulted in a clash with the military authorities; and, besides, the citizens would surely have had to pay for the stockade if they had been permitted to rebuild it.

The annual election of officers of the corporation was held on May 7, 1804, the electors again making a clean sweep in choosing the Board. For Trustees they named Solomon Sibley, James Abbott, Henry Berthelet, Dr. Joseph Wilkinson, Jr., and Frederick Bates. Peter Audrain, as usual, was retained as secretary. The Trustees elected Sibley chairman of the Board. At their first meeting they established the rule that any member absent from the regular sessions "without a reasonable Cause" would be fined one dollar. They also directed the secretary to advertise in French and in English that after Sunday, May 13, the ordinance requiring that streets adjacent to owners' lots be swept, and yards, lanes, and alleys be cleaned would again be in effect; and that the law respecting the market, which also had been suspended during the winter, would be enforced.

On May 17 the Trustees appointed Thomas McCrae, Jr., police officer and clerk of the market.[2] His duties were detailed in an ordinance passed on the same day "to promote regularity and order, to insure Justice & fairness in the market; and for due obedience to the ordinances for the health, Safety & Cleanliness of the town." He was to have the market house repaired "in a reasonable way," to examine weights and measures, to prevent the sale of unsound meat and garden produce, to preserve order in the market, and to report to the Board all frauds or breaches of the peace.

Besides, he was instructed to "perform the duties of a police officer." At least once each fortnight he must "examine all Streets, lanes, allies, & yards, and report to this board all Viola-

---

[2] McCrae was also sheriff of Wayne County and town marshal.

tions of ordinances which may come under his observations." His remuneration for serving in this dual office was seventy-five cents "for each day he may be actually employed."

Repairs to the merchants' wharf cost the town £29 8s. To raise money to pay this bill a town meeting agreed to a head tax of twenty-five cents, the remainder to be raised by a levy on real estate. The Trustees, desiring to provide a fund for continued maintenance of the wharf, established regular rates for the use of this facility. Every vessel of twenty tons burden or more would pay a dollar and fifty cents; *bateaux*, twenty-five cents; pirogues or canoes, twelve and one-half cents. Besides, each freeholder, tenant, or head of a family desirous of filling water buckets from the wharf would pay one dollar annually in advance. This last provision was soon repealed, probably as the result of many protests.

Except for Thomas McCrae, Jr., town marshal and clerk of the market, there was no police force in Detroit. As marshal his duty was limited to collecting fines assessed by the Trustees, and his authority as clerk and police officer was confined to specific matters. Consequently, "in order to insure additional Security to the town from the Danger to be apprehended from Indians, as well as other persons, and from fire, owing to the negligence of the Inhabitants," the Board, on August 31, established the night watch.

The ordinance provided that every night, beginning on September 1, five men from a group which had already volunteered to serve, would assemble at the courthouse at nine o'clock. Under the command of a captain elected by the members of the watch they were ordered to patrol the streets of the town and to arrest "all disorderly and riotous persons," and "all persons of every description, after the hour of eleven o'clock in the evening, who cannot, or who refuse to give a Satisfactory account of themselves," and confine them in the courthouse.

Besides, if a member of the watch noticed a light in any house after eleven o'clock, he was "to enquire the Occasion thereof, lest it Should be burning without the Knowledge of the family." John Dodemead was charged with carrying out the details of the ordinance. He was to "form the Watches, prescribe the order in which they Shall Serve, and in all respects

3

The Henry and Wilkins tannery was probably the largest industry in Detroit. On January 1, 1804, there were on hand leather worth £312 1s. and hides valued at £231 12s. 6d. At the same time there were in the tanning vats about 675 cow hides and 175 skins of various kinds. The finished leather was intended for bootlegs, shoe soles, harness, and shoepacks.

During February and March merchants and individuals sent orders to Robison and Martin in Albany for goods to be delivered by water after the navigation opened. Charles Curry, besides the usual assortment of drygoods, ordered a keg of raisins, a keg of almonds, a box of figs, and twelve pounds of "sugar Candy."[3]

Elijah Brush ordered a barrel of loaf sugar, a barrel of coffee, a chest of hyson tea, and clothing for his wife and his son Edmund, now fourteen months old. For Edmund he ordered a half dozen pairs of shoes. As the only guide to the merchants in their selection Brush wrote: "my Boy has a pretty stout foot for his age."

Mrs. Brush apparently was satisfied with whatever was fashionable in clothing. Without any directions in regard to size or color her husband ordered a "fashionable Summer cloak," a "fashionable Bonnet for Summer," and a dozen pairs of lady's kidskin shoes. About the shoes he did advise the merchants that "Mrs. Brush has not a large foot."

All the women of Detroit and the vicinity must have had small feet. At any rate they preferred small shoes. Alexis Maisonville, a former clerk for John Askin, complained to Robison and Martin that shoes they had sent were too large. He informed them that "women's shoes of every description must not be too long, otherwise they will not sell here."

Two officers of the garrison, Captain John Whipple and Lieutenant Eli B. Clemson, ordered from Robison and Martin *calèches* like the one Elijah Brush had bought the previous sum-

---

[3] This is the first time that candy has appeared in any of the orders that have been examined.

mer. Captain Whipple asked them to send him also a set of plated harness.

John Williams, instead of ordering goods, made a trip to New York, where he bought tea, pepper, and coffee. He was probably purchasing on his own account, since the firm of Campau and Williams had been dissolved in November, 1803.[4] This time, without engaging in any altercations he returned to Detroit with his merchandise by way of the Hudson, the Mohawk, and Lake Erie.

The shipping season opened late in 1804. The first vessel, the *Thames*, was ordered to sail only on April 26, and others were not expected to leave before May 1. Consequently John Askin was surprised when the *Lark*, commanded by Captain Johnson, arrived in the Detroit River on April 30 from Fort Erie.

Askin, who still owned real estate on the American side of the river, heard that the inhabitants of Detroit and of the neighboring farms were alarmed by the prospect of having to buy their land from the United States Government, since few of them had either French or British deeds. As a result of a report made to Congress in 1803, land commissioners were to be sent to investigate the validity of titles to land. The more intelligent people, Askin was told, were hopeful of an equitable decision. They cited the precedent of the Vincennes region, where the same conditions had existed, and where the settlers without titles had not been dispossessed.

There was enough faith in the security of property in Detroit, so that John Askin, as agent, could sell the four small houses facing on the Common, which he had deeded to Todd and McGill. The last one, which he sold in the spring of 1804, brought only £200; but Askin thought this was a fair price, considering the dilapidated condition of the building. He was glad to be rid of these houses, for he had had to keep them occupied even though the tenants did not pay their rent regularly, in order to "prevent Rascals from taking possession of them, which is no uncommon trick among the low class of Americans."

[4] Copy of the decision of "McCrae, Audrain & Moran," arbitrators in the affairs of the partnership, which they found "dissolved & nul," November 26, 1803, Sibley Papers, Burton Hist. Coll.

Robert and Barent Sanders, two young merchants from Albany who arrived at Detroit early in June, found the officers at the Fort and the businessmen in the town very friendly. Although at first the brothers had difficulty in finding a vacant store in which to display their wares, when they began to trade, business was brisk. During the first two days they sold $300 worth of goods at about 50 per cent profit.

Barent wrote to his father that money was very scarce, but that the paymaster was expected any day with $55,000 for Detroit and Mackinac. The young man expressed the opinion that the trip to Detroit would be of great value to the Sanders establishment at Albany. He was sure that a store at Detroit would pay better than the one at home, for, he explained, "the merchants here sell at enormous profits, and no people in the globe for their property live more extravigant."

A month later the brothers sailed for Mackinac with the paymaster, after having sent about £900 worth of furs to their father, and cash with which to buy more merchandise. They were very enthusiastic about their prospects in Detroit.

4

Early in 1804 Father Richard asked permission of Bishop Carroll for Father Jean Dilhet to remove from the River Raisin to Detroit. Father Dilhet, as Father Richard had previously reported to the Bishop, was "a great reformer." He had abolished the custom of the *queteuse*, and he had refused baptism to the children of parents who failed to pay the tithe. Consequently, as the Detroit priest expressed it, he had been "abused by some of his parishioners."

The people on the River Raisin, according to Father Richard, were not worthy of a man so able and so learned as Father Dilhet, who would be very useful at Detroit as an assistant. Besides, Father Dilhet wanted to teach Latin to some boys who might prepare for the priesthood.[5] Father Richard was wholly in accord with this proposal for educating children, and so he asked the Bishop's approval of Father Dilhet's project.

[5] Richard to Carroll, May 1, 1804, Letters to Carroll, 7C5, Archives of the Archbishopric of Baltimore and Washington.

Bishop Carroll consented to the removal of Father Dilhet to Detroit. Since the *habitants* at River Raisin were either unable or unwilling to support a priest, he decided that they should have none, but he requested Father Richard to try to visit them two or three times a year. The Bishop warned the Detroit priest that because Father Dilhet was the older, he might try to assume more authority than an assistant should and thus endanger the peace of the congregation.

At the same time Bishop Carroll expressed his hearty approval of Richard's putting a stop to the taking of offerings in church by girls. Nevertheless, he cautioned the priest not to act hastily. "Peace and a good understanding between a pastor and his flock," he wrote, "are so essential to the increase of piety and religion, that it is better to suffer inconvenience, & even the danger of some abuses not very grievous, than to raise animosities & dissensions."

The Bishop enclosed the pastoral letter which Father Richard had requested. In it he informed the parishioners that the Pope had recommended uniformity of practice in the churches throughout the United States; and so he directed that offerings henceforth be taken only by men. This letter was read to the congregation at the close of the service on November 25, 1804.

Bishop Carroll apparently gave his consent to the establishing of what Father Dilhet called "un collège ou école clericale." Father Richard selected eight or ten boys between the ages of nine and fifteen as the most promising. Even so, few of them could read well, and they scarcely knew how to write. No fees were charged these pupils whose parents were so poor that they could barely afford to provide paper and ink.

In spite of these unfavorable circumstances, Father Dilhet began in October to teach a class of nine boys in rooms that had been especially prepared in the rectory. Besides Latin, he taught them geography, history of religion, sacred music, and the practice of prayer. Perhaps Father Richard also took a hand in teaching these boys. Certainly he was greatly interested in their progress.[6]

[6] Richard to Carroll, March 14, 1805, 7C8, *ibid.*
Sister Mary Rosalita, *Education in Detroit prior to 1850*, p. 65, states that Richard and Dilhet also had a school for girls in 1804. There is no mention of such a school either in Dilhet, État de l'Église, or in Richard's letters to Carroll, during 1804 and 1805.

Other schools at this time were being conducted by John Burrell, M. La Serrières, a "french Gentleman," John Goff, and Matthew Donovan. Donovan, who was reputed to be a classical scholar, had as a pupil in Latin John Askin's youngest son, Alexander. When the Askin family crossed the river to their new home, Strabane, Aleck, as his father called him, remained in Detroit with his brother-in-law, Elijah Brush, to learn Latin so that he might begin the study of law with Mr. Brush.

In the summer of 1804 Donovan reported to John Askin: "I am not ashamed of the progress that Masr. Alick has made while under my care & Tuition and be assured Sir, that I will not be in the least slack or Remiss in advancing him in every degree to the utmost in my power. Masr. Alick has a pretty collection of Books, but unhappily lost his Grammar which is the Key & Instrument to all the Authors. Perhaps you could procure him one Soon."

In the fall of the year the formal education of Isaac Burnett, youngest of the three brothers who had spent a number of years under Detroit schoolmasters, was completed. James, the eldest, informed their father that he could find a place for Isaac, who was old enough to be "put out" to work.

John Burnett, who was James May's indentured clerk, had got himself into so much trouble that his employer decided to send him home. First, however, he wrote to the boy's father explaining the situation. William Burnett was sorry that John had caused May so much worry, and chagrined to hear that his son was "such a vicious character as you represent him to be." He asked May to keep him until his brother James could find a new position for him "upon the other side, if possible." By this means his father hoped to separate him from his evil companions in Detroit.

5

At various times during 1804 there were three Protestant ministers in Detroit. In the spring the Reverend Daniel Freeman, "a venerable-looking man," a local preacher of the Methodist Church, crossed from Canada and remained a few days. He preached only once. A church historian asserts that, as a result of this sermon, "Mrs. Marie C. McCarty [Maria Audrain] received such convictions for sin as never left her until she was converted some years later."[7]

Early in August the Reverend David Bacon and his family, including a baby that had been born at Mackinac on July 4, arrived at Detroit. Ordered by the Missionary Board to return to Connecticut, Mr. Bacon apparently intended to continue his journey; but, because of illness, he remained until the middle of September. His dream of civilizing and Christianizing the Indians had been shattered at L'Arbre Croche and at Mackinac, and the familiar faces in Detroit must have recalled to mind his failure there, too.

While the missionary was waiting for an opportunity to return East, a young and energetic Methodist circuit rider, the Reverend Nathan Bangs, arrived in town. He had recently been appointed to the River Thames circuit in Upper Canada, and intended to include Detroit among his preaching points. Mr. Bacon told him that he had previously preached in Detroit until only a few children came to his meetings. The discouraged missionary added: "if you can succeed, which I very much doubt, I shall rejoice."

Mr. Bangs preached only three times in Detroit. Twice he had large audiences. About his second visit he told the following story:

> I preached in the old council house on a week-day evening. The house was pretty well filled with hearers. While preaching there arose a terrible thunderstorm; the lightning flashed, the thunder rolled through the heavens with awful noise. But I kept on preaching. I was afterwards informed that two young men sat trembling, fearing that God was about to strike them dead for what they had done, as they had put powder into the candles in the expectation that they would burn down to the powder and explode during the sermon. They were disappointed, as I concluded my sermon and closed the meeting without any accident, though they said when I took up the candle to see to read my hymn, they feared the explosion would take place and burn my eyes.

On his third visit, which occurred in the fall of 1804, only a few children came to hear him preach. To the Reverend Mr. Bangs, "Detroit, at that time, seemed to be a most abandoned place." Consequently, "no one appearing to take any interest in hearing the gospel preached there, our missionary shook off

---

[7] Elijah H. Pilcher, *Protestantism in Michigan: Being a Special History of the Methodist Episcopal Church and Incidentally of Other Denominations* (Detroit, 1878), p. 11.

the dust of his feet as a testimony against them, and took his departure from them,"[8] never, apparently, to return.

Before this occurred the Reverend Mr. Bacon and his family had probably left Detroit. For want of a better conveyance they packed their worldly belongings and some provisions into a canoe and paddled down the river and along the shore of Lake Erie to Cleveland, whence they returned to Connecticut.[9]

6

Although the House of Representatives had refused to pass the Senate bill for dividing Indiana Territory, the two Houses passed a law which provided for establishing a land office at Detroit. The act required all persons in the region who had grants from the French or the British Government, or from Congress, to deliver to the register of the land office a notice of their claims with a plot of the tract, and the grant, deed, or other evidence of ownership, on or before January 1, 1805. The register and the receiver of public moneys were to serve as a board of commissioners to hear the claims and to make decisions, which they would then lay before Congress. George Hoffman, a Virginian, was sent to Detroit as register; Frederick Bates was appointed receiver of public moneys.

When the terms of the law were known, the people of Detroit were dismayed. Few of them could show deeds from the French or the British Government, and Congress had made no grants. Consequently, a memorial addressed to the Senate and the House was drawn up and signed. The petitioners protested against the requirement of original deeds and of a "plot." They asserted that changes of government and the consequent carrying away of records made compliance with the first stipulation impossible; and that plots could not be filed because surveys had never been made. As the best title to their holdings, they cited the provision of Jay's Treaty, which guaranteed the right to private property.

Persuaded of the necessity of having an agent in Washington to present their views to Congress, property owners agreed to

[8] Nathan Bangs, *A History of the Methodist Episcopal Church* (New York), II, 170.

[9] Mr. Bacon never visited Detroit again. His later career is sketched by M. M. Quaife in "Detroit Biographies, David Bacon," *Burton Hist. Coll. Leaf.*, IX, no. 3.

raise a fund of a thousand dollars to pay the expenses of Solomon Sibley to act for them. He left during December, carrying with him the memorial on land claims.

Gradually evidences of ownership were deposited with commissioners Bates and Hoffman. The people delayed, as was their custom, until almost the last minute, with the result that a great number of documents were delivered between Christmas and the New Year. Peter Audrain, who was invaluable as a translator of the French papers, served as clerk to the Commissioners.

Another petition requesting that Indiana Territory be divided had been circulated during October after a town meeting had been held to arouse interest. It was presented to the Senate by Senator Worthington on December 5, and the next day he filed a petition from the Democratic Republicans of Wayne County urging the necessity of separation.

Solomon Sibley must have convinced Judge Henry Vanderburgh that a session of the Circuit Court should be held in Detroit, for the Judge, accompanied by Attorney General John Rice Jones, arrived late in October, 1804. The only case known to have been decided by the Court was the suit of Marie Françoise Huc Eberts for separation from her husband. Her lawyer, Solomon Sibley, presented her complaint, in which she asserted that the Doctor had "an ungovernable, cruel and unrelenting temper and disposition"; that he had not provided her and their seven children with the necessities and conveniences of life; and that on several occasions he had beaten her without cause. The Court awarded Mrs. Eberts legal separation, and she went to Montreal to live with relatives.

As divorces were almost unheard of in Detroit, the Eberts case must have occasioned a great deal of talk in the community. Another event of a happier nature must also have been the topic of local conversation, even though it took place out of town; for the most important social affair of Detroit in the fall of 1804 occurred in Chicago. There, during November, were married James Abbott, merchant of Detroit, and Sarah Whistler, daughter of Captain John Whistler, commandant of Fort Dearborn, who had formerly been stationed at Detroit. Another Detroiter, John Kinzie, now a trader in Chicago and a justice of the peace, performed the ceremony. After the wedding the young couple made their honeymoon journey on horse back over the old Sauk Trail to Detroit.[10]

7

The winter of 1804–05 was "uncommonly severe." In December the river was frozen from shore to shore so that people could cross on foot. A few warm days, however, weakened the ice. Elijah Brush, who was walking over to visit his father-in-law, John Askin, found himself on a sheet of ice that had "separated from the land and he had like to be lost." Fortunately he was able to reach the American side again in safety. Cold weather soon returned, and John Askin reported that "Horses and Slays" crossed the river during the whole month of January.

Winter was usually a dreary season for Askin. Because of poor health he remained indoors until the weather became warm. This year, however, he had hope to cheer him in his winter seclusion. At last he expected the dream of the Cuyahoga Associates to come true. The old merchant heard that the United States Government had granted the inhabitants of New London, Connecticut, a preëmption right to half a million acres of land on the south shore of Lake Erie as compensation for their losses when the town was burned by the enemy during the Revolutionary War.[11]

Askin learned also that a Major William Dean, representing the grantees, had come to Detroit to purchase the Indian title. He was reported to have offered the Cuyahoga Associates $10,000 if they would assemble the chiefs and induce them to sign a treaty. The old merchant thought this was not enough. He decided that $10,000 for the Indians and $10,000 for each associate would be a fair return for relinquishing title to the land.

John Askin's dream began to fade when months passed without a direct offer from Major Dean. To protect his partners Askin persuaded the Indians not to go to the Cuyahoga River to make a treaty; but they did assemble late in June at Fort Industry, near the mouth of the Maumee River.

[10] Now U. S. Route 112.
[11] This part of the Western Reserve was later known as the "Firelands."

The only concession Askin had been able to gain from the chiefs was the promise that they would not sell without consulting Elijah Brush, who accompanied them as agent of the Associates.

The Detroit lawyer soon discovered that he was powerless to influence the Indians. Charles Jouett, acting as commissioner for the United States, purchased the 500,000 acres for the Connecticut Land Company for $4,000 cash, $2,000 a year for six years, and $1,000 annually thereafter, the Indians retaining the right to hunt and fish on the tract. On July 4, 1805, the treaty was signed by a number of chiefs, including Nigig (Little Otter), Big Bowl, and Ogonse for the Ottawa; Little Bear and Tonguish for the Chippewa; Tarhee (the Crane), Walk-in-Water, Leather Lips, and Adam Brown for the Wyandots; and Blue Jacket for the Shawnee. Charles Jouett signed for the Government, and William Dean for the Connecticut Company. Whittmore Knaggs, a resident of Detroit, put his name to the document as an interpreter. Witnesses were Israel Ruland, the only Cuyahoga Associate living on the American side of the river, and Elijah Brush.[12]

Brush returned to Detroit on July 7, tired and angry. He reported to John Askin that Jouett had opposed him on every point, behaving "more like a Savage than a Christian." The only financial return to the Associates was $600, which Brush got at the treaty—"all that could be had."

[12] A signed copy of the treaty is in the Burton Historical Collection.

CHAPTER XVII

HOPE FOR BETTER DAYS[1]

ON JANUARY 11, 1805, an act to divide Indiana Territory was approved by President Jefferson. The new territory was called Michigan. Its boundaries were practically the same as those of Wayne County, as established by Governor Harrison's proclamation, except that the western line passed north and south through the middle of Lake Michigan instead of being drawn to touch its most westerly point. The law set July 1, 1805, as the birthday of the territory and made Detroit the capital.

News of the passage of this act and other communications from the States probably reached Detroit more quickly now than previously, for the postal service from Cleveland was better than it had been by the former route from Cincinnati. Mail was usually delivered once a week, the carrier using "a Coasting Vessel" for the journey during the summer and the fall. Although Postmaster General Gideon Granger held the opinion that this means of transportation was better than the route "thro' the Wilderness," he was willing to issue other instructions if Postmaster Bates would make suggestions to improve the service.

Granger expressed the hope that during the winter the carrier, taking the overland trail, would arrive on Sunday and leave the same day. Explaining that poor roads, numerous streams, and inclement weather made this route difficult, he promised that, when summer came, the mail would arrive on Wednesday and leave on Thursday morning.

Besides being postmaster, which probably took little of his time, Frederick Bates was also a land commissioner. He and his colleague George Hoffman worked steadily at their task of hearing claims and making decisions. Early in March they

---

[1] The motto of Detroit is *Speramus meliora. Resurget cineribus.* "We hope for better days. It will arise from the ashes."

completed the job; but Peter Audrain, clerk, interpreter, and translator, was still busy making transcripts. Nevertheless, they expected to forward their report in June. Their calculations were completely upset, however, when they received a new law on land claims, supplemental to the one under which they were acting.

This law permitted persons who were in actual possession of improved land on July 1, 1796, to present evidence of that fact, and it extended the time for filing claims until November 1, 1805. The new law made it necessary that the commissioners reopen their office to claimants. As Bates phrased it, their work was "but *half performed.*"

Solomon Sibley, who had been lobbying for the new land law, was in Washington when the list of officers for Michigan Territory was published. His name was not among them. He wrote immediately to Elijah Brush to inform him that General William Hull of Massachusetts had been appointed governor; Stanley Griswold of New Hampshire, secretary; and Samuel Huntington of Ohio, Augustus B. Woodward of Washington, and Frederick Bates of Detroit, judges.

Bates first learned of his appointment when he saw his name in a newspaper. He was very happy to be a judge, "an honorable and a lucrative" office, in his estimation. When he received his commission on May 27, he addressed a note of acceptance and thanks to James Madison, Secretary of State. At the same time he wrote to Secretary Gallatin asking that he be permitted to continue to serve as land commissioner, since there was still a great deal of work remaining to be done. Bates had earlier decided to close his store; now he resigned his position as postmaster, recommending George Hoffman as his successor. Both resignation and recommendation were accepted. Hoffman was named postmaster on July 29.

President Jefferson's appointment of Frederick Bates to the territorial bench was certainly a wise one. The young Virginian, who had been a resident of Detroit for more than six years, knew the people and their problems. Besides, he had studied law in Goochland County, Virginia, where, as deputy clerk, he had won the approbation of the clerk, the bench, and the bar. In addition, Bates had continued to read law after his arrival at Detroit.

The announcement of the names of the officers of the new territory dashed the hopes of the other local aspirants. Charles Jouett, Indian agent at Detroit, had been very eager to be governor. He had mustered all the influence he could command, and at one time he had been quite certain that he would be chosen. When he learned that Hull had been appointed, he declared that only his Virginia origin had deprived him of the office, and that the President had named a Massachusetts man solely for political reasons.

Frederick Bates thought that Jouett was meddling too much in local politics. He accused the Indian agent of trying to effect the removal of Matthew Ernest, collector of customs, so that Jouett's brother-in-law, Dr. Joseph Wilkinson, Jr., might have the position.[2] The Indian agent denied the charge. As a matter of fact, Ernest was removed in June, 1805, "for delinquency,"[3] and Wilkinson was appointed to his place.

The Board of Trustees held monthly meetings during the winter and spring of 1805. No important ordinances were enacted, but numerous inhabitants were fined for infractions of the fire regulations. In March James Dodemead was appointed to succeed Dr. William McD. Scott as "director of the Engine," and the treasurer was authorized to pay $15 for repairing it. When Isaac Bissell was charged with carrying "fire uncovered thro the Streets," contrary to an ordinance of September, 1803, the offense was considered serious enough to require the calling of a special meeting of the Board, which Bissell was ordered to attend. After several witnesses had testified against him, he was found guilty and fined.

At the annual election of May 6 the voters chose James Abbott, Jr., Joseph Wilkinson, Jr., Frederick Bates, Dr. William Brown, and John Williams trustees. Dr. Wilkinson was elected chairman by the Board; Peter Audrain, secretary; and John Conner, marshal, clerk of the market, and police officer.

The Trustees appointed Elijah Brush and Thomas Jones fire inspectors. They were instructed to make their rounds once each week instead of twice a month, as had formerly been

---

[2] Wilkinson had married Alice Dodemead, sister of Jouett's wife.
[3] Gallatin to Jefferson, November 25, 1806, Henry Adams (ed.), *The Writings of Albert Gallatin* (Philadelphia, 1879), I, 321.
Ernest's accounts were short $7457.77.

the practice, and the Trustees directed Abraham Cook and Conrad Seek to visit the suburbs above and below the town and to report any fire hazards they might find.

2

In 1805 Henry Berthelet was one of the leading businessmen of the town. Besides his store and his ventures in the Indian trade, he had "large tanneries and establishments for manufacturing Pot and Pearl Ashes &c."[4] Berthelet also had a shoemaker in his employ.

Navigation on the Detroit River for the season of 1805 began on March 31. John Askin, at home on the Canadian side of the river, saw Angus Mackintosh's "small vessel" sailing up, bound for the River Thames, and recorded the fact in his diary. The old merchant knew every ship on the Upper Lakes. He watched them as they passed his house and jotted down their names. The *Montreal*, the *General Hunter*, the *Nancy*, the *Contractor*, the *Caledonia*, the *Saguinah*, the *Maria*, the *Charlotte*, and the *Adams* passed his farm during April and May.

Captain Henry Brevoort was still master of the brig *Adams* and commodore of the United States Navy on the Upper Lakes. The other naval vessel, the schooner *Tracy*, was captained by Peter Curry. Besides carrying troops and supplies in the Government service, these vessels carried also merchants' goods at commercial rates, when there was room for extra cargo. Thus the quartermaster general managed thriftily so that even warships partially paid their way.

On April 19 John Askin heard that the *Adams* was sailing for Presqu' Isle with Colonel Thomas Hunt, commandant at Detroit, and a large part of the garrison. All day long he watched the wharf across the river; the *Adams* remained at her mooring. Instead of sailing down the river, the *Adams* sailed up for Mackinac a week later. It was probably during the early part of May that the Colonel and some of the troops did embark, leaving Captain Samuel T. Dyson in command of the depleted garrison.

[4] A copy of Berthelet's sworn Bill of Complaint in Chancery Court, Michigan Territory, November 19, 1833. Henry Berthelet Papers, Burton Hist. Coll.

3

The preparatory school conducted by Father Dilhet did not prosper. Father Richard reported that they had had "great difficulties and oppositions." The greatest difficulty was the lack of pupils. The village priest expected to find some recruits in the school of M. La Serrières; but he was disappointed, soon discovering that they could hope to have "but a few of his pupils for the Clerical State." In the spring of 1805 there were only four students, but Father Richard thought they were "Learning pretty well."

Another difficulty which appeared imminent was that of finding priests to succeed Fathers Richard and Dilhet, who would carry on this educational experiment in spite of discouragements. For Father J. A. Emery, superior general of the Sulpicians, had directed all émigré priests of the order to return to France in 1802. Since Napoleon had made peace with the Catholic Church by the Concordat of 1801, the superior general wanted them to return to their native land. Bishop Carroll begged him to permit them to remain and carry on the good work which they were doing in America. Father Emery acquiesced for a time, but in 1805 he issued a second order. Father Richard, feeling that he and his assistant should obey, asked the Bishop to send a successor to Detroit. If the two priests left, there would probably be no school.

In June, 1805, there was a jubilee celebration at Ste Anne's Church. The faithful flocked to Detroit, even from distant settlements; and the town was filled with people. Special services were held daily. On the morning of June 11 Fathers Richard and Dilhet were celebrating Mass when a messenger brought word that fire had broken out in the town and that three houses were already consumed. Father Richard immediately left the church. Father Dilhet continued to carry on the service, assisted by the *chantre*. When they had finished, the priest and the parishioners hastily removed the vestments and the sacred utensils of the church to a place of safety.

The fire had begun in John Harvey's stable in the western part of the town. According to local tradition, one of Harvey's employees, perhaps the luckless Peter Chartrand, was responsible. A live coal carelessly knocked from his pipe into a pile of hay was said to have set off the conflagration. In a few moments the stable was a blazing torch, and a light wind blowing from the southwest carried the flames to adjacent buildings.

Robert Munro, Indian storekeeper, was in the Government "factory" just opposite the stable. Before any alarm had been given Munro saw the flames burst through the doors and windows of the building. Sensing the imminence of catastrophe, he hastily removed the records and most of the Government goods to the safety of the Common. The Citadel, which was close by on the west, was soon engulfed in flames.

Doubtless James Dodemead and his assistants brought the fire engine into action as soon as possible, and soldiers from the Fort joined the inhabitants to fight the fire. One engine, however, could make little headway against the roaring inferno; and the small garrison now stationed at the Fort was insufficient to resist the relentless march of the flames.

From his home across the river John Askin saw the fire spreading from house to house. Calling his sons and his *engagés* together, he embarked them upon his small ship, the *Surprise*, and sent them to help fight the fire. It was soon evident, however, that the old town was doomed. There was nothing the distracted inhabitants could do but carry as many of their personal belongings as time permitted to the open ground of the Common or load them into boats and canoes on the river.

The flames leaped the narrow streets, embracing in their deadly grip the tinder-dry buildings crowded one against the other. To spectators on the river or upon the ramparts of Fort Lernoult the town seemed to have become a single monstrous torch. The "impenetrable column of smoke and flame ... wafted by the current of air thro' the north and south streets, streamed to a great distance beyond the limits of the houses." One spectator, with understandable exaggeration, described the scene as "at once sublime and painful, exceeding in awful grandeur perhaps almost any spectacle of the kind which has happened since the world began."

By early afternoon Detroit had been reduced to a bed of glowing embers, from which projected here and there naked chimneys of stone or brick. Not a building within the pickets was left standing except the old blockhouse in the extreme southwest corner of the town. Fort Lernoult and the buildings in the old shipyard, a little to the east of the stockade and near the river bank, were unharmed. In spite of the great loss of property no one was killed. Only two persons were seriously injured: one, "a poor woman"; the other, a child who was crippled.

The people were stunned by the suddenness and the extent of the catastrophe. All of them had lost their homes. Many had had to abandon household goods. Some of the merchants had seen their stocks of merchandise or furs consumed in a trice. Quantities of provisions, too, were destroyed. To meet the pressing need for food and shelter, farmers on both sides of the river shared the contents of their limited larders with the hungry and found places in their small houses for some of the homeless. Others had to spend the first night without shelter on the Common. During the next few days, however, they erected "bowers" of branches there and beside the River Road. Nevertheless, in spite of neighborly coöperation, provisions were scarce, and prices were high.

4

A few days after the fire the distressed inhabitants held a meeting in Macomb's orchard and appointed a committee to draw up a petition for financial assistance and to send copies of it to various parts of the United States. They wanted to begin to build their houses; but, since Vincennes, the capital of Indiana, was far away and since the government of Michigan Territory had not yet begun to function, there was no authority at hand to formulate a plan of action. Dissension arose regarding the proper steps to take for rebuilding the town. Some were willing to await the arrival of the new governor; others, impatient of delay, began to erect houses on their former lots. Still others wanted to lay out a new town on the plan of the old one, with the Common included.

Judge Frederick Bates was the only officer of the new territory on the ground. He urged the people to await the arrival of the other officials before taking definite action. The first to reach Detroit was Judge Augustus Brevoort Woodward, who arrived on Sunday, June 30. Woodward's office and his friendship with President Jefferson gave him prestige in the Territory, and his own imperious nature demanded respect. Although neither he nor Bates had any authority, not having taken their oaths of office, they addressed a meeting of the inhabitants who had met on July 1 to plan for immediate action in rebuilding the town. The judges urged the people to await the arrival of the Governor, assuring them that all possible measures would speedily be taken for their relief. The counsel of the judges prevailed, and the people agreed to a fortnight's delay.

While this meeting was in session, Governor Hull was approaching the site of Detroit by water. He was accompanied by his wife; his son, Abraham F. Hull; two of his daughters, Ann and Maria; his secretary, Elisha Avery; and Stanley Griswold, Secretary of Michigan Territory. The Governor had come from his home in Massachusetts by way of Albany, where he took the oath of office before Vice-President George Clinton. He landed at Detroit in the evening of July 1.

Governor Hull was surprised and shocked to find his intended capital in ruins, and the inhabitants encamped round about. Like many of them, he could find no lodgings near by; but Matthew Ernest entertained him for a week in his home at Spring Wells, below Detroit, until he found quarters in a farmer's house about a mile above the ruins.

Governor Hull wasted no time in lamentations over the destruction of Detroit, but immediately set the machinery of the new territory in motion. On the day after his arrival he administered oaths of office to Judges Woodward and Bates and to Secretary Griswold, "in the presence of a number of Citizens who assembled on the occasion."[5] Captain Dyson, commandant at the Fort, had salvos of artillery fired to mark the birth of Michigan Territory. Fortunately for the participants in this outdoor ceremony, the weather was "fair & pleasant."

The Governor and the two judges, who together constituted the legislature, at once convened and prepared plans for rebuilding the town. They engaged Thomas Smith, surveyor, formerly a resident of Detroit, but now living in Canada, to lay out a new town according to their design, which was similar to

[5] Hull to Madison, August 3, 1805, *Mich. Pio. and Hist. Soc. Coll.*, XXXI, 523.
Samuel Huntington of Ohio was appointed judge for Michigan Territory, but he declined the position. William Sprigg, also of Ohio, likewise rejected an appointment. Consequently there were only two judges at first instead of three. C. E. Carter (ed.), *Territorial Papers of the United States*, X, 12.

that of Washington.[6] Judge Woodward, who admired the scheme adopted for the national capital, was the author of this plan.

In spite of the pressure of work to be done, the people found time and means to celebrate the Fourth of July in an appropriate fashion. On that day John Askin heard the firing of cannon and other sounds of the celebration "long after night."

On July 8 Governor Hull called the people together and delivered an address. First, he expressed his sympathy for their losses in the recent catastrophe. Then he assured them that they would be fully remunerated "by the generous bounty" of their fellow citizens in the States, by a liberal policy of Congress toward them, and by the "Judicious and enlarged plan" for rebuilding the town.[7] He promised that other benefits would follow. Their new government, he declared, would guarantee to them the blessings of civil and religious liberty.

The Governor urged the people to give a ready obedience to the laws and to show a proper respect for their Government, assuring them that the new officers would labor zealously for the general welfare. Calling upon "the Supreme Ruler of human Events" for His Benediction, Governor Hull expressed the hope that the new régime might be "commenced in wisdom, conducted with virtue, and in its operation promote the happiness and prosperity of the People."

In conclusion, the Governor predicted that, if the inhabitants of Detroit would make the best use of the favorable location of the town and of the natural resources of the territory, "the most sanguine imagination could form no conception of the number of humane [sic] beings, whose happy destination will be here fixed or of the useful and magnificent Scenes which will here be displayed."[8]

---

[6] A resident of Detroit wrote: "The plan is nearly like that of the city of Washington." *National Intelligencer* (Washington), September 6, 1805.

[7] Governor Hull's expectation of relief from the states was not realized. The only contributions came from other sources: drafts amounting to $765.83, with a promise of $200 more, sent from Mackinac (David Duncan to F. Bates, J. Henry, and R. Abbott, Mackinac, June 25, 1805, Sibley Papers, Burton Hist. Coll.), and a bill of exchange for $1010 sent from Montreal. Farmer, *History of Detroit*, p. 491.

[8] *Mich. Pio. and Hist. Soc. Coll.*, XXXI, 534.
This address was translated into French and read in Ste Anne's Church. Hull to Madison, August 3, 1805, *ibid.*, p. 523.
A French version of the address in the handwriting of Peter Audrain is in the Sibley Papers, Burton Hist. Coll.

The citizens answered the Governor with a polite address in writing on July 15. They thanked him for his interest in the happiness of the people, and promised to coöperate with him and the other officers. Recalling his prediction that financial assistance would be forthcoming from their fellow citizens in the States, they expressed the hope that it would not fail. In closing they requested the territorial government to take early measures to provide means of education.

5

Governor Hull kept his promise to lay out a new town as speedily as possible. Within a month the plan began to take shape. Across the constricted area of old Detroit and across the Common beyond appeared the lines of new streets, the principal ones a hundred and twenty feet wide, with "squares" placed at intersections. Lots sixty feet wide by one hundred feet deep were staked off and offered for sale on credit to former property owners. Since the new plan took no account of their old lots, they were permitted to exchange them foot for foot for new ones and to bid for the additional area.[9] The average price offered was four cents a square foot.

Lots were sold also to those who were inhabitants of Detroit, but not landowners. Nevertheless, since all of these arrangements would be void unless they were approved by Congress, sales were made only to those who were ready to build. Even so, by September 22, according to Governor Hull, thirty houses had already been erected "on a regular plan."

The Governor was sanguine for the future. The two judges, who together with him composed the legislature, were coöperating loyally. He admired Judge Woodward for his talents, his industry, and his zeal; and he characterized Judge Bates as an intelligent young man who needed only experience to render him very useful. The people also were favorably disposed. They appreciated the industry of the territorial officers in their behalf, and apparently they were pleased by the prospect of a new and more spacious town to replace the old one, which had been crowded within a close stockade. An anonymous in-

---

[9] On July 19, 1805, owners of thirty-two lots in the old town gave their "cordial Assent and Approbation" to the plan for the redistribution of lots. *Mich. Pio. and Hist. Soc. Coll.*, XXXVI, 116.

habitant of Detroit praised the new plan because it seemed likely to "promote the health and convenience of the inhabitants as well as improve the beauty of the place."[10] Even John Askin, who certainly loved the old town which had been his home for many years, thought the change would be an improvement.

Officers and citizens were in accord, and, for the moment at least, there was no quarrel with the military authority. The garrison had been greatly reduced, and it was now, perforce, quartered in the Fort, since the Citadel had been destroyed. Consequently there was less likelihood of clashes occurring between soldiers and civilians. Besides, Captain Samuel T. Dyson, who had succeeded Colonel Thomas Hunt as commandant, was a capable and tactful officer. Governor Hull informed Secretary Dearborn that Dyson was very helpful.

The future must have appeared bright to Detroiters during the summer of 1805. Perhaps they even forgot their losses in looking forward to better days ahead. There was every reason to be hopeful. The new government for which they had petitioned so earnestly and so often was established; the officers were capable, sympathetic, active; and a new town with many beautiful features was now springing up about them. Truly, Detroit was arising from the ashes.

6

What changes had American rule effected at Detroit? The most obvious one was certainly in the sphere of government. A county divided into townships had been established, and the people had a greater voice in local affairs than had been possible under British rule. Furthermore, Detroit had been incorporated. It was governed by a Board of Trustees elected by the taxpayers, and wholly conversant with the needs of the community, the Trustees had passed ordinances providing for the health, safety, and moral welfare of the inhabitants. Moreover, in their executive and judicial capacities they zealously enforced the law.

In addition to these developments in local self government, Detroit was now the capital of Michigan Territory. Long and

---

[10] *National Intelligencer*, September 6, 1805.

earnestly the people had petitioned for a government of their own. Their prayer had finally been answered. The Governor, the legislature, and the courts were now in their midst. In the future it would not be necessary to carry an appeal six hundred miles to the territorial supreme court, or to wait two years or more for the arrival of circuit judges.

In spite of the improvement in civil government, the Fort still dominated the town from its position on the rising ground beyond Savoyard Creek; but the Citadel, which had been within the circuit of the stockade, had been destroyed by the fire, and Secretary Dearborn decided that it should not be rebuilt. All troops were to be quartered in Fort Detroit.[11]

The War Department, however, was concerned about the location of the new town. Secretary Dearborn had abandoned his earlier project of moving the Fort. Now he instructed Governor Hull to move the town upstream so that the ground between the Fort and the river would be clear. The letter probably arrived too late to affect the laying out of the new town; but Governor Hull promised to try to prevent building on that area as far as possible. In happy contrast to the quarrels of past years, amicable relations existed between the civil and the military authorities.

A second notable change resulting from the transfer of sovereignty was the partial shifting of the channels of commerce. Although there was still a considerable trade with Montreal, the imposition of tariff duties by the United States Government had compelled the merchants of Detroit to purchase in American markets. Pittsburgh, Albany, and New York became important sources of supply. One result of the duties was that American whisky replaced West Indies rum as a staple in the Indian trade, and distilleries were established in Detroit.

Nevertheless, in 1805 the fur trade, the greatest industry in the region, was still largely in the hands of the British. The great North West Company was the dominant organization. When its agent, Angus Mackintosh, moved across the river,

---

[11] Dearborn to Capt. Dyson, August 5, 1805, C. E. Carter (ed.), *Territorial Papers of the United States*, X, 27.
The Fort was henceforth to be called "Detroit." *Ibid.*

Detroit lost part of the traffic that had formerly passed over its wharves.

During the British régime Dr. Hermann Eberts was the only physician in Detroit. After the American occupation several physicians from the States came to live in the village. In addition to Dr. Eberts, four others were practicing there in 1805: Dr. William Brown, Dr. William McDowell Scott, Dr. William McCoskry, and Dr. Joseph Wilkinson, Jr.[12] The more adequate medical services which the larger number of physicians could provide and the measures taken by the Board of Trustees to keep the village clean probably improved the health of the inhabitants.

In regard to education, there seems to have been little change during the first decade of the American régime. The number of teachers increased somewhat. Perhaps there were more children in school. Nevertheless, the basic condition was unchanged—all the schools were private. Education was available only for those who could pay tuition fees.

Since a considerable number of Americans had settled in Detroit and its vicinity, the English language was certainly heard more frequently than before in the stores and in the taverns; but French was still the speech of the majority of the inhabitants. Few of these people, apparently, took the trouble to learn English; and many were unable to read or write their own language.[13] It is likely that their native insouciance was a principal reason for their illiteracy; but because of their extreme poverty education was for many a luxury beyond their means.

The American occupation made little impression upon the age-old customs of the French element. The ordinance establishing a regular market, it is true, had outlawed their Sunday morning trading; but that was the extent of legal interference with their habits. They still were free to celebrate numerous saints' days and other religious fêtes; and Ste Anne's Church was still the center of their social life. The village priests, Fathers Levadoux and Richard, had labored earnestly to make

[12] Dr. Eberts moved across the river after the fire.

[13] Of 179 Frenchmen whose names were attached to the petition to Congress, March 20, 1803, 50 made their marks. Every American and every Englishman signed his name.

loyal Americans of their French-speaking parishioners. The extent of their success in this endeavor is difficult to measure; but the *habitants* were apparently satisfied with the new régime. So long as accustomed practices were not interfered with, they were happy; and the United States Government had not tried to change their traditional way of living.

In religious activities no change had occurred as a result of the American occupation except that the priests were now directed from Baltimore instead of from Quebec. They were still French, however. Both Father Richard and his assistant, Father Dilhet, were preparing to return to their native land. Father Dilhet had aroused hostility among the parishioners in Detroit as he had previously done in the River Raisin Settlement. When he departed for Baltimore on October 14, 1805, he left Father Richard alone to face a group of hostile *marguillers*. On some pretext or other they filed suit against the Curé. The court issued a writ which Father Richard declared was "grounded only upon talk and calumniatory report."[14] However baseless the charges may have been, the writ forced Father Richard to change his plans for leaving the town at that time. In fact, he remained in Detroit until his death. Thus the lawsuit was the means of keeping Father Richard in Detroit, where he gave many years of devoted service as a leader in religious and civic activities.

Although the influx of Americans must have increased the number of people in Detroit who were nominally Protestant, no effort had been made to organize a church. Perhaps the variety of denominations to which these people had at one time belonged made such an establishment impractical. Nevertheless, the treatment which had been accorded to the several Protestant preachers who had visited Detroit would indicate rather a lack of interest in organized religion. More than ten years were to elapse before the Reverend John Monteith, a Presbyterian, became the first resident minister in Detroit.[15]

Zion Lodge was still the only fraternal organization. In spite of applications to the Grand Lodge of New York, it had

---

[14] Richard to Carroll, September 10, 1805, Letters to Carroll, 7C9, Archives of the Archbishopric of Baltimore and Washington.

[15] Mr. Monteith preached for the first time in Detroit on June 30, 1816. He was supported by a nondenominational body, the "First Evangelic Society of Detroit."

not been able to acquire an American charter. Although the Grand Lodge of Lower Canada retained jurisdiction, it had become American in membership. Moreover, in addition to the British element, which had formerly constituted the entire brotherhood, and Americans from the States, who were now the majority, some French-speaking citizens were being initiated. Following the lead of Joseph Campau and Gabriel Godfroy, half a dozen others had entered the order by 1805. Thus Zion Lodge was helping to unify and Americanize the dissonant elements in Detroit.

There were other factors, too, which were assisting in this dual process: the slow but continuous influx of Americans from the States; intermarriage of the newcomers with natives of the town; an improved postal service; commercial relations with other American cities; the presence of territorial officers; and the necessity of appealing to the United States Government for attention to local concerns.

In 1805, after a decade of American rule, Detroit was still predominantly French in speech, in manners, and in point of view; to a certain extent, it was British in sentiment; but potent influences were at work which would make it eventually a truly American city.

BIBLIOGRAPHICAL ESSAY

MANUSCRIPTS were the principal source of materials for this book. By far the greatest number were found in the Burton Historical Collection of the Detroit Public Library. Other important holders of papers dealing with the history of Detroit from 1796 to 1805 are the Michigan Historical Collections, the William L. Clements Library, and the Legal Research Library on the campus of the University of Michigan; the Historical Society of Pennsylvania in Philadelphia; the Archives of the Archbishopric of Detroit; the Archives of the Archbishopric of Baltimore and Washington, in Baltimore; and the Missouri Historical Society, in St. Louis.

The manuscripts in these depositories provided a pretty complete story of the first decade of the American régime in Detroit. Some of them were particularly useful as sources for special subjects. For instance, the John Askin Papers in the Burton Historical Collection, including letters, diaries, journals, and ledgers, are indispensable for the study of commercial activities. John Askin, one of the most substantial merchants in the town, had widespread interests in the fur trade. He also kept a retail store, dealt in lumber, bricks, and farm produce, had a farm, gristmills, and several ships. The great volume of his papers which have been preserved contain almost a day-by-day account of the business life of Detroit.

Other manuscripts which contributed valuable information about commercial practices were the papers of Joseph Campau, John R. Williams, Solomon Sibley, Angus Mackintosh, and James May in the Burton Collection. The rise of Joseph Campau, a young merchant when the Americans occupied Detroit, is reflected in his correspondence and business accounts. Before his death he was accounted the richest man in Michigan. His nephew and sometime partner, John R. Williams, was almost as successful as his uncle. Williams' papers for this period show his great attachment to Detroit. The story of his duel and subsequent imprisonment is contained in correspondence between John and his uncle. Many letters written in English several years before the duel disprove the legend that Williams learned to write English in prison. Some of his papers are in the Michigan Historical Collections in Ann Arbor.

Solomon Sibley, a New England lawyer who established himself in Detroit in 1798, was the sort of man in whom the historian delights—he apparently never discarded a scrap of paper with writing on it. In the dozens of boxes which contain his manuscripts there are letters and all sorts of important legal and commercial documents—and receipted bills, on odd bits of paper, for games of billiards played at Dodemead's tavern and for the ale he drank there. An attorney for James Henry and other local merchants, Sibley looked after their legal affairs and filed many of their papers with his.

Angus Mackintosh, agent of the great North West Company, wrote numerous letters to his principals, which contain many details about business activities at Detroit. His letter books in the Burton Historical Collection are photostats of the originals in the possession of Mr. George F. Macdonald of Windsor, Ontario.

James May was a shipowner, merchant, boardinghouse keeper, auctioneer, and landowner. His account books and ledgers contain innumerable entries of business transactions, some of them providing answers to century-old questions about Detroit history. For instance: Was Father Richard's printing press the first one in Detroit? May's Day Book, 1798–1804, proves that it was not. An entry dated July 14, 1800, mentions the shipping of a press from Detroit (see note 6, Chapter VII). Again, historians have expressed the opinion that Governor William Henry Harrison had never visited Detroit while it was in Indiana Territory. Proof that he was there in 1803 was found in the same Day Book under the date May 14; on that day the Governor purchased a number of items in the store.

For details about ships and shipping the most important sources are the papers and account books of Askin, Mackintosh, and May. Names of ships, tonnage and other specifications, names of officers and sailors, and their annual salaries or wages, all may be found in these manuscripts. John Askin, who knew all the ships on the Upper Lakes, recorded in his diary their passage up and down the Detroit River.

Information about military affairs is most abundant in the J. F. Hamtramck Papers, which include an orderly book of the First United States Infantry; in the Wayne-Wilkinson Letter Book; and in General John Wilkins' Cash Book and his Letter Book, all in the Burton Historical Collection. In addition, there are the correspondence of General Anthony Wayne and his general orders issued at Detroit, in possession of the Historical Society of Pennsylvania. Photostats of these papers are in the William L. Clements Library, Ann Arbor.

The most valuable sources for the study of the religious life of Detroit are the records of Ste Anne's Parish—the Registre de Ste Anne, which contains entries of baptisms, marriages, and burials from 1704 onward; and the Livre des Assemblées de la Paroisse Ste Anne, minutes of the congregational meetings. Both are kept in the rectory of the present Ste Anne's Church. There are copies in the Burton Historical Collection. The Burton Collection also has a manuscript copy of Father Jean Dilhet's "État de l'Église Catholique ou Du Diocese des États-Unis de l'Amérique Septentrionale." The original is in the library of St. Mary's Seminary, Baltimore, Maryland.

Other important papers which contain information about the religious life of Detroit are in the Chancery Archives of the Archbishopric of Detroit and in the Archives of the Archbishopric of Baltimore and Washington, Archbishop's House, Baltimore, Maryland. The latter collection has many letters written by Bishop John Carroll, Father Michel Levadoux, and Father Gabriel Richard. A few letters written to and from Detroit are in the library of Notre Dame University, and in the Archives of the Archbishopric of Quebec.

The principal manuscript sources for the history of law and the courts are the Northwest Territory Records in the Legal Research Library of the University of Michigan Law School, Solomon Sibley's Docket Books and Papers, the Gabriel J. Godfroy Papers, and the papers of François Navarre. The last three are in the Burton Historical Collection. The records in the Legal Research Library are largely lawyers' briefs and court orders. There are a great many which were issued by the Court of Common Pleas and by the Court of General Quarter

Sessions; records of the infrequent sessions of the Territorial Circuit Court are meager. Solomon Sibley, the leading lawyer in Detroit, and assistant prosecutor of the Territory, had a great variety of legal business. His practice of preserving all his documents makes his collection especially valuable. Gabriel J. Godfroy's papers contain a number of "Presentments of the Grand Jury," and François Navarre's correspondence from the River Raisin Settlement, where he was a justice of the peace, contains a great deal of information about judicial affairs.

The political life of the community is mirrored in the papers of Solomon Sibley, Peter Audrain, James May, George McDougall, and François Navarre, in the Burton Historical Collection. These men were actively engaged in politics. Their correspondence proves that elections were lively affairs, with the former British subjects who spoke English on one side; the French-speaking element and the newly arrived Americans on the other. There were, however, exceptions; for George McDougall, whose mother was French, stood with the Americans, and some of the French detested Americans, whom they later characterized as *sacrés cochons de Bastonnais*—"damned Bostonian [i.e. New England] pigs."

Information about the social life of Detroiters may be found in the papers of all men previously mentioned. An additional source is the correspondence of Frederick Bates with his brothers Richard and Tarleton, and his sister Sally. These delightfully intimate letters describe the French people, their customs, and their attitude toward the Yankees. Bates also wrote frankly of the pastimes of the young men about town. The original papers are owned by the Missouri Historical Society, St. Louis. Photostatic copies are in the Burton Historical Collection.

The most valuable work for tracing family lines of Detroiters is the monumental Genealogy compiled by Father Christian Denissen, in twenty-five volumes. Remarkably accurate and comprehensive, it is an indispensable aid to anyone who is interested in the origins of Detroit families. The Genealogy is in typescript because funds for publishing have not been available. It may be consulted in the Burton Historical Collection.

Among the printed collections of contemporary documents

the most important are the two volumes edited by Milo M. Quaife under the title *Burton Historical Records: The John Askin Papers* (Detroit, 1931). Consisting of the most significant and interesting letters and other papers selected from the vast store of Askin manuscripts, these books provide information about the social, political, commercial, and religious life of the community. Liberally supplied with footnotes, many of them biographical sketches of Detroiters and their neighbors, the volumes are also a rich repository of genealogical lore.

Another valuable book for the study of conditions in the village is *Corporation of the Town of Detroit. Act of Incorporation and Journal of the Board of Trustees, 1802–1805* (Detroit, 1922), edited by Clarence M. Burton. This little volume contains the first charter of Detroit and the proceedings of the Trustees. Ordinances regulating the weight of bread, the speed of horses in the streets, the marketing of meat and vegetables, the keeping of taverns, and many other matters are found in it, and penalties imposed on residents for infractions of these laws are set down.

Volumes II, III, VII, and X of the *Territorial Papers of the United States* (Washington, 1934–42), compiled and edited by Clarence E. Carter, a collection of official documents, are an indispensable source of political and social information on the Northwest Territory, Indiana Territory, and Michigan Territory.

Jacob Burnet, a Cincinnati lawyer who frequently went to Detroit to practice in the courts, in later years wrote a book entitled *Notes on the Early Settlement of the North-Western Territory* (New York, 1847). His account of the social and political life of the town is extremely interesting and, in general, trustworthy; nevertheless, there are misstatements of fact resulting from the long span of years between the events and the writing.

Although the title is forbidding enough to repel the casual reader, *The Correspondence of Lieutenant-Governor John Graves Simcoe, with Allied Documents Relative to His Administration of the Government of Upper Canada* (Toronto, 1923–31), in five volumes, edited by E. A. Cruikshank, will richly repay anyone interested in the history of Detroit for his time spent in leafing through them. The excellent index in each volume makes easy the locating of material about individuals or events. In this work one will find the British point of view on the occupation of the Western posts, Indian relations, and international problems. Many of the letters printed in this work were written by Colonel Richard England, commandant of Fort Lernoult at Detroit, and many others were addressed to him. Several volumes of the *Michigan Pioneer and Historical Collections*, notably XII, XX, XXIII, XXIV, and XXV, which contain hundreds of documents from the Canadian Archives, also reflect the British interest in the West and are very useful as a source of information on conditions in Detroit.

Two other volumes of these *Collections* are worth mentioning here. In Volume XXXIV "General Wayne's General Orders" show vividly how the Commander in Chief whipped his army into shape for the decisive western campaign. Although the orders issued during General Wayne's stay in Detroit are missing, later orders give a graphic picture of military life in the Fort and the Citadel. Another view of Detroit is presented in Volume XVII, which contains the "Account of a Journey to attend the Indian Treaty proposed to be held at Sandusky, in the year 1793, interspersed with various observations, remarks, and circumstances that occurred on this interesting occasion," by Jacob Lindley, and the "Journal of a tour to Detroit, in order to attend a Treaty, proposed to be held with the Indians at Sandusky," by Joseph Moore. These men were Quakers from Philadelphia, intelligent and inquisitive. Greatly interested in the strange environment in which they lived for some weeks, they investigated, asked questions, and wrote, in their quaint style, the most complete contemporary account of Detroit and its people in the 1790's. These Journals are also in the *Friends' Miscellany*, Vols. II and VI (Philadelphia, 1832).

Two books by foreign travelers who visited Detroit in 1796 are extremely interesting. Isaac Weld's *Travels through the States of North America during the Years of 1795, 1796, and 1797* (London, 1799), in two volumes, has many details on the social and commercial life of Detroit. Although the author, an Irishman, was somewhat prejudiced against Americans, his narrative is well worth reading. The other book is Constantin F. Volney's *Tableau du Climat et du Sol des États-Unis d'Améri-*

que (Paris, 1803). It has been translated and published under the title *A View of the Soil and Climate of the United States of America* (Philadelphia, 1804). The author traveled extensively in the United States. His detailed analysis of the character of the French in the Illinois country may, with some reservations, be profitably applied to the French in the vicinity of Detroit. Volney's visit to Detroit unfortunately occupies little space in his book because he fell ill of the prevalent malaria and spent most of his time in bed.

Father Jean Dilhet's "État de l'Église Catholique," which has been mentioned among the manuscripts, has been edited by Patrick W. Brown and published under the title *Beginnings of the Catholic Church in the United States* (Washington, 1922). This work gives the reader an insight into the character of Father Dilhet as well as information on the subject with which he deals. Actually only Father Richard's assistant in Detroit, he was, to judge from his own account, the central figure in the religious life of the community.

As stated in the Preface, very little has been printed about Detroit in the first decade of American occupation. Accordingly, few books can be cited as sources of information. Some, however, must be mentioned. First among them is Silas Farmer's *The History of Detroit and Michigan, or The Metropolis Illustrated* (Detroit, 1884). This work contains much social, political, and military history. The author quite diligently gathered and consulted all the documents he could find; but there was no Burton Historical Collection to work in, and the Anthony Wayne Papers were not then available. Consequently there is no complete account of the period, and there are some errors. The two-volume work, *The City of Detroit, Michigan, 1701–1922* (Chicago, 1922), by Clarence M. Burton, who gathered and gave to the city the collection which bears his name, contains some useful material which was not known to Silas Farmer.

Interesting biographical sketches of several Detroiters of this period written by Milo M. Quaife may be found in the *Burton Historical Collection Leaflets*. The most pertinent are: "John Harvey," IV, No. 1; "John Askwith," VII, No. 4; "David Bacon," IX, No. 3; "Daniel de Joncaire de Chabert," VI, No. 1; "Alexander Macomb," X, No. 1; and "John Whistler," V, No. 1. Other *Leaflet* articles by the same author, which may profitably be read, are "Detroit's First Election," II, No. 2; "Early Detroit and Early Chicago," V, No. 3; and "The 'Old Brigg' Adams," II, No. 4.

If one would understand the French *habitants* of Detroit and the vicinity, he must know their pastimes and their traditions. No one else has written about these matters so delightfully as Mrs. M. C. W. Hamlin in *Legends of Le Détroit* (Detroit, 1884). In this book one may become acquainted with the French people at play, and he may read of the werewolf, *Le Nain Rouge*, *Les Dames Blanches*, and other local apparitions. Although Mrs. Hamlin's historical references are not always exact, her local lore is authentic; for she was a descendant of one of the old French families, and she had heard these stories over and over again during her childhood.

Two authors who give a comprehensive view of the most important business at Detroit are Ida A. Johnson, *The Michigan Fur Trade* (Lansing, 1919), and Wayne E. Stevens, *The Northwest Fur Trade, 1763–1800* (Urbana, Illinois, 1928).

Sister Mary Rosalita's *Education in Detroit prior to 1850* (Lansing, 1928) may be consulted for information about schools and teachers.

For military affairs in which General Anthony Wayne and General James Wilkinson were engaged, Harry E. Wildes, *Anthony Wayne, Trouble Shooter of the American Revolution* (New York, 1941), and James R. Jacobs, *Tarnished Warrior* (New York, 1938), are excellent. The latter work is a biography of Wilkinson. Both have been drawn on extensively in writing this book. The details in Chapter V about the personal affairs of General Wayne were taken from Mr. Wildes' book; and the information about General Wilkinson's dealings with the Spaniards, in Chapter VIII, was obtained from Major Jacobs' narrative.

The foregoing are the most important sources from which materials for this book were drawn. They are also the ones which will be useful to readers who may wish to do some research of their own; for most of the personal papers, such as those of John Askin, cover a much longer period than the one treated here.

INDEX

Abbott, James, merchant, 26; business interests of, 31–32; appointed justice of the peace, 56; entertains Rev. David Jones, 67; in Miamis Company, 74; fined, 213; orders goods, 214; trustee, 223

Abbott, James, and Sons, 31–32

Abbott, James, Jr., merchant, 31–32; married, 232; trustee, 237

Abbott, Robert, 138, 163, 190; merchant, 31–32; fined, 197, 213; trustee, 213; orders goods, 214

Act Passed at the First Session of the Fourth Congress of the United States of America, An, printed at Detroit, 93, 94, 94 n.

Adams, President John, 109, 120, 124, 135, 150, 163, 174; proclaims day of prayer, 128-129; receives chiefs, 136

Adams, galley on the Ohio, 199

Adams, U. S. brig; see *President Adams*

Adhemar, Miss, schoolmistress, 91

Albany, 37, 64, 154–155, 214

Allegheny River, 62, 217

Allen, Ebenezer, 13

Ambassador Bridge, 36

Americans, hostility of, to Indians, 39

Amherst, Lord Jeffrey, 5

Amherstburg, 214; Ft. Malden at, 2; beginning of, 17

Amusements, 95-98, 162, 180

Anderson, John, 76, 151; complains of cut-throat trade, 127

Aniquiba, Potawatomi chief, 88, 171

Annette, 73, 152; wrecked, 134

Apprentices, 129 n., 187, 213

Ariadne, 128

Armstrong, Capt. Hamilton, 60

Arpent, defined, 33

Ash, Sylvester, 125

Askin, Adelaide (Alice), 90; wife of Elijah Brush, 191

Askin, Alexander, 183; studies Latin, 229

Askin, Charles (Charley), studies music, 90; attends school, 183

Askin, Eleanor, 183

Askin, James, 183

Askin, John, Sr., 2, 32, 73, 76, 78, 94, 117, 124, 143, 152, 154, 159, 174, 182, 194, 220, 225; friend of Col. England, 3; and Cuyahoga Purchase, 12, 13, 14; letter by, delivered to Wayne, 13; attempts to buy Lower Peninsula of Michigan, 13; tan yard of, 26; merchant, 26; accepts American régime, 30; early life of, 30; half-breed children of, 37; commends Hamtramck, 42; intends to remain British, 56; in Miamis Company, 75; transfers land to Todd and McGill, 75; losses in fur trade, 75; business transactions of, 81; bookkeeping of, 83; pays tuition for children, 89; supports school, 90; lends books, 92; protests against martial law, 115; advises British subjects, 115–116; issues orders to militia, 120; illness of, 151; pessimistic about business situation, 165–166; characterized, 166; contract with schoolmaster, 170; writes to McCoskry, 184; sends slave to May, 187; trustee, 190; praises Brush, 191; praises Williams, 193; buys farm machinery, 195; praises court, 195 n.; fined, 197; moves across river, 197; expects better business, 199; optimism of, 217; sells houses, 226; tries to save Cuyahoga Purchase, 233; loses claim, 234; sends help to Detroit, 240; approves new plan of Detroit, 245

Askin, Mrs. John, 184

Askin, John, Jr., 37; agent of Ottawa and Chippewa, 13; confined in Ft. Jefferson, 13; in battle of Fallen Timbers, 13; in charge of fire engine, 86

Askin farm, 35, 189

Askwith, John, favors Americans, 10; and Cuyahoga Purchase, 12, 13, 14; at Ft. Wayne, 13; books of, 91; tavern bills of, 96

Astor, John Jacob, 165, 188

Athabasca, 73

Atlee, Margaretta Wayne, 70

Atlee, Will, 70

Audrain, James, 138

Audrain, Marie Catherine, 202

Audrain, Peter, 116, 138, 140, 144, 179, 180, 190, 223, 237; accompanies Wayne to Detroit, 47-49; naturalized Frenchman, 55; appointed clerk of General Quarter Sessions, 56; appointed prothonotary, 56; appointed judge of Probate, 56; appointed recorder, 57; death of, 57; announces court session, 83; reports work of court, 84; rents court room, 85 n.; orders pickets, 86; borrows

259

INDEX

book, 92; records land claims, 107; takes census, 137; supports May's candidacy, 142; reports on election, 145-146; reports interest in education, 158; nicknamed Talleyrand, 162; notifies judges of suspension, 169; seeks secretaryship, 221; clerk to commissioners, 232; makes transcripts, 236
Au Glaize River, 76
Avery, Elisha, 242

Bacon, Rev. David, at Detroit, 174-176; preaches, 183; conducts school, 182-183; discouragements of, 186-187; visits Maumee, 200; goes to L'Arbre Croche, 200; in Detroit, 230; leaves Detroit, 231
Bacon, Mrs. David, conducts school, 182-183; bears son, 200
Bacon, Leonard, 200, 200 n.
Badger, Rev. Joseph, 187 n.
Baker, Capt. William, master of *Charlotte*, 73
Baldwin, Abraham, 221
Baltimore, 51
Band, First Infantry (First Sub-legion), 46
Bangs, Rev. Nathan, 230-231
Bariau, Joseph, 81
Barkle, Mary, wife of James Abbott, Sr., 31
Barthe, Marie Archange, wife of John Askin, Sr., 30
Barthe, Thérèse, wife of Commodore Grant, 32
Bates, Frederick, 139, 222; in quartermaster's department, 123; opinion of French girls, 140; defends Col. Strong, 148; on politics, 163; verses of, 191-193; opens store, 199; appointed postmaster, 202; Republican again, 210; wants to be secretary, 212; fined, 213; recommended by Curry, 214; seeks secretaryship, 221; trustee, 223; in land office, 231; postmaster, 235; hears land claims, 235-236; judge, Michigan Territory, 236; accuses Jouett, 237; trustee, 237; urges patience, 241
Bates, Richard, 163 n.
Bates, Sally, 141
Bates, Tarleton, promises to help Frederick, 212; reports aid for Frederick, 221
Bates, Thomas Fleming, 123
Batiscan, 34
Baudry, Marie Archange, wife of Angus Mackintosh, 30
Beaubien, Antoine, 144, 195
Beaubien, Jean Baptiste, 66; signs Treaty of Greenville, 15
Beaubien farm, 35, 189

Beaufait, Louis, Sr., 137, 148, 162, 168; signs Treaty of Greenville, 15; appointed judge of Common Pleas, 56; appointed justice of the peace, 56; judge of election, 145
Beaufait, Louis, Jr., 144, 194; candidate for representative, 145; charges murder, 195
Beaufait, Teresa, wife of William Groesbeck, 37
Beaufait family, 36
Beaver, 73, 84
Belanger, Philip, 125-126
Belestre, François Marie Picoté (father), officer at Detroit, 34
Belestre, François Marie Picoté (son), last French commandant at Detroit, 35
Belle Isle, 211, 211 n.; owned by William Macomb, 10
Bellecour, François D^x, 34, 83; appointed notary public, 57; county commissioner, 84
Bellecour, Mme François D^x, schoolmistress, 91, 154 n.
Berthelet, Henry, 194; trustee, 223; business interests of, 238
Berthelet family, 36
Big Beaver, 196 n.
Big Bowl, Ottawa chief, 234
Billet, Ignatius, 81
Bissell, Isaac, 237
Bizaillon, François, 203
Black Betty, 41
"Black Snake," Indian name for Wayne, 49
Bloody Bridge, 96; Capt. Dalyell defeated at, 23
Blue Jacket, Shawnee chief, assists Wayne, 11; greets Wayne, 48-49; leaves for Philadelphia, 64; signs treaty, 234
Boat mill, 95 n.
Bois Blanc Island (Bob-Lo), British blockhouse on, 17
Bond, Lewis, 139, 140, 145, 170; appointed sheriff, 133; posts election notice, 137; calls election, 145
Bond, Mrs. Lewis, 140
Bonnecamps, Fr. Pierre Jean de, describes Detroit, 22
Bounty, paid to recruits, 45
Bouquet, Col. Henry, 5
Bourbon, Anthony of, Duke of Vendôme and King of Navarre, 36
Bowyer, Lieut. John, 60
Brevoort, Lieut. Henry B., commands *President Adams*, 199, 238
Brickyard, on River Rouge, 152
Britons at Detroit, 29-32
Brock, Capt. Joseph, 60, 71

INDEX 261

Brown, Adam, white chief of Wyandots, 10; signs treaty, 234
Brown, Dr. Charles, describes Detroit, 22; characterizes merchants, 29; reports on Indians at Detroit, 39–40; reports soldiers ill, 69–70
Brown, James, silversmith, 76 n.
Brown, Dr. William, 161, 161 n., 194, 247; attends Lasselle, 204; fined, 213; trustee, 237
Brunson, Isaac, silversmith, 76 n.
Brush, Edmund, 225
Brush, Elijah, 139, 162, 163, 178, 179, 194, 229, 233, 236; marries Adelaide Askin, 191; occupies Askin homestead, 197; trustee, 213; orders goods, 215, 225; attorney for Williams, 220; agent of Cuyahoga Associates, 234; signs treaty, 234; fire inspector, 237
Brush, Mrs. Elijah, clothing ordered for, 225
Burbank, Capt. Jesse, escapes from *Charlotte*, 135
Burbeck, Maj. Henry, to command at Mackinac, 59
Burke, Rev. Edmund, accuses British subjects, 9–10; characterized, 11; detested by American officers, 54
Burnet, George, 161
Burnet, Jacob, lawyer, 50–51, 148, 158, 159, 161, 169, 170, 171
Burnett, Abraham, 171
Burnett, Isaac, 171, 229; completes schooling, 182
Burnett, James, 89, 91, 157, 171, 229; pupil of Burrell, 88
Burnett, John, 89, 157, 171, 182; pupil of Burrell, 88; apprenticed to May, 187–188; in trouble, 229
Burnett, Nancy, 171
Burnett, Rebecca, 171, 182
Burnett, William, fur trader, 88, 187, 229
Burrell, John, schoolmaster, 32, 91, 157, 229; school of, 88; tutors Campau, 89; sues Campau, 122
Burton Historical Collection, 12 n.

Cabassier, Charles, 85 n.
Cadillac, Antoine de la Mothe, 29, 61; land granted by, 32; interested in fur trade, 74
Cain, John, tailor, 81
Caldwell, Capt. William, commands Detroit militia, 7
Calèche, defined, 215 n.
Caledonia, 153, 199, 238
Callahan, Hugh, 157
Camden, 211
Camp Deposit, 3

Campau, Miss, seamstress, 81
Campau, Denis, 205
Campau, Jacques, 35, 162
Campau, Joseph, merchant, 26, 35, 209, 249; studies English, 89; sends Williams to school, 89; claim of, against Burrell, 122; advises Williams, 154; offers partnership, 167; urges return of Williams, 172–173; joins Zion Lodge, 178 n.; pledge to Ste Anne's, 186; trustee, 190; affection for, for Williams, 193; fined, 197; partnership with Williams, 199; illness of, 205; attends lodge, 217; offers bond, 219
Campau, Marie Cecile, 89
Campau, Nicholas, *dit* Niagara, 34, 188
Campau, Toussaint, 203
Campau Alley (St. Antoine St.), 24
Campau and Williams, firm established, 199; firm dissolved 226, 226 n.
Campbell, Major William, denies aid to Indians, 8
"Canadian Godefroy"; *see* Godfroy, Jacques
Canoe, description of, 77 n.
Cariole, defined, 97
Carondelet, Baron, 111, 119
Carroll, Mr., 203
Carroll, Bishop John, 69, 99, 103, 125, 156, 171, 183, 227; Ste Anne's in jurisdiction of, 51; approves Levadoux's program, 100, 102; transfers Richard, 131; pastoral letter of, 219, 228; transfers Dilhet, 228; wants French priests to remain, 239
Cass farm, 31
Casse, Jean, *dit* St. Aubin, 33
Cemetery, new, on Common, 149, 149 n.
Chabert, François de Joncaire de, 98, 160, 188, 195; career of, 35; appointed county treasurer, 57; lieutenant colonel, 57; signs address, 72; candidate for representative, 145; files election claim, 146; candidate for representative, 177; elected representative, 178; pledge to Ste Anne's, 186
Chapell, Braddock, 92
Chapin, Dr. Cyrenius, 204
Chapman, Nathaniel, 84
Chapoton, Dr. Jean, 36
Chapoton, Jean Baptiste, 8
Chapoton, Louis, 129 n.
Chapoton, Louise Clotilda, second wife of Jacques Godfroy, 37
Chapoton, Marie Catherine Angélique, wife of George Meldrum, 29
Charlotte, 73, 153, 156, 238; damaged by fire, 135
Chartrand, Peter, 176 n., 239–240; sues

INDEX

Saunders, 160, 160 n.; sues William Smith, 196; liberated, 218
Chartrand, Rebecca, 160
Chatham, blockhouse at, moved, 127
Chauvin, Louis, 186
Chêne, Mme Charles, 81
Chêne, Capt. Isidore, 35
Chêne, Marie Josette, 35
Chêne, Pierre, 189, 219
Chêne, Toussaint, 59
Chêne family, 36
Chicago, 208, 232
"Chief-who-never-sleeps," Indian name for Wayne, 48
Chillicothe, 179, 188
China, 75
Chippewa, 39, 64; in battle of Fallen Timbers, 7–8; sign Treaty of Greenville, 15; menace Lindley, 38; grant land, 107; receive annuity, 120; language, 182, 183; cede land, 234
Chippewa, 74 n.
Choate, Samuel, 94
Cicotte, Agatha, wife of Jacob Visger, 37
Cicotte, Jean Baptiste, 72
Cicotte family, 36
Cincinnati, 6, 7, 46, 59, 61, 65, 144, 158, 160, 161
Circuit Court, Territorial, 158, 169; first session of, 1798, 130; session of, 1800, 170; session of, 1804, 232
Cissne, Joseph, 146; supports May, 163; suspended, 169; candidate, 177; contests election, 179
Citadel, at Detroit, 21, 24, 42, 113, 246; houses troops, 19; description of, 20; guard house in, 43; commandant's quarters in, 43; Rev. David Jones preaches in, 67; repairs to, 86; destroyed by fire, 240
Clark, George Rogers, 35
Clark, Thomas, 219–220
Clemens, Christian, 146
Clemens, Jacob, tanner, 26, 190, 197
Clements Library, McNiff's map in, 14 n.
Clemson, Lieut. Eli B., 225
Cleveland, 12
Clinton, Vice-President George, 242
Clinton River, 89
Clymer, George, 64
Coates, Mrs. Ann, tavern keeper, 189 n.
Cole, Sergeant, abducts Poquette, 176–177
Collot, Gen. Victor, 65, 108, 136
Commander in chief, British, 44
Common, 23, 201 n., 222; bowers built on, 240, 241
Communication and transportation, expresses, 59, 125; routes to Detroit, 61–62; uncertainty of, 61, 95, 98, 99, 124, 125, 202; Indian runners, 125, 156; postal service, 181, 222, 235, 249
Company of the Colony, 74
Congress, 51
Connelly, Capt. John, 184, 219; commands *Senator Tracy*, 199
Conner, John, marshal, 237
Connor, Lydia, 113–114
Conspiracy of Pontiac, 35, 37
Contractor, 238
Cook, Abraham, 238
Corps of Artillerists and Engineers, 70–71
Coté, Joseph, 186
Coté, Prisque, 186
Côte du Nord-Est, 23, 194
Côte du Sud-Ouest, 23, 36
Council House, 182; balls held in, 97; election in, 178
Court House, 84 n., 85, 85 n.
Court of Common Pleas, 84, 162, 169; established by Sargent, 56; Burrell vs. Campau in, 122; judges appointed to, 133; lacks quorum, 138; judgment by, upheld, 159; praised by Askin, 195 n.; Chartrand sues in, 196; smugglers sued in, 216
Court of General Quarter Sessions, 103, 157, 195; established, 56; first session of, 83; appoints officers, 84; summons Askin and Park, 117; McNiff accuses judges of, 138; few persons tried by, 159; judges discharge commissioners, 162; judges of, suspended, 169; liberates Chartrand, 218
Coventry, Dr., 122 n.
Crow, John, 204
Cuillerier, Angélique, 35
Cuillerier, Antoine, *dit* Beaubien, 35
Cuillerier, Jean, 34
Cuillerier, Jean Baptiste, *dit* Beaubien, 35
Curry, Charles, 218; reports conditions at Detroit, 188; quotes fur prices, 198; trustee, 213; turns business to Albany, 214; orders goods, 215, 225
Curry, Capt. Peter, 61, 74 n.; master of *Detroit*, 19; a Mason, 94; establishes shipyard, 125; directs shipbuilding, 133; master of *President Adams*, 167; master of *Senator Tracy*, 238
Curtis, Eli, 87, 95
Custom of Paris, 32
Cuyahoga Associates, entertain Indians, 64; lose claim, 233, 234
Cuyahoga Purchase, 12–14; not confirmed, 14

Dalyell, Capt. James, 23
David, Moses, 215
Deal, Corp. John, 138

INDEX

Dealy, William, 134, 152
Dean, Maj. William, 233
Dearborn, Henry, Secretary of War, 196 n., 211; orders fort built, 208; orders Burbeck to Detroit, 209; considers moving Ft. Lernoult, 210; changes name of Ft. Lernoult to Ft. Detroit, 246
DeButts, Capt. Henry, 16, 61, 65; procures ships at Detroit, 2; reports evacuation and occupation of Detroit, 18–19; borrows flour, 43; warns Wayne of bad road, 62; assistant quartermaster, 62; agent of O'Hara, 62; borrows pork from British (second loan), 62–63; leaves Detroit, 72
Deer Park, 31
Delaware River, 50
Delawares, in battle of Fallen Timbers, 7–8; sign Treaty of Greenville, 15
Delisle, ——, schoolmaster, 89
Delisle, Alexis, 129 n.
Delisle François, 213
Denaut, Monseigneur Pierre, Bishop of Quebec, 183
Denissen, Father Christian, genealogist, 36
Denny, Col. Ebenezer, 155, 155 n.
DePeyster, Col. Arent S., 97 n.
Dequindre, Antoine, 84, 162
Derineau, Capt. Louis, master of *Weazell*, 16, 73, 152 n.
Deserters, American, 44; reward offered for arrest of, 59; punishment of, 59; in Canada, 126–127
Deserters, British, 44, 127
Desnoyers, Peter, silversmith, 76 n.
Detroit, 3, 6, 10, 11, 16, 29, 30, 31; Ft. Lernoult at, 1; in hands of British, 1; troops from, garrison Ft. Miamis, 7; British militia from, at Fallen Timbers, 7–8; rumors of evacuation of, 8; disaffection of British at, 8–9; McNiff shows plan of, 13; map of, 14 n.; ceded by Treaty of Greenville, 15; view of, from river, 18; British evacuate, Americans occupy, 18–19; Citadel at, 19; defenses of, 21; descriptions of, 22; view of, from Ft. Lernoult, 22–25; number of houses of, 23 n.; number of stores in, 23 n.; description of houses in, 25; streets, description of, 25–26; population of, 27; population reported by Sargent and Weld, 27 n.; nationalities at, 28; farms at, 32–33; feudal tenure at, 32–33; physicians in, 37, 38, 122 n., 194, 247; in Northwest Territory, 42; description of, 50; headquarters of U. S. Army at, 58–59; routes to, 61; first Protestant service in, 67; description of, 67; funeral procession in, 69; inhabitants of, address Wayne, 72; stock of stores in, 80; printing at, 93 n.; winter at, 95, 95 n.; legends about, 95–96; winter amusements at, 95–98; balls at, 97; first celebration of Washington's birthday at, 100–102; Mardi Gras at, 102–103; furs shipped from, 1797, 106; first celebration of Fourth of July at, 111–112; martial law at, 113; British subjects at, retain allegiance, 116; Forts Mackinac, Miamis, Defiance, Wayne, Knox, and Lorimers, dependent on, 118; annuity distributed to Indians at, 120; furs shipped from, 1798, 127; 1792 election in, 143; 1798 territorial election in, 143–144; 1799 territorial election in, 145; new cemetery at, 149, 149 n.; description of, 155; politics in, 163–164; "funeral" of Washington in, 164; customs duties collected at, 165; Second Regiment leaves, 166–167; First Regiment returns to, 166; petition from, 173; description of, 175; 1800 territorial election in, 177; charter of, 189–190; market in, 190, 190 n.; slaves in, 194; value of houses in, 194; Board of Trustees of, 196; first annual town meeting, 197; election of town officers, 197; Indian "factory" at, 198, 240; price of furs at, 198; in Indiana Territory, 207; people of, dislike transfer, 207; town meeting, 212–213; election of town officers, 213; new postal route to, 221–222; finances of, 222; town meeting, 223; election of town officers, 223; Richard and Dilhet open school in, 228; people send agent to Washington, 231; land office opened in, 231; petitions from, 232; capital of Michigan Territory, 235; election of town officers, 237; fire destroys, 239–241; plan of, like that of Washington, 242, 243, 243 n.; Hull predicts great future for, 243; assistance for sufferers by fire at, 243 n.; inhabitants of, promise coöperation, 244; Askin approves new plan of, 245; changes in, under American régime, 245–249
Detroit, 74 n., 124; purchased by DeButts, 2; carries troops to Detroit, 19; carries troops to Mackinac, 59; Capt. Curry commands, 61; carries Wayne, 72; carries Wilkinson, 118; Capt. Guthrie commands, 125; carries Fr. Richard, 156; unfit for service, 167, 167 n.
Detroit River, voyage up, 17
Detroit Township, 84, 193–194
Dickson, Thomas, 220
Dilhet, Father Jean (John), 131; at River Raisin, 219; reforms of, 227; teaches

school in Detroit, 228; has few pupils, 239; leaves Detroit, 248
Dillon, Peter Joseph, schoolmaster, 157, 170
Dodemead, Alice, 237 n.
Dodemead, Elizabeth, 217
Dodemead, James, 237, 240
Dodemead, John, 32, 144, 149, 179, 217; and Cuyahoga Purchase, 12-14; tavern keeper, 26; defies Col. Strong, 147; sues Col. Strong, 148; trustee, 190; owns slaves, 194; fined, 197; head of night watch, 224
Dodemead's tavern, guard stationed at, 114, 114 n.; polling place, 145; courts sit in, 147
Dolson, Matthew, tavern keeper, 26
Donaldson, James, tavern keeper, 26, 32, 94, 96
Donovan, Matthew, schoolmaster, 32, 91; teaches Burnett boys, 89; Askin removes children from school of, 170 n.; teaches Latin, 229
Dorchester, Lord, 9 n., 18; predicts war with United States, 7; offers to evacuate Detroit, 16; orders detachment to Bois Blanc, 17
Doyle, Maj. William, commands at Mackinac, 52
Drake, Capt. John, 96
Drouillard, Simon, 186
Dubois, Etienne, *chantre*, 201
Dufaux, Father François Xavier, at Sandwich, 53; describes Levadoux, 53; visits Hamtramck, 54, dines with Wayne, 54; reports hostility of Wayne toward Fr. Burke 54; death of, 69
Dundas, Henry, disapproves building of Ft. Miamis, 7
Dunmore, 74 n.
Dutch at Detroit, 37
Dyson, Capt. Samuel T., commandant at Detroit, 238; fires salute, 242; assists Hull, 245

Eberts, Dr. Hermann Melchior, 138, 194, 247, 247 n.; surgeon in Hessian regiment, 37, 38; appointed coroner, 56; acts as sheriff, 83; troubles as sheriff, 84; removed as sheriff, 132
Eberts, Mrs. Hermann (Marie Françoise Huc), 232
Elections in Detroit, 1792, 143; territorial, 1798, 143-144; 1799, 145; 1800, 177; town, 1802, 197; 1803, 213; 1804, 223; 1805, 237
Elliot, Matthew, 14, 108, 177; loyalist, 4; controversies with Col. England, 6; at battle of Fallen Timbers, 8; Indians hired to murder, 10; Tory refugee, 38; removed from office, 150
Emery, Father J. A., recalls Sulpicians, 239
Engagé, 37, 73, 81, 152, 156; defined, 33
England, Lt. Col. Richard, 4, 10, 14, 19, 20, 116; commandant of Ft. Lernoult, 1; career of, 1; writes to Gen. Wilkinson, 2; receives evacuation order, 3; address to, by townspeople, 3-4; troubles with Indian agents, 6; expects Wayne to attack Detroit, 8; accuses British subjects, 9; deports LeDru, 9 n.; unable to check disloyalty, 11-12; and Cuyahoga Purchase, 12; evacuates Ft. Lernoult, 18-19; letter from Askin to, 30; deports Irvine (Irwin), 38; letter to, from Askin, 42; orders loan of pork, 43
England, Richard, Jr., 3
Enos, Indian runner, 125
Ernest, Matthew, 130, 139, 140, 145, 193; assistant quartermaster, 118; builds shipyard, 124; justice of the peace, 133; judge of Common Pleas, 133; inspector of revenue, 165; contract with schoolmaster, 170; owns slave, 194; collector, asks advice, 197-198; recommends Bates, 199; sues Lasselles, 216-217; removed as collector, 237, 237 n.; home of, at Spring Wells, 242
Ernest, Mrs. Matthew, 140
Esplanade (Grand Parade), 24, 112, 164; reviews held on, 46; maneuvers on, 101; guard-mount on, 42
Euretta, 128

"Factories," government trading posts, 79-80
Fallen Timbers, battle of, 7-8, 11; Hamtramck cited for bravery in, 20; Blue Jacket commands Indians at, 48-49; Wayne describes, 48
Farquharson, Lewis and Company, 199
Fearing, Paul, 184-185
Fearson, John, master of *Saguinah*, 73
Felicity, 74 n.
Feudal tenure at Detroit, 32-33
Fields, Capt. Daniel, 120
Fire, Detroit destroyed by, 239-241; regulations for prevention of, 85-86, 190
Fire engine, 85, 85 n.
Fontenoy, Antoine, 129 n.
Fontenoy, Mariane, 129 n.
Forsyth, Richardson and Co., 82, 214
Forsyth, William, Jr., and Cuyahoga Purchase, 12-14
Fort Dearborn, 208, 209
Fort Defiance, 59, 61, 105; Wayne at, 47; supplied from Detroit, 62
Fort Deposit 48; *see* Camp Deposit

INDEX 265

Fort Detroit, new name for Ft. Lernoult, 246
Fort Erie, 153, 203
Fort Greenville, 5, 12, 70; named for Gen. Nathanael Greene, 7 n.; Wayne retires to, 10; McDougall goes to, 13; Indian delegation at, 14; Col. Strong commands, 46; Wayne at, 46
Fort Hamilton, 46
Fort Industry, treaty of, 233–234
Fort Jefferson, 13, 46
Fort Knox, built by Hamtramck, 20
Fort LeBoeuf, 62
Fort Lernoult, 2, 16, 18, 42, 43, 211; Col. Richard England, commandant of, 1; McNiff shows plan of, 13; map of, 14 n.; Col. England evacuates, Capt. Porter occupies, 18–19; number of troops in, 19; description of, 21; Wayne describes, 49–50; Wayne orders repairs to, 50; repairs to, 86, 118; not damaged by fire, 240–241; becomes Ft. Detroit, 246
Fort Mackinac, 62; British garrison at, 43; British retain, 59; Maj. Burbeck sent to, with garrison, 59
Fort Malden, 59, 79, 127, 149–150, 152, 176, 177; building of, 2, 17; British at, lend pork, 43, 62–63
Fort Miamis, 3, 7, 8, 43, 46, 59, 61, 62, 105; location of, 2; Capt. Shortt commands, 17; Captain Marschalk commands, 19; British evacuate, 19; Wayne at, 48
Fort Pitt, 5
Fort Pontchartrain, 33, 34
Fort St. Clair, 46
Fort Washington, 61
Fort Wayne, 13, 59, 61; built by Hamtramck, 20
Fourth of July celebration, 111–112, 243
Francis, 74 n.
Fraser, James, 32, 115; convicted by court-martial, 113–114
Frechette, Father Pierre, 51
Freeman, Rev. Daniel, 229
Freeman, Edmund, 93 n.
Freeman, Ezra Fitz, lawyer, 93 n., 139, 144; visits Zion Lodge, 94; opens office, 122; attorney for McDougall, 133; waits for Symmes, 159
Freeman, Dr. James C., 122 n.; deported from Detroit, 38
Freeman, Samuel, 93 n.
Freeman's Journal, 92, 93 n.
French, houses of, 17; farms of, 17; costumes of, 26–27; at Detroit, 32–37; characterized, 33; nicknames of, 33–34; favor American régime, 56; lack interest in self-government, 56, 65; opinion of, of Americans, 140; literacy of, 247 n.
French Creek, 62, 217
Fur trade, characteristics of, 76; uncertainty of, 78; attempts to regulate, 78–80; subsidized by governments, 79; "factories" provided for, 79–80
Furs, price of, 198

Gallatin, Albert, Secretary of Treasury 198, 236
General Hunter, 238
"General Wabang," Indian name for Wayne, 63
General Wilkinson, 93 n.; runs ashore, 123
Gentle, John, 217
Germans at Detroit, 37–38
Gilkinson, William, master of *Thames*, 73; marries Isabella Grant, 206
Gilman, Judge Joseph, 117; holds court, 130
Girardin, Charles François, 137, 148, 162, 163, 168; appointed judge of Common Pleas, 56; signs address, 72; trustee, 190
Girardin family, 36
Girty, Simon, loyalist, 4; at battle of Fallen Timbers, 8; Tory refugee, 38
Gladwin, Maj. Henry, 35
Godfroy, Gabriel, 97, 105, 186, 249; owns slave, 194
Godfroy, Jacques, 36–37
Godfroy family, 36
Goff, John, schoolmaster, 229
Good Intent, 187
Gouie, Robert, tailor, 81; county commissioner, 84
Gouin, Thérèse, wife of William Park, 29
Government wharf, 18, 24
Grahames, Mrs., seamstress, 81
Grand jury, presentments of, 85, 103–104, 129; petitions legislature, 157–158; complaint of, 169; indictments by, 176–177
Grand Marais, 23, 180
Grand Parade, the (Esplanade), 21
Granger, Postmaster General Gideon, 202 n.; promises better service, 235
Grant, Col., 218
Grant, Commodore Alexander, 121, 211; early life of, 32; "Castle" of, at Grosse Pointe, 32; plans to cross river, 32; daughters of, in school, 90; sails for York, 184; farm of, 194; owns slaves, 194
Grant, Mrs. Alexander, 184
Grant, Alexander, Jr., 90, 183
Grant, Isabella, 184; 206
Grant, Jean (John), 90 n.
Graverat, Gerrit, merchant, 37
Great Miami River, 61
Green, Maj. James, 177

Greene, Gen. Nathanael, 7 n.
Gregg, Lieut. Aaron, 60
Griffin, Judge John, 211
Griswold, Stanley, secretary of Michigan Territory, 236, 242
Groesbeck, William, merchant, 37
Grosse Ile, 17, 211; owned by William Macomb, 10
Grosse Pointe, 23, 33, 121, 178, 194; Grant's "Castle" at, 32
Gruenist, Joseph, 37
Grummond, Peggy, 134
Grummond, Timothy, master of *Annette*, 73; abandons ship, 134
Guignier, Louis, *dit* Bourguignon, constable, 159-160
Guthrie, James, master of *Detroit*, 125; fights fire, 135

Habitants, 23 n., 74, 177, 178, 248; defined, 33; befriend Indians, 39; Sunday, observance of, by, 68; customs of, 97-98
Hagerstown, 123
Haldimand, Gen. Frederick, 22 n., 38
Halifax shilling, 82
Hamburg, 165
Hamilton, Alexander, 14, 135, 149
Hamilton, Henry, Lt. Governor, 35
Hamilton, Robert, 151
Hamsher, John, 181
Hamtramck, Alexis H., 209
Hamtramck, Henriette, 19, 209
Hamtramck, Lt. Col. John Francis, 25, 30; on Maumee River, 3; saves life of Antoine Lasselle, 11; stops McNiff, Askwith, and Ruland at Fort Wayne, 13-14; characterizes McNiff, 14; reports McKee's failure with Indians, 14-15; on Maumee River, 16; sends Capt. Porter to Detroit, 16; reaches Detroit, 19; family of, 19; wife dies, 19; description of, 19-20; sketch of early life of, 20; commands First Sub-legion, 20; builds Ft. Wayne, 20; inspects defenses of Detroit, 21; views town, 23; account of, with James Abbott and Sons, 32; reports number of Indians, 39; needs food for Indians, 40; asks coöperation of Detroiters, 42; issues orders for safety of Detroit, 42-43; brings supplies to Detroit, 43; receives loan of pork from British, 43; gives reasons for desertion, 44-45; urges pay for fatigue duty, 45; sends detachment to Huron River, 46; sends *Swan* to Ft. Miamis, 46; welcomes Fr. Levadoux, 52; introduces Levadoux to Wayne, 52; at Vincennes, 52; quoted, 63; Wayne suspicious of, 65; appointed commandant, 71; commands First Regiment, 71; hastens repairs, 86; borrows book, 92; issues New Year's greeting, 98; tribute of, to Wayne, 99; observes Washington's birthday, 100-102; transferred to Ft. Wayne, 112; commands Western Army, 153; altercation with Mackintosh, 153; at Pittsburgh, 168; pledge to Ste Anne's, 186; arranges to build Ft. Dearborn, 208; death of, 208; books of, 209; tomb of, 209, 209 n.
Hamtramck, John F., Jr., 209
Hamtramck, Julienne, 19, 209
Hamtramck, Rebecca Mackenzie, 209 n.
Hamtramck Township, 84, 193 n., 194
Harffy, Dr. William, 90, 92, 217
Harlequin, 187
Harmar, Gen. Josiah, 6, 20
Harpsichord, 90
Harrison, William Henry, secretary Northwest Territory, 144-145, 164; delegate to Congress, 161, 161 n.; proclaims Wayne County Indiana, 207; governor of Indiana, visits Detroit, 211; contrasted with St. Clair, 212
Harsen, Bernhardus, 175
Harsen, Jacob, 107
Harsen's Island, 87, 175
Harvey, John, 176
Harvey, Sarah, 176
Hastings, Seth, 210, 216
Hay, Jehu, Lt. Governor, 38
Hayes, John, 156
Heath, Capt. John, 64
Henry, Alexander, 191, 217; attorney for Cuyahoga Associates, 14; competes for furs, 165; predicts better business, 199
Henry, James, 139, 165; employe of O'Hara, 99; supplies forts from Detroit, 105; wants cattle, 106; opens store, 123; hires tanners, 123; opens tannery, 129-130; justice of the peace, 133; judge of Common Pleas, 133; attends celebration, 140; buys in Montreal, 154; manufactures leather, 155; quoted, 164; at Pittsburgh, 172; orders stills, 181; pays tuition, 183; trustee, 190; conducts hearing, 195; prepares statement, 201-202; "adventure to Pitt," 202; fined, 213; buys in Montreal and Albany, 214; seeks secretaryship, 221
Henry, William, 99
Heward, Hugh, 94
Hivernants, defined, 76
Hoffman, G., register of land office, 231; hears claims, 235-236; postmaster, 236
Hog Island; *see* Belle Isle
Houghton, John, musician, 90
Houses, number of, in Detroit, 23 n.; description of, in Detroit, 25
Hubert, Bishop Jean François, of Quebec, 51, 51 n., 53-54; sends Burke to Michigan, 9 n.

INDEX

Hudson River, 61
Hughes, Rev. Thomas E., 187 n.
Hull, Abraham F., 242
Hull, Ann, 242
Hull, Maria, 242
Hull, William, Governor of Michigan Territory, 236, 246; asks pardon for Indian, 196 n.; arrives at Detroit, 242; entertained by Ernest, 242; administers oaths, 242; addresses inhabitants, 243; predicts great future for Detroit, 243; reports new buildings, 244; characterizes Bates, 244; admires Woodward, 244
Hull, Mrs. William, 242
Hunot, Gabriel, 83
Hunt, Maj. Thomas, commandant, 166–167; entertains Bacon, 174; orders stockade removed, 222; leaves Detroit, 238
Huntington, Benjamin, merchant, 139, 174; member of committee, 144; quoted, 161; appointed commissioner, 163; candidate for representative, 177; opposes McDougall, 178; leaves Detroit, 193
Huntington, Samuel, appointed judge Michigan Territory, 236; rejects appointment, 242 n.
Huron, 39; *see also* Wyandots
Huron River, 48

Illinois country, 9 n.
Indian Council house, location of, 24
Indian Department, British, 4, 5, 7, 9, 11, 79, 150, 177; complains of Capt. Mayne, 63
Indian "factory," established in Detroit, 198; merchants hostile to, 198; burned, 240
Indiana Territory, Detroit in, 207, 208, 231, 235
Indians, 1, 11, 13; extermination of, suggested, 5; in battle of Fallen Timbers, 7–8; hired to murder Elliot, 10; hate Americans, 38; cool toward English, 39; trust *habitants*, 39; welcome Wayne to Detroit 48; rôle in fur trade, 77; beg food, 107–108; collect annuity, 135, 136
Innis, Robert, 83, 154
Insurance, 74, 128
Irvine (or Irwin), William, deported by England, 38
Isle aux Cochons (Belle Isle), 23

Jail, insufficiency of, 84, 84 n.
Jay, John, negotiates treaty, 9
Jay's Treaty, 17, 40 n., 56, 79, 110, 115, 177, 198, 231

Jefferson, President Thomas, 198, 236, 242; policy of, 209–210
Johnson, Capt., master of *Lark*, 226
Jones, Rev. David, 67
Jones, John Rice, attorney general, 222; in Detroit, 232
Jones, Thomas, fire inspector, 237
Jouett, Charles, Indian agent, 194 n., 198; recommends fort on Belle Isle, 211; marries, 217; purchases land from Indians, 234; explains appointment of Hull, 237

Kakima (Mrs. William Burnett), 88, 157; visits sons, 171
Kelly, Corp. William, 114
Kennedy, James, tanner, 123, 130, 139
Kentucky, 7, 38, 40
Kimberly, Zenas, 185
Kingston, 89
Kinzie, John, 12–14, 232
Kish-ku-kon, Chippewa chief, charged with murder, 195; escapes, 195 n.; later career of, 195 n.
Knaggs, George, 32
Knaggs, Whittmore, interpreter, 64; signs treaty, 234
Kremer, Lieut. Jacob, 60

Labadie, Pierre Descomps, tailor, 81
Labadie family, 36
La d'Ignolée, 98
La Fontaine, François, favors Americans, 11; signs Treaty of Greenville, 15; owns slave, 194
Lafoy, Augustine, 86
Lake Champlain, 32
Lake Erie, 61, 62
Lake Huron, 13
Lake Ontario, 61
Lake Superior, 78
Lancaster, 99
Land, law on claims to, at Detroit, 231; new law on claims to, at Detroit, 236
Land, Indian, to be purchased only by government, 12, 14; traffic in, 12; attempt to purchase, 13
Land office, opened in Detroit, 231
Lanman, James H., alleges vandalism by British at Detroit, 19 n.
Lansdane, Lord [Lord Shelburne, Marquis of Lansdowne], 22
L'Arbre Croche, 174, 175, 200
Lark, 226
LaSerrières, M., schoolmaster, 229, 239
Lasselle, Antoine, captured, 8; favors Americans, 10; assists Wayne, 11; leads Indians to Greenville, 14; signs Treaty of Greenville, 15
Lasselle, François, 203, 216–217

268 INDEX

Lasselle, J. F., 186
Lasselle, Jacques, influences Blue Jacket 11; fights Williams, 202–204; convicted of smuggling, 216–217; recovery of, 219; sues Williams, 220
L'Assumption Parish, Sandwich, 53
Lauzon, Antoine, 195
Lauzon, Jacques, 89
Leather Lips, Wyandot chief, 234
Le Canot du Nord, 98
Le carême, 102–103
Le Chemin du Ronde, 24
Le Dru, Father Thomas, on River Raisin, 9 n.; deported by British, 9 n.
Lee, William, 41
Le feu follet, 96
Legion of the United States, 70
Leith, Jameson and Co., 154, 214
Leith and Shepherd, in Miamis Company, 74
Le jour de l'An, 97–98
Le Lutin, 96
Le Nain Rouge, 95–96
Lernoult Street, 20, 21
Les Dames Blanches, 96
Levadoux, Father Michel, vicar general, 68, 103, 182, 191, 247; journey of, to Detroit, 52; arrives at Detroit, 52; early life of, 52; at Vincennes, 52; sings Te Deum, 52–53; asks Bishop to approve his policy, 53; opinion of, of Detroit, 53; salary of, 69; asks for assistant, 69; reports deaths from malaria, 69; signs address, 72; loyal to U. S., 99–100; reads eulogy of Washington, 102; sells flour, 105; reports dissension, 125–126; holds special service, 129; wants Richard as assistant, 130–131; recalls Richard, 156; signs petition, 173; pledge of, to Ste Anne's, 186; leaves Detroit, 200, 200 n., 201
L'Eveille, Frances, first wife of Jacques Godfroy, 36
Lewis, Capt., 16
Lewis, Ensign Meriwether, 71
Light dragooons, 70
Lindley, Jacob, 96; describes Col. England, 1; complains of insects in Detroit, 26 n.; on Askin, 30; menaced by Chippewa, 38; impressed by orchards, 66; his opinion of French, 68; characterizes *voyageurs*, 76; quoted, 77
Liston, Robert, 110
Little, John, 38
Little Bear, Chippewa chief, 234
Little Cedar, Chippewa chief, 196 n.
Little Turtle, Miami chief, greets Wayne, 48; leaves for Philadelphia, 64
Livingston, Henry Brockholst, 124
London, 73, 78, 165

Lootman, Marie, *dit* de Barrois, wife of Robert Navarre, 36
Lorimer's (Piqua, O.), 61
Louis XIV, 27
Louis, XV, 36
Loup Garou, 96
Lower Canada, 3, 38
Lucas, J. B. C., 221
Luxemburg, 20

McCall, John, printer, 93
McCarty, Mrs. Marie (Marie Audrain), 229
McConnell, Stephen, 59
McCoskry, Dr. William, 184, 194, 206, 247
McCrae, Robert, 125
McCrae, Thomas, Sr., tailor, 81
McCrae, Thomas, Jr., recommended by Curry, 214; appointed police officer, 223, 224
McDonnell, Ronald, at Ft. Defiance, 127; sued by McDougall, 133
McDougall, Lieut. George, 30
McDougall, George, merchant, 11, 26, 36, 84, 117; charged with plotting murder, 10; favors Americans, 10; delivers Askin's letter to Wayne, 13; early life of, 30; appointed sheriff, 56; militia captain, 57; "Miamis Adventure" of, 76; financial transaction of, 82; transfers office of sheriff, 83; success of, as trader, 106–107; at Ft. Defiance, 127; sues McDonnell, 133; supports Sibley candidacy, 143; candidate for representative, 177; accused of arousing people, 178; elected representative, 178–179; attends session of legislature, 188
McDougall Alley, 24
McFall, Matthew, 114
McGill, Andrew, 151
McGill, James, 151; urges Askin to reduce debt, 75; wealth of, 78
McGregor, John, 202–203
McHenry, James, Secretary of War, 14, 18, 110; forwards evacuation documents, 16; informs Wayne of Wilkinson's charges, 47; instructs judges, 149
McKee, Col. Alexander, 14, 38, 136; loyalist, 4; attributes Indian deaths to Americans, 5; controversies of, with Col. England, 6; directs Indian raids, 7; at battle of Fallen Timbers, 8; accuses British subjects, 11; unable to influence Indians, 14–15; accused by Sargent, 63; death of, 150
McKenzie, Alexander, 11
Mackinac, 29, 30, 52, 109, 156, 174
Mackintosh, Angus, merchant, 26, 73,

INDEX

155, 246; early life of, 30; factor of North West Company, 30; dinner at house of, described, 51; intends to remain British, 56; in Miamis Company, 74; agent of North West Company, 78; on business conditions, 151; moves to Sandwich, 153; altercation of, with Hamtramck, 153; orders stills, 181; gives testimony, 195

McLean, Capt. Hector, 152, 177; characterizes Indian officers, 6 n.; commandant at Malden, 127; prepares defenses, 149-150; accuses Indian Department, 149-150

McMurtrie, Douglas C., 93 n.

McNiff, Patrick, 137, 139, 139 n. 145, 162, 168; favors Americans, 10; and Cuyahoga Purchase, 12-14; shows plan of Ft. Lernoult and Detroit, 13; at Ft. Wayne, 13; characterized by Hamtramck, 14; Wayne pays, for maps, 14, 14 n.; gives Wayne secret code, 14; fails in mission to Ft. Greenville, 14; is paid $100 for maps, 14 n.; appointed judge of Common Pleas, 56; appointed surveyor, 57; a Mason, 94; buys land from Chippewa, 107; appointed conductor of military stores, 116; removed as surveyor, 133; accuses May, 138; accuses judges, 138; accused by May, 138; acquitted, 138; instructs representatives, 146; removal of, urged, 195; death of, 195 n.

McNiff, Robert, 12-14, 138
Macomb, Alexander, 30, 31 n., 136
Macomb, Edgar, and Macomb, 30
Macomb, Sarah Dring, wife of William Macomb, 31
Macomb, William, favors Americans, 10; owner of Grosse Ile and Belle Isle, 10; career in Detroit, 30; slaves of, 41; books of, 92; may have owned press, 93 n.
Macomb farm, 31, 31 n., 189
McTavish, Simon, 79
Madison, James, Secretary of State, 236
Maisonville, Alexis, 225
Malaria, 4, 8, 65, 185, 188; Volney ill with, 65; epidemic of, 69-70
Malcher, Paul, silversmith, 76 n.
Mangeurs de lard, defined, 77
Mansion House, 31
Maple sugar, 107
Marchand, Father J. B., 208
Mardi Gras, 102-103
Maria, 74 n., 211, 238
Marietta, 184
Market, location of, 190, 190 n.
Marsac, Sergeant Jacob, 33

Marsac, Jean Baptiste, 33
Marsac, Louise, wife of Robert Navarre, 36
Marschalk, Capt. Andrew, commands Ft. Miamis, 19
Mash-i-pi-nash-i-wish, Chippewa chief, 64
Masonic Order; *see* Zion Lodge
Matthews, Maj. Robert, 22
Maumee River, 13, 16, 17, 84; Ft. Miamis on, 2; Hamtramck camps near, 3; McKee's store on, 5; Simcoe builds fort on, 7; land on, ceded, 12; *Detroit* on, 19; Wayne descends, 47; called "Miami of the Lakes," 61; furs from valley of, 74
May, Betsey, 88
May, James, 86, 97, 137, 148, 157, 158; rents schooner, 2; business interests of, 31; appointed judge of Common Pleas, 56; appointed justice of the peace, 56; militia captain, 57; signs address, 56; owner of *Swan*, 73; financial transactions of, 82; signs petition, 84; orders new ship, 87; boards Burnett children, 88; borrows book, 92; ships printing press, 93 n.; a Mason, 94; buys land from Chippewa, 107; E. F. Freeman boards with, 122; acquitted, 138; accuses McNiff, 138; called "Sir James" by Sibley, 139, 139 n.; candidate for representative, 142; protests election of Sibley, 144, 145; reports counterfeiting, 159; petition to remove, 162; discharges commissioners, 163; suspended, 169; candidate, 177; hears charges, 179; loses *Harlequin*, 187; sells slave, 187, 187 n.; owns slave, 194; trustee, 213; jails slave, 218
May, Capt. Joseph, master of *Swan*, 16, 32, 73; drowned, 187
Mayne, Capt. William, commandant of Ft. Malden, 117, 127; pardon signed by, 44; troubled by desertion, 44; lends pork to Wayne, 62-63; reprimanded for loan of pork, 63
Meigs, Col. Return Jonathan, Sr., clothier general, 120
Meigs, Judge Return Jonathan, Jr., holds court, 130; advises Sibley, 132; blamed by Sibley, 207
Meldrum, George, 29, 133; sends daughter to school, 91; a Mason, 94; contract with schoolmaster, 170; owns slaves, 195; trustee, 197; fined, 213
Meldrum, Nancy, 91
Meldrum and Park, 2, 26, 73, 86, 133; in Miamis Company, 74
Meloche family, 36
Melvin, James, clerk for McDougall, 76
Merchants, characterized by Dr. C. Brown, 29; as bankers, 83

INDEX

Merchants' wharf, 18, 24
Meredith, Archange Askin, letters of, to Askin family, 27 n.; in England, 90; reports London fashions, 97 n.
Meredith, Capt. David, 90
Mettez, René, tailor, 81
Miami, 39, 64; in battle of Fallen Timbers, 7–8; sign Treaty of Greenville, 15
Miami of the Lakes; *see* Maumee River
Miamis, 74 n.
Miamis Company, organized, 74
Michigan, Lower Peninsula of, speculators attempt to purchase, 13
Michigan Territory, Legislature of, meets, 242
Militia, American, organized by Sargent, 57
Militia, British, from Detroit at Fallen Timbers, 7–8, mutinous, 8; useless, 12; John Askin captain of, 30; François de Joncaire de Chabert captain of, 35; Askin commands, 120
Miller, Christopher, interpreter, 64
Mills, 18, 105 n., 194
Mills, Capt. William, master of *Nancy*, 73; a Mason, 94; fights fire, 135
Miro, Gov. Esteban, 110
Mitchell, William, 113
Mocock, defined, 40 n., 107
Mohawk River, 61
Money, Halifax, 14, Halifax shillings, 82; Sterling shillings, 82; New York shillings, 82; scarcity of, 82; variety of, 82; local currency, 82; scarcity of, 159, 199
Monteith, Rev. John, 248
Montigny, Louvigny, books of, 91–92
Montreal, 27, 74, 152, 155; trade goods from, 73; merchants at, 77; furs sold in, 78; Campau sails for, 154; Alexander Henry in, 165; Williams leaves, 202–203; Henry buys in, 214
Montreal, 238
Moore, Joseph, 37, 38, 68, 77; notices many nationalities in Detroit, 28; companion of Lindley, 30; impressed by orchards, 66; describes Detroit, 67
Moran, Charles, 186
Moran, Maurice, 194
Morris, Capt. Thomas, 37
Mt. Clemens, 89
Muirhead, Dr. James, 204
Mulholland, Charles, 44
Munro, Robert, fined, 213; Indian storekeeper, 240
Myers, Martin, 213

Nagot, Father Francis, 201
Nancy, 73, 238; caught in ice, 95
Nanga, Chippewa chief, 175
Nationalities at Detroit, 28

Navarre, King of; *see* Bourbon, 36
Navarre, Miss, 202
Navarre, François, 83, 117, 124; favors Americans, 10; attacked by Fr. Burke, 10; signs Treaty of Greenville, 15; on River Raisin, 36; appointed justice of the peace, 56; militia captain, 57; signs address, 72; hauls army supplies, 105; ill, 162; protests action of May, 163
Navarre, Marie Françoise, wife of Lieut. George McDougall, 30, 36
Navarre, Robert, Sr., career of, 36
Navarre, Robert, Jr., Potawatomi grant land to, 36; appointed justice of the peace, 56
Navarre, Touton, 203
Negroes, slaves, 40, 218; free, 41
Nelson, Capt. Jonathan, master of *Beaver*, 73
Newman, Michael, tanner, 130, 139
New York City, 30, 61, 64, 165
New York currency, 82
Niagara, 64, 66
Nichol, Robert, clerk, 32; buys prayer book, 92; visits Williams 204, 204 n.
Nigig (Little Otter), Ottawa chief, signs treaty, 234
North West Company, 73, 246; Angus Mackintosh factor of, 30; extent of operations, 78
Northwest Territory, Detroit in, 42, 47, 55, 137, 157, 158, 188, 207
Nowlan, Sgt. Thomas, 124

O'Brian, Patrick, shoemaker, 124
Ogonse, Ottawa chief, 234
O'Hara, James, 123, 139; asks loan of pork, 43; commissary contractor, 62; orders salting of meat, 87; employs Henry, 99; Williams employed by, 173
Ohio River, 6, 61; Wayne sails down, 46
O'Neal, Antoine, silversmith, 76 n.
Oneida Lake, 61
Oni-g-wi-gan, 156
Ordinance of 1787, 137, 142
Oswald, Richard, 22
Oswego, 64
Ottawa, 39, 152, 174, 175; in battle of Fallen Timbers, 7–8; John Askin, Jr., agent of, 13; sign Treaty of Greenville, 15; carry Yax and wife to Detroit, 38; receive annuity, 120; cede land, 234
Ottawa, 74 n., 184

Panis, Indian slaves, 40
Paoli, 70
Papineau, Miss, schoolmistress, 91
Parent, Major, 120
Parent family, 36
Parent's Creek, 23

INDEX

Paris, 27
Park, William, 117; justice of the peace, 29; expresses attitude of British toward American régime, 29; intends to remain British, 56
Parkman, Francis, *Conspiracy of Pontiac*, 35, 37
Parks, Beaumont, 182, 200
Pasteur, Capt. Thomas, 108
Patrick McNiff's Plan of the Settlements at Detroit, 14 n.
Pattinson, Mrs., schoolmistress, 90
Pawnee, 40; *see* Panis
Pekin, 80
Pelletier (Peltier), Isidore, pledge to Ste Anne's, 186
Pelletier (Peltier), Jacques (father), 186; owns slave, 194
Pelletier (Peltier), Jacques (son), 86
Pelletier (Peltier), Louis, 190
Pennsylvania, 38
Pennsylvania Line, 51
Pepin, François, Wayne's emissary to Indians, 11; leads Indians to Greenville, 14; signs Treaty of Greenville, 15
Perrot, Marie Edeline, first wife of Hamtramck, 20
Perrot, Nicholas, 20
Persie, Mme, dressmaker, 80
Phelps, Oliver, 221
Philadelphia, 47, 50, 59, 72; capital city, 5; Joseph Moore from, 28; Mrs. J. Abbott, Sr., from, 31; chiefs sent to, 63; Volney in, 64
Physicians in Detroit, 37, 38, 122 n., 194, 247
Piano, 217
Pierson,———, 125
Pike, Capt. Zebulon, prefers charges against Lieut. Gregg, 60; assumes command, 208
Pinckney, Charles C., 109
Pinckney, Thomas, 109
Pinckney's treaty, 109, 119
Piquette, J. B., 203
Piquette family, 36
Pittsburgh, 59, 64, 72; Wayne at, 6; Wayne leaves, 46; route from, 62
Pittsburgh *Gazette*, 124
Point Industry, 129 n.
Pollard, Richard, 92
Pontiac, Ottawa chief, 37, 64
Pontiac Gate, 24; guard house inside, 43; removed, 222
Pontiac War, 35
Poor relief, 180-181
Population of Detroit, 27, 27 n.
Poquette, François, 176-177
Porter, Capt. Moses, 38, 168; embarks for Detroit, 16; occupies Ft. Lernoult, 18-19; makes estimate for repairs, 50; leaves on furlough, 71; at Mackinac, 118
Post office, petition for, 173 n.; established, 202
Postal service, 181, 222, 235, 249
Potawatomi, 36, 39, 64; in battle of Fallen Timbers, 7-8; sign Treaty of Greenville, 15; village at Spring Wells, 171
Poulins, Mary, 138
Powder magazine, location of, 24
Powell, Judge William Dummer, Sr., 8
Powell, William Dummer, Jr., 219
Power, Thomas, 65, 108; visits Wilkinson, 111; agent of Spaniards, 119
Powers, David, lawyer, 123-124, 139
Prescott, General Robert, 136
President Adams, launched, 152-153; description of, 167, 167 n.; Williams commands, 183; offered at auction, 211; carries merchants' goods, 238
Presqu' Isle (Erie, Pa.), 62, 64, 72, 153, 217; *Russell* winters at, 124
Printing press, at Detroit, 93 n.

Quaife, Milo M., 208
Quebec, 16, 27, 74; British headquarters in, 3; Hamtramck born in, 20
Queen's Rangers, at Malden, 44
Quilleriez, 35

Rameau de Saint-Père, Edmé, 68-69
Randall, Robert, 13
Ransom, Daniel, 218
Razice, François, 118
Red House on Common, 81
Reed, John, 218
Richard, Father Gabriel, 69, 217, 247; at Cahokia, 52; printing press of, 93 n.; journey of, to Detroit, 131; characterized, 131, 132; at Mackinac, 156; fears he will forget English, 171; distressed by condition of Indians, 172; signs petition, 173; serves as *chantre*, 182; pledge to Ste Anne's, 186; pastor, 201; bargain of, with Campau, 205; conducts funeral service, 208; trouble of, with parishioners, 218-219; asks transfer of Dilhet, 227; opens school, 228; reports lack of pupils, 239; detained by writ, 248; remains in Detroit, 248
Richardson, John, 183
Rivardi, Maj. J. J. U., 102, 112; in charge of construction, 86; characterizes French, 116; transferred to Niagara, 118; quoted, 119
River Raisin settlement (Monroe, Michigan), 10, 23, 145; Rev. Edmund Burke at, 9-10; disloyalty at, 9-10

River Road, 23, 24, 48, 241
River Rouge, 180; settlement at, 23; races on, 97; shipyard on, 125, 133, 152-153; voters from, 145; brickyard on, 152
Robertson, David, 32, 44
Robertson, William, merchant, 26, 32, 83, 170, 178; predicts lower prices for furs, 75; business career of, 75 n.; warns Askin of speculators, 124; offers house for school, 157
Robison, William, 215
Robison and Martin, 188, 191, 215; orders to, 214, 225
Roe, Walter, lawyer, 32; Wayne occupies house of, 49
Rogers, Maj. Robert, 34, 74
Romain, Jean Baptiste, *dit* Sans Crainte; *see* Sans Crainte
Roucour, Jean Baptiste, schoolmaster, 89; *chantre*, 90; death of, 182
Rough, Capt. James, master of *Russell*, 135
Rowe, Joseph, schoolmaster, 89; a Mason, 94
Royal American Regiment, 30
Royal Engineers, 4
Royal Navy of Upper Lakes, 32, 74 n. 184
Rudhart, George Jacob, 37
Ruffin, William, 222
Ruland, Israel, silversmith, 37, 38, 76 n.; at Ft. Wayne, 13; a Mason, 94; signs treaty, 234
Rumors of war, 108-109, 117-119, 149-150
Russell, Peter, 113, 114-115; orders arms for militia, 108; moves blockhouse to Sandwich, 127; issues militia orders, 136
Russell, William, merchant, 202 n.
Russell, 73, 124, 125

Sabrevois, Capt. Jacques Charles, 211 n.
Saginaw, 74, 195
Saginaw Bay, 134
Saguinah, 73, 238; carries Maj. Swan, 68; damaged, 134; repairs to, 152
St. Antoine Street (Campau Alley), 24
St. Aubin, Jacques, 183
St. Aubin family, 33
St. Clair, Arthur, 144, 163, 195, 212; defeated by Indians, 6; Gov. Northwest Territory, feud between, and Wayne, 47; announces return to Territory, 57; decides not to go to Detroit, 58; removes Eberts, 133; removes McNiff, 133; orders census, 137; orders election, 137, 145; intention of, to visit Detroit, 158; suspends judges, 169; reports murder, 177; opposition to, 188
St. Clair, Arthur, Jr., 181; attorney general, 132; friend of Sibley, 161; member of commission, 169; at Detroit, 170
St. Clair River, pinery on, 152
St. Clair Township, 84
St. Cosme, Rose, wife of James May, 31
St. David's, Radnor, 70
St. Honoré Street, 24
St. Jacques Street, 24
St. Joseph River, 61, 88
St. Joseph Street, 24
St. Lawrence River, 61
St. Louis Street, 24
St. Mary's River, 61
St. Mary's Seminary, 52, 201
St. Petersburg, 80
Ste Anne's Church, 69, 182, 247; location of, 24; Fr. Frechette leaves, 51; under jurisdiction of Bishop Carroll, 51; bells of, ring, 52; observance of Washington's birthday in, 101-102; dissension in, 125; confirmation at, 183; plans for new building, 185-186; enlarged, 201; jubilee celebration in, 239
Ste Anne Street, 20, 35; principal thoroughfare, 23-24; stores on, 26; Wayne's quarters on, 49
Salmon, Capt. George, commandant at Malden, 43-44
Sanders, Barent, merchant, 227
Sanders, Robert, merchant, 227
Sandusky, 74
Sandusky Bay, 12
Sandwich, laid out by Russell, 114-115; called "Smugglingburg," 115; militia to assemble at, 120; courthouse and jail at, burned, 126; Chatham blockhouse moved to, 127; Mackintosh moves to, 153; ball at, 180; goods smuggled from, 216
Sans Crainte, Jean Baptiste Romain *dit*, Wayne's emissary to Indians, 11; leads Indians to Greenville, 14; signs Treaty of Greenville, 15; origin of name, 34
Sargent, Winthrop, 83, 94, 207; reports population of Detroit, 27 n.; secretary Northwest Territory, 47; accompanies Wayne to Detroit, 49; acting governor, 55; establishes Wayne County, 55; establishes Court of General Quarter Sessions, 56; establishes Court of Common Pleas, 56; organizes militia, 57; receives letters from St. Clair, 57-58; replies to St. Clair, 58; sails for Mackinac, 59; accuses McKee, 63; township named for, 84; reports lack of education, 88; reprimands Chabert, 98; quoted, 117
Sargent Township, 84
Saunders, George, 160, 160 n., 196
Savoyard Creek, 21, 23, 24, 246
Schabel, ———, 125

INDEX

Schenectady, 37, 199
Schieffelin, Jacob, 217
Schieffelin, Jonathan, merchant, 37, 38, 188, 217; appointed Indian agent, 116–117; distributes annuity to Indians, 120; conducts chiefs to Philadelphia, 136; letter of, to Sibley, 161 n.; advises Bacon, 174; candidate for representative, 177; elected representative, 178–179; defends St. Clair, 189; in New York, 193; honored, 213
Scott, Dr. William McDowell, 237, 247; attends Cole and Poquette, 176, 176 n.; practices in Detroit, 194; marshal, arrests Indian, 196 n.; trustee, 213
Second Regiment, in garrison, 112; leaves, 166–167
Seek, Conrad, tailor, 37, 238
Selby, Prideaux, 6, 93, 177
Senator Tracy, 211; built at River Rouge, 167 n.; first voyage of, 184; carries troops and supplies, 199; carries Capt. Whistler, 209; carries merchants' goods, 238
Sevey, Henry, 60, 111–112
Shank, Maj. David, 44, 110
Sharp, George, tavern keeper, 26, 32
Sharp and Wallace, in Miamis Company, 74
Shaumburgh, Capt. Bartholomew, 2, 121
Shaw, Private Angus, 44
Shaw, John, brickmaker, 186
Shawnee, 39, 64; in battle of Fallen Timbers, 7–8; sign Treaty of Greenville, 15; cede land, 234
Shipyard, U. S., on River Rouge, Ernest establishes, 125; ships being built in, 133; *President Adams* built in, 152–153; *Senator Tracy* built in, 167 n.
Shipyard on River Rouge (John Askin's), 152
Shoepack, defined, 155 n.
Shortt, Capt. C. W., 2, 17
Showalter, Conrad, 37
Shower bath, 142
Sibley, Solomon, lawyer, 138, 140, 168, 190; early life of, 132; opinion of Detroit, 132; opinion of French girls, 132; deputy attorney general, 132, 139; characterizes French, 141; candidate for representative, 142–143; elected representative, 144; attends session of legislature, 144; writes legal opinion, 148; expects Indian attack, 150; petition to, 158; reports scarcity of money, 159; in legislature, 160–161; quoted on judges, 163; journey of, from Cincinnati, 169; at Chillicothe, 179, 179 n.; considers leaving Detroit, 181; in legislative council, 181, 188–189; courtship of, 184–185; in Marietta, 191; Huntington writes to, 193; urges removal of McNiff, 195; vote of thanks to, 197; marries Sarah Sproat, 205–206; dislikes transfer of Detroit to Indiana, 207; fearful for country, 210; asks recommendation, 212; sends petitions, 212; pessimism of, 216; brings wife to Detroit, 217; suggests sale of slaves, 218; attorney for Lasselle, 220; seeks secretaryship, 221; J. R. Jones writes to, 222; trustee, 223; attorney for Mrs. Eberts, 232; in Washington, 232; sends names of officers, 236
Sibley, Mrs. Solomon, 218
Simcoe, John Graves, Lieut. Governor, 14, 38; Col. England reports to, 4, 12; constructs Ft. Miamis, 7; suspicious of Americans, 17; agrees to lend pork, 43
Slaves, 187, 187 n., 194, 195; Panis (Indians), 40; Negroes, 40, 218
Smart, George, silversmith, 76 n.
Smilie, John, 221
Smith, Lieut. David W., 143
Smith, Thomas, surveyor, 32, 242
Smith, Thomas, tavern keeper, 26, 83, 94; borrows book, 92; Askwith's account with, 96
Smith, William, 196, 197
Smith, Col. William S., agent of land speculators, 124
"Smugglingburg," 115
Social life, dances, 3, dinners, 3, sleighing, 3
Soldiers, American, punishment of, 6; pay of, 45; deliver address to Wayne, 51
Soldiers, British, pay of, 45
Spencer, Oliver M., 1 n.
Spring Wells, Wayne lands at, 48; Indian village at, 171; Ernest's home at, 242
Sproat, Col. Ebenezer, 185
Sproat, Sarah Whipple, 184, wife of Solomon Sibley, 206
Sterling, James, 35
Sterling shilling, 82
Stores, number of, in Detroit, 23 n.
Strabane, 197
Streets, description of, in Detroit, 25–26
Strong, Col. David, 86, 118, 127, 140, 153, 168; commander at Ft. Greenville, 46; commandant at Detroit, 112; writes to Navarre, 124; organizes bucket brigade, 135; sends chiefs to Philadelphia, 136; posts guard at Dodemead's tavern, 147; expects Indian hostilities, 149; leaves Detroit, 166–167; promises Williams commission, 167
Strong, Warham, 139
Stuart, Charles, 105
Surprise, 152, 240
Swaine, Thomas, 87

INDEX

Swan, Maj. Caleb, paymaster general, 65, 68, 118
Swan, 17, 32, 48, 73, 95; chartered by DeButts, 2; carries advance detachment to Detroit, 16; carries Indians, 64; lost, 87
Swan Creek, 19
Swearingen, Lieut. James S., 209
Symmes, Judge John Cleves, 207; characterized, 158–159, 159 n.; member of commission, 169; at Detroit, 170; quoted, 182

Talleyrand-Perigord, Charles Maurice de, 128, 135, 150
Tallman, Lieut., 118
Tannery, 26, 123, 129, 155, 201, 225
Tarhee (the Crane), Wyandot chief, 234
Territory Northwest of the River Ohio; *see* Northwest Territory
Testard, Pierre Jean Baptiste, Sieur de Montigny de Louvigny; *see* Montigny, Louvigny
Thames, 73, 203, 206, 226
Thames River, 134
Tiffany, Sylvester, 93 n.
Todd, Isaac, 128, 197; predicts low prices for furs, 75; prepares memoir, 79
Todd and McGill, 75, 128, 226
Toledo, 2, 12
Tonguish, Chippewa chief, 234
Topinabee, 88
"Tornado," Indian name for Wayne, 49
Toys, 215–216
Tracy, Senator Uriah, at Detroit, 174–175; describes Detroit, 175 n.
Trade goods, 76, 188
Traineau, defined, 97, 105
Transportation; *see* Communication and transportation
Treaty of Greenville, 15, 63, 120
Treaty of Paris, 1
Tremblé, Louis, 186, 194
Trotier de Beaubien, 34
Trotier de Bellecour, 34
Trotier de la Rivière de Loup, 34
Trotier de l'Isle Perrot, 34
Trotier des Ruisseaux, 34
Trotier, Antoine, de Beaubien, 34
Trotier, Antoine, des Ruisseaux, 34
Trotier, François X., *dit* Bellecour, 34
Trotier, Julius, 34
Trotier, Marie Catherine, de Beaubien, 34
Trustees, Board of, ordinances of, 190; passes safety ordinance, 196; fines officials, 197; levies tax, 224; establishes night watch, 224
Tupper, Samuel, 221
Tuttle, Christopher, merchant, 202 n.

Tuttle and Russell, 202 n.
Twenty-fourth Infantry, 1, 4, 59

Upper Lakes, Royal Navy of, 32, 74 n., 184

Valley Forge, 51
Vance, Capt. Samuel C., 161, 210
Van Derhyden, David, 218
Vanderburgh, Judge Henry, 222, 232
Vincennes, 25, 26, 155; Ft. Knox at, 20; Hamtramck and Levadoux at, 52; capital, Indiana Territory, 208
Visger, Jacob, merchant, 37, 158, 160; candidate for representative, 145; elected representative, 146; candidate for representative, 177; hears charges, 179
Visger, Joseph, 162
Volney, Constantin François, 108; at Detroit, 64; suspected by Wayne, 65; ill with malaria, 65
Voss, John, 59
Voyageurs, 73, 156; characterized, 76
Voyer, Joseph, 145, 148, 169; appointed justice of the peace, 56; signs address, 72
Voyer family, 36

Wabash River, 74
Walk-in-Water, Wyandot chief, 234
Wallace, George, Jr., 139, 140, 141; clerk for Henry, 130; likes Detroit, 202
Wallen, Elias, 139, 182; appointed sheriff, 170; trustee, 190; requests militia detail, 195
Washington, George, 53, 71; appoints Wayne, 6; Indians to visit, 63; "funeral" of, 164
Washington's birthday, first celebration of, in Detroit, 100–102
Water blockhouse, 18
Waterville, 3
Wayne, General Anthony, 2, 5, 9, 18, 30; commands western army, 6; called "Mad Anthony," 6; defeats Indians, 7–8; engages Canadians to bring Indians to Greenville, 11; agents of speculators visit, 12–14; confines Askin, Jr., 13; receives secret code from McNiff, 14; pays McNiff for maps, 14, 14 n.; signs Treaty of Greenville, 15; Indians await arrival of, 39; quoted, 40; orders Mulholland released, 44; orders pay for fatigue duty, 45; sends compliments to Col. England, 46; at Ft. Greenville, 46; describes Wilkinson, 47; describes battle of Fallen Timbers, 48; called "Chief-who-never-sleeps" by In-

dians, 48; lands at Spring Wells, 48; welcomed to Detroit, 48-49; called "Black Snake" by Indians, 49; called "Tornado" by Indians, 49; lives in Roe's house, 49; praises Washington's policy, 49; describes Ft. Lernoult, 49-50; orders repairs for Ft. Lernoult, 50; describes Detroit, 50; entertained by Detroiters, 50; receives address from "The American Army," 51; welcomes Fr. Levadoux to Detroit, 52; establishes headquarters at Detroit, 58-59; offers reward for arrest of deserters, 59; approves sentences of court-martial, 60; thanks Capt. Mayne, 62-63; sends Indian chiefs to Philadelphia, 63; called "General Wabang," 63; gives presents to Indians, 63; suspects Volney, 65; suspects Hamtramck, 65; suspects Burbeck, 65 n.; buys cider, 66; ill with malaria, 69; reorganizes U. S. Army, 70-71; appoints Hamtramck commandant, 71; receives address, 72; replies to address, 72; leaves Detroit, 72; petition addressed to, 84; death of, 99; warns McHenry, 108; suspects France and Spain, 109; has boat intercepted, 111
Wayne, Isaac, 70
Wayne, Polly, 70
Wayne County, Indiana, 207
Wayne County, Northwest Territory, 57, 144, 160, 169; established, 55; extent of, 55; St. Clair never visited, 58; townships of, 84; trouble expected in, 117; census of, 137; election, 1798, 143; election, 1799, 145; representatives of, 158; judicial machinery of, 168; election, 1800, 177; tax roll of, 193-194
Waynesborough, 70
Wea, sign Treaty of Greenville, 15
Weazell, 17, 73, 152, 152 n.; chartered by DeButts, 2; carries advance detachment to Detroit, 16; wrecked, 134
Weld, Isaac, Jr., estimates population of Detroit, 27 n.; reports nickname for Wayne, 63; at Detroit, 65; opinion of Americans, 65-66; pleased with country, 66
Wells, Capt. William, 64
West Gate, 18, 24
Wheaton, John, 94
Whipple, Lieut. John, 168, 225-226
Whistler, Capt. John, 208-209, 232
Whistler, Sarah, marries James Abbott, 232
White, Capt. John, master of *Russell*, 73
White, Margaret, 176
Whitney, Charles, 13
Wilkins, John, Jr., 154, 202; quarter-

master general, 47; accompanies Wayne to Detroit, 47-49; competence of, 60; responsibilities of, 61; pays for printing, 93 n.; with Wilkinson at Detroit, 118; partner of Henry, 123; orders ship built, 124-125; quoted, 125; advises Henry, 130; instructs protégé, 141; asks for accounting, 155; demands accounting, 201
Wilkinson, Gen. James, 67, 168; writes to Col. England, 2; Hamtramck reports to, 43; at Ft. Greenville, 46; files charges against Wayne, 46-47; jealous of Wayne, 47; retained as brigadier-general, 71; intimacy of, with Power, 108; in the West, 110-111; relations of, with Spaniards, 110-111; at Detroit, 111-121; proclaims martial law, 113; posts guard at Dodemead's tavern, 114, 114 n.; appoints McNiff, 116; reassures Capt. Mayne, 117-118; goes to Mackinac, 118; orders gunpowder to magazine, 119; meets Power at Detroit, 119
Wilkinson, Dr. Joseph, Jr., 194, 247; trustee, 223, 237; appointed collector, 237
Wilkinsonville, 193
Williams, Elizabeth, 154 n.
Williams, Isaac, Jr., 96
Williams, James, tanner, 123, 129-130, 139
Williams, Capt. John, master of *Adams*, 183, 183 n.
Williams, John (John R. Williams), 122, 219; pupil in Burrell's school, 89; boyhood of, 89; partner of Joseph Campau, 154; leaves for Pittsburgh, 167; homesick, 168; in Pittsburgh, 172; employed by O'Hara, 173; returns to Detroit, 193; partnership with Campau, 199; in Montreal, 200; fights duel, 202-205; release of, 220; sued by Lasselle, 220; wins verdict, 220; goes to New York, 226; trustee, 237
Williams, Nathan, 138; appointed justice of the peace, 56; appointed judge of Common Pleas, 56; signs petition, 84; a Mason, 94
Williams, Thomas, 89
Windmills, 105 n., 194; description of, 18
Winston, Maj. William, tavern keeper, 132, 139, 139 n., 140
Winston's Tavern, courts sit in, 148
Winter amusements at Detroit, 95-98
Wiswell, Oliver, merchant 123, 123 n., 139, 160, 179; candidate for representative, 145; elected representative, 146; refuses to serve, 146
Wolcott, Oliver, Jr., Secretary of Treasury, 62
Woodward, Judge Augustus Brevoort,

rules on slavery in Michigan, 40 n.;
judge, Michigan Territory, 236; arrives
at Detroit, 241; urges patience at Detroit, 242; plans new town, 243
Worthington, Thomas, 207, 212, 232; presents memorials, 221
Wright, Thérèse, 184
Wright, Thérèse Grant, death of, 184
Wright, Dr. Thomas, death of, 184
Wyandots, 10; in battle of Fallen Timbers, 7-8; sign treaty of Greenville, 15;
receive annuity, 120; cede land, 234

Yax, Jean, 186
Yax, Jean Michel, 213
Yax, Michel, 37, 38
Yax, Simon, 186
York (Toronto), 43
York currency; *see* New York currency
York shilling; *see* New York currency

Zion Lodge, No. 10, A. F. & A. M., 139,
164, 180, 248-249; organization of, 94,
94 n., 95; Campau, officer of, 205; seeks
new charter, 217, 217 n.

UNIVERSITY OF MICHIGAN PUBLICATIONS
HISTORY AND POLITICAL SCIENCE

(*The first three volumes of this series were published as "Historical Studies," under the direction of the Department of History. Volumes IV and V were published without numbers.*)

VOL. I. A HISTORY OF THE PRESIDENT'S CABINET. By Mary L. Hinsdale (*o.p.*)

VOL. II. ENGLISH RULE IN GASCONY, 1199–1259, WITH SPECIAL REFERENCE TO THE TOWNS. By F. B. Marsh. Pp. xi + 178. $1.25.

VOL. III. THE COLOR LINE IN OHIO: A HISTORY OF RACE PREJUDICE IN A TYPICAL NORTHERN STATE. By F. U. Quillin. Pp. xvi + 178. $1.50.

VOL. IV. THE SENATE AND TREATIES, 1789–1817. THE DEVELOPMENT OF THE TREATY-MAKING FUNCTIONS OF THE UNITED STATES SENATE DURING THEIR FORMATIVE PERIOD. By R. Hayden. Pp. xvi + 237. $1.50.

VOL. V. WILLIAM PLUMER'S MEMORANDUM OF PROCEEDINGS IN THE UNITED STATES SENATE, 1803–1807. Edited by E. S. Brown. Pp. xi + 673. $3.50.

VOL. VI. THE GRAIN SUPPLY OF ENGLAND DURING THE NAPOLEONIC PERIOD. By W. F. Galpin. Pp. xi + 305. $3.00.

VOL. VII. EIGHTEENTH CENTURY DOCUMENTS RELATING TO THE ROYAL FORESTS, THE SHERIFFS AND SMUGGLING: SELECTED FROM THE SHELBURNE MANUSCRIPTS IN THE WILLIAM L. CLEMENTS LIBRARY. By Arthur Lyon Cross. Pp. xvii + 328. $3.00.

VOL. VIII. THE LOW COUNTRIES AND THE HUNDRED YEARS' WAR, 1326–1347. By Henry S. Lucas. Pp. xviii + 696. $4.00.

VOL. IX. THE ANGLO-FRENCH TREATY OF COMMERCE OF 1860 AND THE PROGRESS OF THE INDUSTRIAL REVOLUTION IN FRANCE. By A. L. Dunham. Pp. xiv + 409. $3.00.

VOL. X. THE YOUTH OF ERASMUS. By Albert Hyma. Pp. xi + 350. $3.00.

VOL. XI. UNIVERSITY OF MICHIGAN HISTORICAL ESSAYS. Edited by A. E. R. Boak. Pp. vii + 182. $2.25.

VOL. XII. THE SIEGE OF CHARLESTON, WITH AN ACCOUNT OF THE PROVINCE OF SOUTH CAROLINA: DIARIES AND LETTERS OF HESSIAN OFFICERS FROM THE VON JUNGKENN PAPERS IN THE WILLIAM L. CLEMENTS LIBRARY. Translated and edited by B. A. Uhlendorf. Pp. xi + 445. $4.00.

VOL. XIII. THE MICHIGAN CONSTITUTIONAL CONVENTIONS OF 1835–36: DEBATES AND PROCEEDINGS. By Harold M. Dorr. Pp. xi + 626. $5.00.

VOL. XIV. FEDERAL COÖPERATION WITH THE STATES UNDER THE COMMERCE CLAUSE. By Joseph E. Kallenbach. Pp. viii + 428. $4.00.

UNIVERSITY OF MICHIGAN PUBLICATIONS

Vol. XV. JOHN STUART AND THE SOUTHERN COLONIAL FRONTIER: A STUDY OF INDIAN RELATIONS, WAR, TRADE, AND LAND PROBLEMS IN THE SOUTHERN WILDERNESS, 1754-1775. By John Richard Alden. Pp. xiv + 384. $4.00.

Vol. XVI. DETROIT'S FIRST AMERICAN DECADE, 1796-1805. By F. Clever Bald. Pp. xi + 276. $4.50.

Vol. XVII. THE IDEA OF ECONOMIC UNIFICATION IN GERMANY BETWEEN 1815 AND 1833, AND THE FOUNDATION OF THE ZOLLVEREIN. By Arnold Hereward Price. (*In press.*)

www.ingramcontent.com/pod-product-compliance
Lightning Source LLC
Chambersburg PA
CBHW021137230426
43667CB00005B/147